PROF. H. KLING'S

MODERN ORCHESTRATION
AND INSTRUMENTATION

OR

THE ART OF INSTRUMENTATION

CONTAINING DETAILED DESCRIPTIONS OF THE CHARACTER AND
PECULIARITIES OF ALL INSTRUMENTS AND THEIR PRACTICAL
EMPLOYMENT, FOR EITHER SOLO, ORCHESTRA, OR MILITARY
BAND PURPOSES. PROFUSELY ILLUSTRATED WITH EXAMPLES
IN NOTES AND FULL SCORE EXTRACTS FROM THE WORKS OF
THE GREATEST CLASSIC AND MODERN MASTERS, TOGETHER
WITH PARTICULAR AND PRACTICAL INSTRUCTIONS REGARDING
ARRANGEMENTS FOR MODERN MILITARY BANDS ∴ ∴ ∴

COMPLETE DIRECTIONS FOR CONDUCTING

THIRD EDITION
REVISED AND ENLARGED BY THE AUTHOR
AND
TRANSLATED FROM THE ORIGINAL GERMAN EDITION
BY

GUSTAV SAENGER

CARL FISCHER, INC.
COOPER SQUARE, NEW YORK, N. Y.

Stanhope Press
F. H. GILSON COMPANY
BOSTON, U.S.A.

PREFACE TO THE AMERICAN EDITION.

THE extraordinary popularity achieved in Germany, Italy, Switzerland, etc., by the present treatise on Modern Orchestration and Instrumentation, and the friendly reception accorded it by the musical profession at large, together with most flattering comments by European art critics in general, have prompted its publication in a specially prepared American edition.

Instrumentation, in its proper sense, is the ability to reproduce musical impressions and ideas in writing, and imparting to them an outwardly comprehensive and audible expression through the employment of one or more musical instruments. In proportion to the number of instruments employed, or their particular combinations, we find the different groupings designated as *Solo*, *Duo*, *Trio*, *Quartett*, *Quintett*, *Sextett*, or ultimately *Orchestra*. In a broader sense, and comparatively speaking, Instrumentation, and particularly Orchestration or Orchestral Instrumentation, might be interpreted as signifying that which the painter designates as color-compilation or combination. As a fact, the idea of *Tonal-color* (as applied to painting) and *Vibratory or Sound-Color* (as applied to music), although impossible in a strictly comparative sense, has become entirely *en vogue*, as through it the intervals or tones (either individually or collectively) of the various Stringed, Wood, Brass or Percussion Instruments can be best and most appropriately designated. It has even been claimed that certain tones correspond exactly with certain colors, in-so-far that both — one through agency of the organs of hearing, the other through the organs of sight — combine and affect the brain in such a manner as to bring about the same impressions and feelings. Without desiring to investigate into the detailed and scientific foundation of these analogies at this point, it may be set down as an absolute certainty that for instance *A flat* or *D flat* will fittingly correspond to the idea of *dark* or *sombre*, and *D* or *E* rather to the idea of *light* or *bright ;* and in the same way as the expressions of *hard* and *soft*, etc., are applied to individual or a combination of colors, and in turn to individual tones of an instrument or to entire tonal successions of different instruments.

From the foregoing may be gathered that instrumentation must be considered from both a *technical* and *æsthetic* stand-point and that both are inseparable. The former above all demands a thorough and complete knowledge of the individual instruments, their tonal-character and compass, treatment, employment, capabilities and tonal-color in the various registers. To gain this knowledge and executive ability, continued application and absolute mastery of instrumental detail must form the foundation, which in turn can only be achieved through incessant and conscientious study. A different proposition presents itself when considering the *æsthetic* side, which embodies and treats of the beauty, effectiveness, and at the same time originality of the compilation of tonal-colors. This faculty is dependent upon natural or inborn capabilities, traceable only to innermost feeling and expressiveness, and which in general is designated as *Talent*, and, if possessed to a greater degree, as *Genius*. Naturally where inborn capabilities are possessed to such an unusual degree, rules and maxims, in fact teaching and learning in the accepted and ordinary sense, are out of the question, development and ultimate mastery being brought about in such a case solely through systematic absorbing of existing material, continual encouragement towards higher ideals, and through the careful and minute study and hearing of master-works by great composers, such as Haydn, Mozart, Beethoven, Mendelssohn, Brahms, Berlioz, Richard Wagner, etc., whose achievements in this particular field will assimilate with the endeavors of the new composer, we might say comingle with them to such an extent that their combination with the composer's own ideal will bring about the formation of a new and original whole. Therefore instrumentation, from a technical stand-point demands *Knowledge*, and from æsthetic considerations *Art*, consequently belonging to both realms.

In conclusion, I will add a few excellent remarks and hints which Richard Wagner expressed in some of his letters addressed to the president of the Royal Music School at Naples, Italy (Duke of Bagnava), relative to the development of young composers and singers. While these hints were originally intended for dramatic music only, they may be used to equal advantage for music in general, and particularly for our present subject. His remarks in part were as follows:

"According to my opinion students in vocal and dramatic composition can only be launched successfully upon the path you wish them to follow through the earnest, conscientious, and ceaseless study of a master-work, say like Mozart's *Marriage of Figaro*. As a natural consequence, through such study, correct declamation, pure and truthful expression of melody, thorough knowledge of the means of instrumentation, and their appropriate methods of employments, would be imparted; and if some day the Conservatory could bring about a perfect performance of the above-mentioned master-work, it would render a great and lasting service, not only to the operatic stage, but would fulfil its mission, which undoubtedly consists in guarding its students against the reigning slip-shod methods of present-day conditions, through encouraging the actual performances of great examples, making the students colaborators of our great masters, in a certain sense.

"All the faulty and absurd habits acquired in such countless numbers in our operatic institutions, for instance, those of our singers, who make a point of forgetting or ignoring everything which passes upon the stage, in order to attract the attention of the audience and challenge its applause and admiration with a showy closing-cadenza more or less brilliantly executed; I feel justified in claiming that such habits would not be accepted or developed by students who have been trained, and who have acquainted themselves only with works of the rank and artistic importance of the above. As to the study of the tragic *genre*, I should recommend the two 'Iphigenien' by Gluck, and the 'Vestalin' by Spontini, to begin with.

"Only after these operas have been thoroughly memorized, analyzed, rehearsed, and fully appreciated and understood in accordance to their true worth, the students of the Conservatory should be allowed to attempt compositions of their own, as only then could we rest assured that they would not fall a victim to the exaggerations and faulty mannerisms so prevalent upon our present-day operatic stages, and in consequence of which it is only through hearsay that we know of those great singers who at one time established the fame of Italian Opera.

"Just as in life, there is such a thing as *good company* in art; and it is the plain duty of parents and guardians to introduce their inexperienced children and pupils entrusted to them, only into this good company, till they themselves are competent and able to discriminate between the true and false in art, and to withstand the temptations of flimsy and shallow effects. If after this they feel inclined to associate with what I can only designate as musical vagrancy, is of secondary consideration; because if they have once acquired the capabilities of judging how the latter is produced, they will, through coming in contact with it, gather so much experience and consciousness as to enable them to discriminate between that *which draws down the masses* and *that which is good.*"

The difficult and most exacting task of translating this work into the English language was entrusted to the hands of *Mr. Gustav Saenger*, well-known throughout the United States as an accomplished composer and musical scholar; and thanks to his energetic zeal and untiring efforts, as well as to the liberal and enterprising assistance of *C. Fischer*, the prominent New York Publisher, this latest and most modern Method on Instrumentation and Orchestration, based on strictly artistic, thorough, concise, and practical principles, is in readiness for the English-speaking world at large.

That this special American Edition, prepared with such infinite care by the author, translator and publisher, may be accorded an equally favorable reception, and install itself as lastingly in the good opinion of the English-speaking profession and musical public in general, as the original German edition, is the earnest and sincere wish of

H. KLING,

Professor at the Geneva Conservatory,

Officier d'Académie.

GENEVA, SWITZERLAND,
    Sept. 1, 1902.

INTRODUCTORY REMARKS ON INSTRUMENTATION.

INSTRUMENTATION consists of the art of combining the instruments in such a way that they will assist and enrich the melody, besides lending strength, volume, and tonal coloring to the harmony. It furthermore brings about a clear and systematic grouping of the various instruments, with particular attention that the different tonal-colors are most effectively contrasted and blended, in order that a composition will be transmitted to the ear in an equally clear, concise, and pleasing manner. This art requires great skill and experience, and even greater taste, on the part of the composer; it is a science, the methods of which are well-known and teachable, but which, above all, is principally dependent upon the imaginative powers of the writer.

The score of an instrumental composition offers endless variety and diversity; its contents may present themselves alternately in a terrible, tremendously-strong, soft, playful, clumsy and light, brilliant or dull, dramatic or romantic, impulsive or quiet, sad or frivolous way, exactly according to the idea the composer wishes to express.

Every instrument possesses its particular tonal-color, peculiar to itself; sometimes more than one coloring can be obtained, according to the different registers employed.

If the instruments are grouped in different ways an endless variety of combinations can be obtained; but to begin with, it is highly necessary and of greatest importance to study the tonal-range and the different registers of every instrument in order to know exactly what will sound good or bad, whether this or that passage can be executed upon an instrument, in short, we must understand to write in such an appropriate manner, that the beautiful and particular characteristics of every individual instrument will appear to best advantage.

Only such instruments have been included in this work as are employed in our modern orchestras, and will be presented in the following five groups.

GROUP I. — Stringed Instruments.

A. INSTRUMENTS PLAYED WITH A BOW.—1, Violin; 2, Viola; 3, Viola alta; 4, Viola d'amoure; 5, Violoncello; 6, Double-Bass.

B. INSTRUMENTS, THE STRINGS OF WHICH ARE PLUCKED WITH THE FINGERS.—1, Harp; 2, Guitar; 3, Mandolin; 4, Zither; 5, Banjo.

C. INSTRUMENTS, THE STRINGS OF WHICH ARE STRUCK BY MEANS OF KEYS, ETC.—1, Piano; 2, Dulcimer.

GROUP II. — Wind Instruments.

A. WOOD WIND INSTRUMENTS.—1, Piccolo; 2, Flute; 3, Flute d'Amour; 4, Flageolet; 5, Oboe; 6, Oboe d'Amore; 7, Oboe di Caccia; 8, English Horn; 9, Clarinet; 10, Bass Clarinet; 11, Basset-Horn; 12, Bassoon; 13, Double-Bassoon.

B. BRASS INSTRUMENTS.—1, Horn; 2, Trumpet; 3, Cornet; 4, Trombone; 5, Saxophone; 6, Ophicleide; 7, Bass-Tuba.

C. INSTRUMENTS WITH KEYS.—1, Organ; 2, Harmonium.

GROUP III.—Instruments of Percussion.

1, Tympani; 2, Small or Side Drum; 3, Bass Drum; 4, Cymbals; 5, Triangle; 6, Tambourine; 7, Tamtam; 8, Glockenspiel; 9, Steel Xylophone; 10, Glocken-Accordion; 11, Large Bells; 12, Xylophone; 13, Castagnets.

GROUP IV.—Different Smaller Instruments.

As employed in Comic Scenes, Dance-Music, Potpourries, etc.: 1, Whip; 2, Bells; 3, Thunder; 4, Railroad; 5, Waldteufel; 6, Nightingale Whistle; 7, Quail Whistle; 8, Shrill or Trill Whistle; 9, Cuckoo Whistle; 10, Railroad Whistle (Locomotive and Conductor Whistle); 11, Spurs; 12, Rattle; 13, Storm; 14, Fireman's Horn; 15, Post Horn; 16, Hunting Horn; 17, Alpine Horn; 18, Czakan; 19, Anvil; 20, Wind-machine; 21, Rain-machine, etc.

GROUP V.—Instruments Employed in Military Bands.

1, Piccolo; 2, Flute; 3, Clarinet; 4, Oboe; 5, English Horn; 6, Bassoon; 7, Double Bassoon; 8, Horn; 9, Trumpet and Bass Trumpet; 10, Piccolo Cornet; 11, Cornet and Flügel-Horn; 12, Alt Horn; 13, Tenor Horn; 14, Baritone (Euphonion); 15, Trombone; 16, Saxophone; 17, Sarusophone; 18, Ophicleide; 19, Bass Tuba; 20, Helicon; 21, Instruments of Percussion, etc.

Following these five groups special chapters have been added treating of

"The Human Voice,"

Girls' voices, Women's voices, Boys' voices, Men's voices, and

Practical Directions for Conducting.

KLING'S MODERN
INSTRUMENTATION AND ORCHESTRATION.

GROUP I.
STRINGED INSTRUMENTS.

A. Instruments Played with a Bow.

1. THE VIOLIN.

(VIOLINE, VIOLINO, VIOLON.)

Music for the violin is written in the G clef, and its strings, of which there are four, are tuned in perfect fifths.

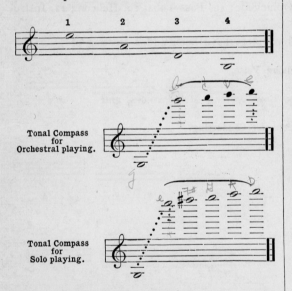

Tonal Compass for Orchestral playing.

Tonal Compass for Solo playing.

The effects to be obtained with this magnificent instrument are inexhaustible and applicable to every conceivable variety of musical composition. The effective application of the qualities offered by the violin must be left to the talent and imagination of the composer, as it is a difficult matter to lay down positive rules therefor. In the first place it is necessary to study the scores of Haydn's, Mozart's and Beethoven's quartettes and quintettes, in order to acquire ability and proficiency in writing for both the violin, the viola, and the violoncello in an artistic manner. We will begin with detailed explanations of a few of the manifold qualities and peculiarities of the violin.

Bowing. This is undoubtedly one of the chief factors in the art of violin playing. If the violin-bow is applied near the bridge and drawn with strength and firmness, a more or less voluminous tone can be produced. Contrary to this, if a soft and pleasing tone, smooth rendition of passages, and delicacy in melodic work is to be produced, the bow must be applied at a distance from the bridge. Opposite effects are produced by drawing the bow near to, or at a distance from the bridge.

Sul ponticello (very near to the bridge) bowing, with very light pressure of the bow, produces a whistling and nasal tone, which can be used to good advantage for bringing about special effects.

With the opposite bowing, *Sulla tastiera* (above the finger-board), soft and flute-like tones are produced. The *flautato* (or *strascinato*) bowing is produced by applying the bow at its tip about an inch away from the end of the finger-board; it must be drawn very delicately and evenly, and every note should be slightly extended. This bowing, with its flute-like effect, can be produced to best advantage in the middle of the D and A string.

Detached Bowing. Executed with long strokes, according to the tempo.

Hammered Bowing. Executed at the nut of the bow, in a short and decided manner.

Staccato Bowing. Executed in one stroke.

Light Staccato Bowing. Usually executed with the up-stroke, the bow rebounding from the strings after each note in a light and elastic manner.

Light Rebounding Strokes. The bow rebounding from the strings in an exceedingly light manner.

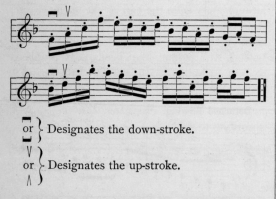

⊓ or } Designates the down-stroke.

V or } Designates the up-stroke.
∧

Brilliantly Detached Strokes. For use in quick movements, necessitating an exceedingly fine and delicate interpretation.

Vivace.

Ricochet, or Jumping Bow. With rebounding strokes, the groups separated by small pauses in which the bow is raised from the strings.

Grazioso et pp.

Dragging Stroke. Executed with the upper half of the bow.

Moderato.

Arpeggio Bowing. Executing the notes of a broken chord in a harp-like manner.

etc., in different keys.

Saccade Bowing. By accenting each 2d, 3d, or 4th note with an additional pressure of the bow, a rough but excellent effect (for orchestral use) is produced.

Strong Sustained Intervals. Vigorously drawn notes and passages executed with whole bows.

The Trill can be executed upon every note of the entire tonal compass of the violin.

Easy Double-trills. (Are never introduced in orchestral writing to be executed by one instrument.)

The Vibrato. The Vibrato is produced by moving the finger in a trembling manner slightly above and below the perfect intervals.

The following sign is used for its designation.

It is very effective for any of the Stringed Instruments if used in passages of a *recitative* nature; but care must be taken not to use it to excess.

In his *recitatives* Gluck has used it to excellent advantage.

Double, Chromatic-Double, Triple and Quadruple-stops possible upon the Violin.

DOUBLE STOPS.

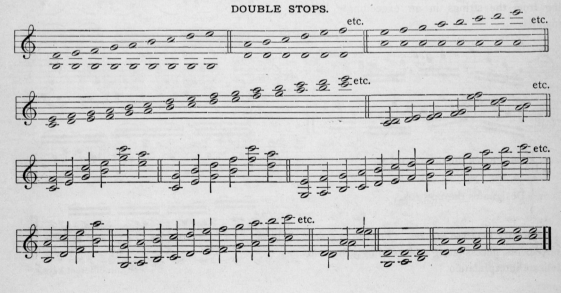

CHROMATIC DOUBLE STOPS.

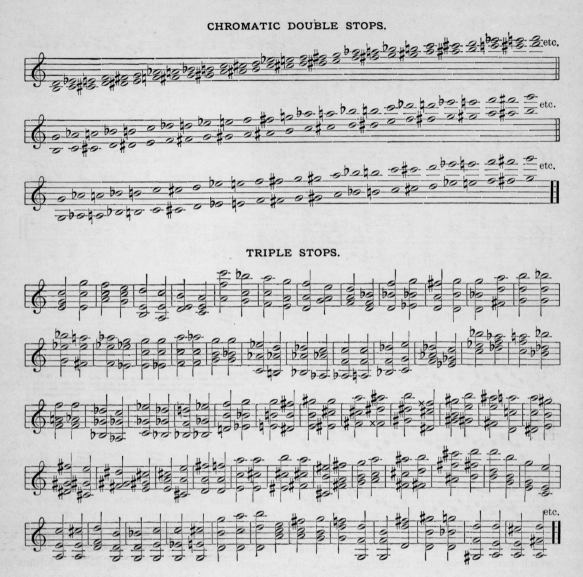

TRIPLE STOPS.

QUADRUPLE STOPS.

QUADRUPLE STOPS (Continued).

Broken Chords. Used for the second Violin. (Viola and Violoncello.)

Tremolo Bowing. A trembling movement which may be executed either with single or double-stops.

Tremolo Bowing.

Harmonics or Flageolet-tones are produced by placing the fingers lightly upon the strings instead of pressing them down in the firm manner necessary for the ordinary intervals; in consequence the string is capable of more vibrations and a flageolet-like tone is produced.

Natural Harmonics.   Artistic Harmonics.

The Sordino or Mute, effects the production of a mysterious, veiled and voluptuous tonal character, which, while possessing undoubted charm, should not be used too often.   In scoring, the Italian term "con sordino" (with mute) is used. If its use is to be discontinued the words "senza sordino" (without mute) are written in advance of the particular place where the effect is to stop.   The necessity of allowing ample time in which to set and again remove the mute must always be borne in mind; this is very important in order that the even flow of a composition will not be interrupted.

Pizzicato is produced by plucking the strings with a finger of either the right or left hand; it can be executed either in single or double stops as well as in arpeggio-like manner.   It is designated by the term "Pizzicato" (generally abbreviated "Pizz."); if the effect is to be discontinued the term "coll arco" (with the bow) or simply "arco" is used.

Pizzicato played with the *right hand*.

Pizzicato executed with the *left hand*.

Pizzicato in which all the notes are executed by the fourth finger of the left hand.

In the following examples the first note (᾿) is played with the bow, the second (+) is plucked with the 4th, and the third (+) with the 2nd finger of the left hand.

The accompaniment plucked with the 4th finger and the melody played with the bow.

It is also possible to execute trills pizzicato.

In case the student is not a violin-player himself, he would derive the greatest benefit through the study of some excellent violin-school, say the one by Ferd. David, in order to acquaint himself thoroughly with the different effects which can be produced upon this unsurpassable instrument.

The Violin is principally adapted for the interpretation of *cantabile-passages*, embellishments and richly elaborated melodies.

Extraordinary Manner of tuning the Violin.

This device is only employed when the violin is used as a Solo-instrument; we find an example in *Saint-Saëns' Danse Macabre*, in which the first Solo-Violin must be tuned in the following manner:

Mozart, Tartini, Lolli, Baillot, Paganini, and others employed this device and tuned their violins in a different manner. It is the privilege of every virtuoso to introduce changes of this kind as seem best suited to his special purpose, but for orchestral playing it is preferable to retain the ordinary manner of tuning in perfect fifths.

Divisi-playing in the Orchestra. Usually the violins are divided to interpret a first and second part, but as each instrument, in any moderately sized orchestra, is represented by numerous players, each part can again be sub-divided. Many of our modern composers, such as Berlioz and especially R. Wagner, sometimes divide the violins to interpret as many as eight different parts; the beautiful Prelude to "Lohengrin" contains a masterly example of how to use the violins in this manner.

EXTRACT FROM THE VORSPIEL TO "LOHENGRIN."

R. WAGNER.

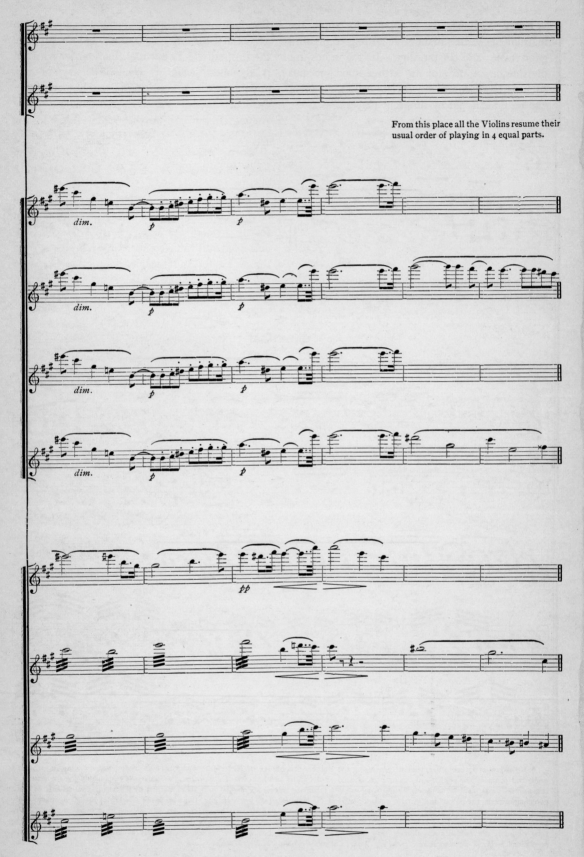

From this place all the Violins resume their
usual order of playing in 4 equal parts.

Every composer is at liberty to apply the instruments in this manner according to his own good taste and inspiration. If the notes for division or sub-division are written upon one staff such parts are marked "divisi" (div.), meaning "to be interpreted by different players."

The Solo Violin-part in the orchestra is usually interpreted by the Concert-master or Assistant Conductor. A well-written solo executed by an accomplished artist will never fail to produce the desired effect; but the situation, for which it is intended, whether dramatic or symphonic, must be fittingly and appropriately pictured in musical sounds. Especial attention and study should be devoted to the Violin solos in the following operas: *Faust* (Gounod), *The Merry Wives of Windsor* (Nicolai), *A Night in Granada* (Kreutzer), *Le Pré au Clercs* (Herold), etc.

In the following example I present a Cadenza composed for the last-named opera (Introduction to the Aria of the 2nd Act) by A. Heps (Concert-master at the Geneva Stadtorchestra). With the aid of this, an idea may be gathered, as to the possibilities upon this instrument by an accomplished soloist.*)

CADENZA.

Introduction to Aria (Act II.) from "Le Pré au Clercs," by Herold.

* Nowadays every composer, without possessing the slightest knowledge or idea of the organism of the violin, writes violin-concertos and orchestral compositions with a solo violin-part, brimful of thankless and unheard-of difficulties. Beethoven is responsible for the efforts of these professional pianistic heroes; Mendelssohn was his fortunate successor. In the enthusiasm aroused by the beauties and merits of these two compositions, the proper and suitable characteristics of the instrument are lost sight of. But what is the offering of these epigones? Only criticism devoid of the real sense of genuine violin-playing can simulate admiration for such concertos. Allowed, that some may lay claim to being very good and interesting compositions, violin-compositions such as their title declares them to be, they are certainly not. In addition to this, violinists are suddenly abandoning their claim of being virtuosi, but wish to be considered solely as interpreters of higher artistic revelations. — H. M. SCHLETTERER: *Ludwig Spohr, Collection of Musical Recollections.*

The most effective keys for the Violin in orchestral writing are C, G, D, A, E, and B Major and Minor.

For Solo-playing the keys of D, A, and E Major are the best, owing to their brilliant and high-sounding notes.

Furthermore it must be remembered that every string of the Violin possesses its own peculiar timbre, similar in some respects to the tonal character of certain wind instruments; accordingly the tonal quality of the 4th string may be compared with that of the Horn, that of the 3d string with the Bassoon, that of the 2nd string with the Oboe, and that of the 1st string partly with the Flute and Piccolo.

If the composer desires a certain passage or

movement to be executed upon one string, he indicates it by means of numerals (E string 1, A string 2, D string 3, G string 4) and a dotted line drawn over the respective notes, as in the above-shown examples.

The fourth string is the most expressive. In the beautiful prelude to the 5th Act of his opera "L'Africaine" (the scene of the Manzanillo tree) Meyerbeer has used it successfully by combining all the Violins, Violas, and Violoncellos, with the Clarinets and Bassoons in one grand *unisono*. Certainly a very flash of genius. The effect is impressive and grand, the quality of tone produced by this combination of instruments resembling that of one enormous Viola.

The Violin as used in dance-music. The Violins are divided into two groups, of which the first usually takes the melody, and the second, in connection with the Viola, the rhythmical accompaniment, as will be seen further on.

2. THE VIOLA.

(BRATSCHE, VIOLA ALTA, ALTO.)

Music for the Viola is written both in the Alto (C-clef, 3d line) and in the Violin or G-clef. The strings are tuned in perfect fifths.

(In his opera "Le Pré aux Clercs," Herold has the 4th string tuned down to B in one instance.)

The various bowings of the Violin, as explained in the preceding chapter, apply to the Viola in every respect.

ARPEGGIOS.

etc.

THE TRILL

Can be executed upon every note of the entire tonal-compass.

Easy Double-trills.

DOUBLE STOPS WITH TWO, THREE, AND FOUR NOTES.

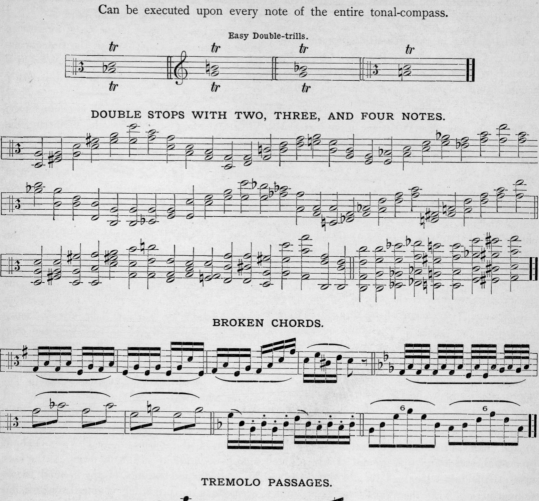

BROKEN CHORDS.

TREMOLO PASSAGES.

HARMONICS.

The **Pizzicato** and **Sordino** are used in the identical manner as upon the Violin.

Divisi-playing in the orchestra. For the production of special effects, the Violas may be divided to interpret 2, 3, or 4 different parts, according to the pleasure or intentions of the composer.

The Viola as a Solo-instrument offers material of wondrous charm, its soft, yearning tonal-character being imbued with extraordinary beauty.

Méhul, misled by the intimate similarity existing between the tonal-character of the Violas and the dreamy character of the Ossianic poetry, decided to use them solely in his opera "Uthal," excluding the Violins entirely. But the tonal-coloring created thereby proved too monotonous, and resulted in a tiresome effect upon the listeners.

Weber used the Viola in his opera "Der Freischütz," to excellent advantage, entrusting it with an important solo. In the 3d Act of his charming opera "The Hermit's Bell," Maillart introduced a short but very expressive solo for the Viola. Gluck, Beethoven, Méhul, Meyerbeer, Mendelssohn, Berlioz, R. Wagner and many others have repeatedly given prominence to the Viola in a marked manner, both in orchestral and solo work. Cantabile-passages upon the higher strings of the Viola create a wonderful effect in scenes of a religious and antique character, as for instance in the beautiful prayer in Spontini's opera "The Vestal."

The best keys for solo-playing are G, D, E♭ and A♭ major.

Used in Dance-music the Viola fills up and completes the accompaniment in connection with the 2nd Violin.

The tonal characteristics of the different strings of the Viola may be described as follows: the 4th and 3d strings possess a soft, earnest and sonorous quality, which in their middle registers are very similar to the tones of a French Horn. The 2nd string possesses a Bassoon-like, and the 1st string an Oboe-like tone.

3. THE VIOLA ALTA.

The Viola alta is tuned, played and employed in the exact manner as the ordinary Viola, differing only in the build of its body (reso-nance-box) and tone, the latter possessing more volume, brightness and carrying-powers.

Before proceeding, it might be of interest to state the reason which led to the transformation of the ordinary Viola, as well as to look into the principles of construction of this newly improved instrument.

Among the group of stringed instruments the Viola takes its place between the Violin and the Violoncello; according to its tonal-register it is a major fifth lower than the Violin and a full octave higher than the Violoncello. In view of certain defects of the ordinary Viola, the possibility of improving the instrument in various ways presented itself.

Never could the Viola compete with the Violin or Violoncello as an independent musical instrument; its inadequate and limited means of expression have ever prevented musicians and soloists from choosing it as a medium through which to portray their artistic sentiments, to such a degree as has been the case upon the Violin or Violoncello. The ordinary Viola possesses a dull and nasal tone. There can be no doubt that the instrument is deficient in free and clear emission of tonal volume and consequently in brilliancy and strength. We might express ourselves in such a manner as to claim that the ordinarily-used Viola cannot sing freely and unrestrainedly owing to the lack of a sound and healthy body; in its hitherto existing form it appears as a narrow-breasted concern.

The wish of the regenerator * was therefore directed towards constructing a Viola which would not alone be improved in this respect, but which in its tonal-register would possess the same general qualities as the Violin, namely: volume, intensity, carrying quality, sonority, and beauty of tone. As the tone of the Violin is brought about by aërial vibrations, which in their turn are produced by the joint action of certain factors (strings, bridge, and resonance-box), the construction of the Viola alta was based upon that of the Violin. Comparison of the two instruments will present them in the propor-

* Hermann Ritter, Esq., Grand-ducal chamber virtuoso of Mecklenburgh-Schwerin, and teacher of the History of Music at the Royal Music-school in Würtzburg, author of a voluminous school, "The Study of the Viola alta," "History of the Viola alta," "Repertorium of the History of Music," Concerts for Viola alta, with orchestral accompaniment, many solo compositions, as well as founder of a literature for the Viola alta, etc.

tion of tonic to sub-dominant; consequently, as this proportion appears as 2 : 3, or 1 : $\frac{3}{2}$, the dimensions and aërial capacity of two vibratory spaces (resonance-boxes) of similar shape, must be in accordance with such proportionate figuring. Based upon this fundamental rule of tonic and sub-dominant, a real foundation for the construction of the Viola alta had at last been laid, offering the advantage of proceeding with the aid of principles and methods as applied in Violin construction. Aided by the personal directions and drawings, etc., of the inventor, this Tenor-violin (Alt-Geige) as Richard Wagner named it in German, was constructed by the violin-maker, Karl Adam Hörlein (pupil of the celebrated Vauchel) in Würzburg, 1875. Now that the proper and real Tenor-violin has been produced, constructed according to scientific principles, and answering all requirements as to tonal color and carrying powers, the question presents itself: Can this new-born instrument be played and manipulated with ease?

By the successful introduction of this instrument in his concert-tours throughout Switzerland, Germany, Holland and Russia, the regenerator, who is a Viola-player himself, has undoubtedly proven so far, that the technical manipulation of the Viola alta has in no way been interfered with by its improved and correct manner of construction. In the production of his tetralogy "The Ring of the Nibelung" in 1876, Richard Wagner immediately added the instrument to his orchestra in preference to the ordinary Violas. Since then this newly constructed and improved Viola alta has been successfully introduced in many German and Russian orchestras in place of the usual Violas.

4. VIOLA D'AMOUR.

(LIEBESGEIGE, VIOLA D'AMORE.)

Unluckily this beautiful instrument, which possesses a lovely and bewitching tone, can be found in only a few privileged orchestras. It is a difficult matter to explain and hardly comprehensible, that an instrument possessing expressive force to such a degree as the Viola d'amour, should have been done away with; the perpetual and everlasting endeavor to improve has resulted in replacing it by an over-abundance of Trombones and Bass-Tubas, with which the modern orchestra is crowded; true it is, we succeed in producing more noise, but a double loss in charming loveliness is entailed.

Music for this instrument is written in the Alto and Violin-clef, and is strung with the following 7 strings:

Its tonal-compass is:

As with the Viola the higher notes are written in the Violin-clef.

Everything remarked as to technique, double-stops, arpeggios, tremolo, pizzicato, and sordino in connection with the Violin, is equally applicable to the Viola d'amour.

The following example is a charming solo, expressly written for it by Meyerbeer, and introduced in his celebrated opera "The Huguenots."

EXTRACT FROM THE OPERA "THE HUGUENOTS."

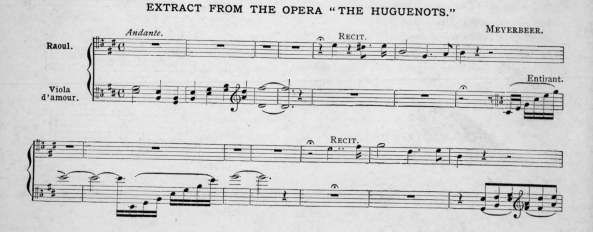

Most conductors, more ambitious to earn money, or save a little for their respective theatrical or operatic managers, than respectful to the ideas and interests of a man of genius or the real interests of art, allow this important solo to be played upon an ordinary Viola. But the effect produced cannot compare to that intended by Meyerbeer, as the Viola can in no way imitate the bewitching quality of sound which constitutes the chief characteristic of the charming Viola d'amour.

5. THE VIOLONCELLO.

(VIOLONCELL, VIOLONCELLO, VIOLONCELLE.)

Music for the Violoncello is usually written in the Bass and Tenor, and sometimes in the Violin or Treble-clef. Its strings are tuned in perfect fifths an octave below those of the Viola.

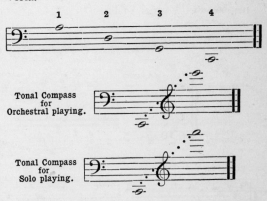

Tonal Compass for Orchestral playing.

Tonal Compass for Solo playing.

The Bowings are identical with those used for the Violin, the following kinds presenting the greatest difficulty :

a staccato.

saltato, martellato, jumping bow.

Three and Four Stringed Arpeggios are used in various forms and bowings.

The Trill can be executed upon every note of the entire tonal-compass.

Double-trills are extremely difficult ; they are rarely used in orchestral, and occur mostly in instructive works.

Double-stops composed of 2, 3, and 4 notes.

Broken Chords.   Applied in the same manner as upon the Violin.

The Tremolo produces an excellent effect.

Sometimes the notes of the higher positions are written in the Treble-clef, although in reality they sound an octave lower, as is illustrated by the following extract from a string-quartette by Mozart; but notation in accordance to the real sounds is gradually becoming the custom; it is certainly preferable and mistakes are avoided thereby:

In reality the written notes sound as below.

Harmonics are produced and applied in the same manner as upon all stringed instruments.

NATURAL HARMONICS.

Artistic Harmonics can only be used to advantage upon the first (a) string, in the following manner:

Pizzicato and Sordino are applied with equal success as in connection with the Violin. Violoncello parts may be sub-divided for interpretation by 2, 3, 4, and 5 different 'Cellos, as may suit the intentions of the composer. In the following example the introduction to the overture of "William Tell" is shown, in which Rossini has made use of 5 Solo-Violoncellos:

EXTRACT FROM OVERTURE TO WILLIAM TELL.

But this passage is so well known that it will probably be more interesting to give another and perhaps even finer example by the greatest master of instrumentation that ever lived, Richard Wagner. It will be seen that the melody is played by a Solo 'Cello, and each part of the accompaniment is doubled.

EXTRACT FROM "DIE WALKÜRE."

R. Wagner.

Méhul in his overture to " Joseph," and Cherubini in his operas and masses have sometimes made use of 4 Violoncellos ; the works of Berlioz and R. Wagner also show numerous examples of this kind.

The Violoncello is a beautiful Solo-instrument, especially well-adapted for pathetic scenes, as in the celebrated Duett of the 4th Act in "The Huguenots," where it is used to answer the voices of the two lovers, in an echo-like manner.

EXTRACT FROM THE OPERA "THE HUGUENOTS."

MEYERBEER.

Melodies of a broad and sustained character are better adapted to the Cello than light and trifling ones ; nevertheless the Violoncello possesses flexibility of expression to such an extent as to make it applicable to nearly any variety of musical composition. In Zerlina's Aria " batti, batti, o bel Masetto" ("Don Juan"), Mozart has written a beautiful and expressive solo for the Violoncello. Sustained passages and melodies are sometimes executed together with the Violas, which adds volume and strength to the tonal-quality of the Violoncellos. An excellent effect is produced by the graceful Cello-part in the " Air de Ballet " (" Scènes pittoresques " for orchestra) by the eminent French composer, Jules Massenet.

EXTRACT FROM "SCENES PITTORESQUES."

JULES MASSENET.

The following example presents a cadenza, kindly offered for use in this work by an excellent European Violoncellist (H. Holzmann). With its aid an idea may be formed as to the manner of writing an effective solo-part for this instrument.

H. HOLZMANN.

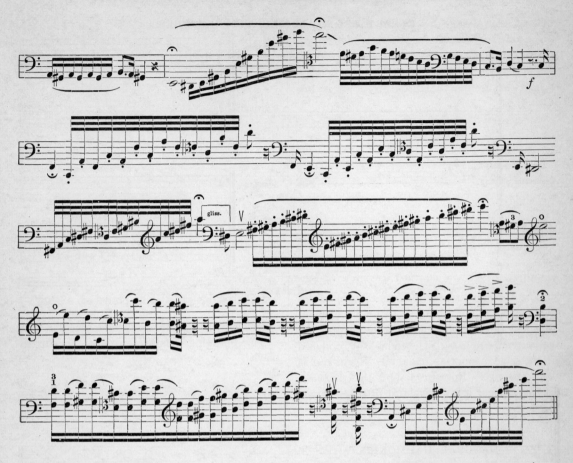

The most Effective Keys, both for orchestral and solo use, are those with few sharps or flats, and where the open strings, which sound exceedingly full and brilliant, can be frequently used.

The Violoncello as used in Dance-Music. Usually a part is written for it together with the Double-bass; but it is of frequent occurrence, that it assists in doubling the melody or some accompanying melody or prominent figure; for instance, pizzicato is assigned to it; the latter produces an excellent effect, especially in a waltz:

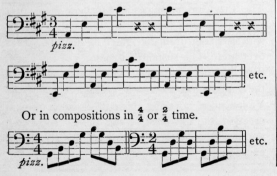

Or in compositions in $\frac{4}{4}$ or $\frac{2}{4}$ time.

The special tonal-character or timbre of each string of the Violoncello may be described as follows: the 4th string serious, the 3rd of clearer quality, the 2nd responsive, vibrating, and the 1st very expressive, especially in the higher positions.

6. THE DOUBLE-BASS.

| BASSGEIGE | { CONTRA-BASSO | } CONTREBASSE. |
| KONTRABASS | { CONTRA-VIOLONE | |

Music for the Double-bass is written in the F-clef and its strings are tuned in the following manner:

But these notes sound an octave lower than they are written.

Double-basses with three strings are tuned in the following manner:

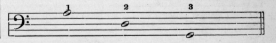

For Solo-playing the Double-Bass is sometimes tuned in a different manner. Beethoven, Cherubini, R. Wagner and others, have written Bass-parts for some of their works which make it necessary to tune the 4th string down to low C or C ♯.*

Tonal-Compass for Orchestral playing.

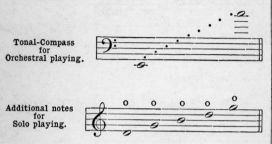

Additional notes for Solo playing.

The bowings are the same as those used for the Violin and are treated in the same manner. The trill can be executed upon any note of the entire tonal-compass. The tremolo is produced in the same manner as upon the Violin, and is very effective. Notwithstanding the thickness of the strings, it is possible to produce harmonics.

NATURAL HARMONICS.

Sounds:

E String.

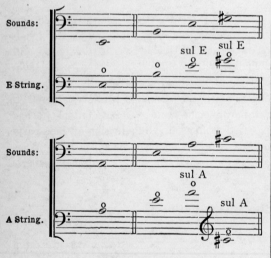

Sounds:

A String.

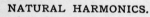

Sounds:

D String.

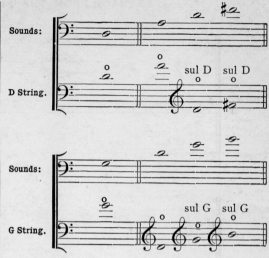

Sounds:

G String.

Double-stops can also be produced.

Double-Stops with two and three notes.

The following examples are not difficult to play:

The Sordino is also used for the Double-bass. The Pizzicato produces an excellent effect, providing it is used judiciously ; Weber has used it with excellent dramatic effect in his Freischütz overture. The sustained low notes of the Clarinets together with the convulsive trembling of the Violins and Violas, the pathetic voice of the Violoncellos, hovering above this gloomy musical creation, the Pizzicato of the Basses, supported and doubled by the Timpani, all this creates an exceedingly impressive effect.

* Mr. Carl Otho, a member of the Leipzic Gewandhaus orchestra, has invented an appliance for the Double-bass, which makes it possible to produce the Contra C upon the instrument ; with its aid the intentions of composers in this special direction can be satisfactorily fulfilled without necessitating the re-tuning of the instrument by the player. He has simply added a fifth string to the Double-bass and the result has been a very successful one. Hans von Bülow made use of these 5 stringed Double-Basses in his cycles of Beethoven concerts.

EXTRACT FROM THE FREISCHÜTZ OVERTURE.

C. M. von Weber.

Easy skips are shown in the following examples :

Sometimes the Bass-parts are sub-divided into 2, 3, and 4 independent parts, but as the tonal-character of the Double-bass is so very low and voluminous, I would suggest not to use a sub-division of this kind too frequently, as the real effect which the composer achieves therewith will hardly come up to the expectations he has pictured to himself. Sub-division of Bass-parts in this manner has been made use of by Wagner, Berlioz, Liszt, Meyerbeer and many others.

EXTRACT FROM THE OPERA "THE PROPHET."

Meyerbeer.

For their symphonies, Haydn, Mozart and Beethoven have oft-times written very interesting and prominent Bass-parts, necessitating excellent players.

Considered as a Solo-instrument, the Double-bass is also capable of shining to advantage, as well as the Viola or the Violoncello. I have heard the celebrated Double-bass soloist, Bottesini, perform the most complicated solos and concertos in a most effective manner. Verdi in one of his latest operas ("Othello") has entrusted a noble, majestic solo to the Double-bass, which when executed unisono by all the Basses of the orchestra produces an exceedingly impressive effect.

EXTRACT FROM VERDI'S OPERA "OTHELLO."

The following composition might be mentioned as a very effective solo for the Double-bass: Variations on a Tyrolean Song by Eisengräber.

Used in Dance-Music the Double-bass usually executes the first beat of each measure.

THE STRINGED INSTRUMENTS COMBINED.

COMPARATIVE TABLE OF THE TONAL-COMPASS OF ALL THE STRINGED INSTRUMENTS.

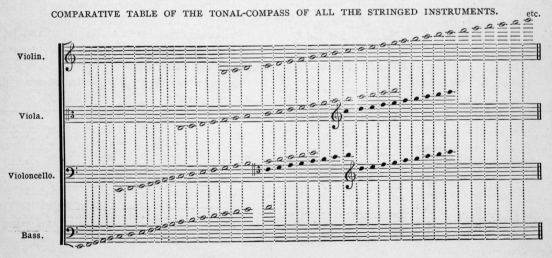

Various effects of a mysterious nature can be produced upon these instruments with the help of Mutes (Sordinos). Nothing more beautiful can be imagined than a well-written Adagio performed with Mutes.

EXTRACT FROM THE OVERTURE TO "EURYANTHE."

C. M. von WEBER.

For additional examples of this class we call attention to the remarkable Entre-acte from C. Reinecke's "Manfred" and the "Adagietto" from G. Bizet's orchestral suite "Arlésienne." A sustained melody performed by the 1st Violin without Mute and accompanied by a muted 2nd Violin, Viola and Violoncello is very effective. The muted String-quartette together with several wind-instruments like the Flute, Clarinet, Horn and Bassoon, makes up a very fine combination. The Introduction to Weber's "Oberon" overture presents an example of this kind. Pizzicato is used to imitate the Harp in serenades, prayers, etc. For dramatic and mysterious scenes a very characteristic effect is produced, by letting the Violoncellos and Double-Basses execute melodious pizzicato passages; they will sound especially well in the Minor Keys.

In scoring pizzicato movements it is of frequent occurrence to introduce certain notes, special motives or parts of bars to be played with the bow, in order to heighten the intensity of tonal-coloring:

Nothing more original and effective can be conceived than an Adagio performed by the 1st Violin, the accompaniment consisting of arpeggio-like passages for the 2nd, sustained notes for the Viola and pizzicato in the Basses. Pizzicato used for all the Stringed Instruments simultaneously produces the effect of a large Guitar; if executed very pianissimo the effect is a very charming and graceful one. For an excellent example see "Chanson d'Amour" (Love song) for String-quartette by Taubert, as well as the following example from "Sylvia, Orchestral suite" by Léo Delibes.

EXTRACT FROM SYLVIA. BALLET. SUITE D'ORCHESTRE.

LEO DELIBES.

EXTRACT FROM RHEINGOLD. FOURTH SCENE.

R. WAGNER.

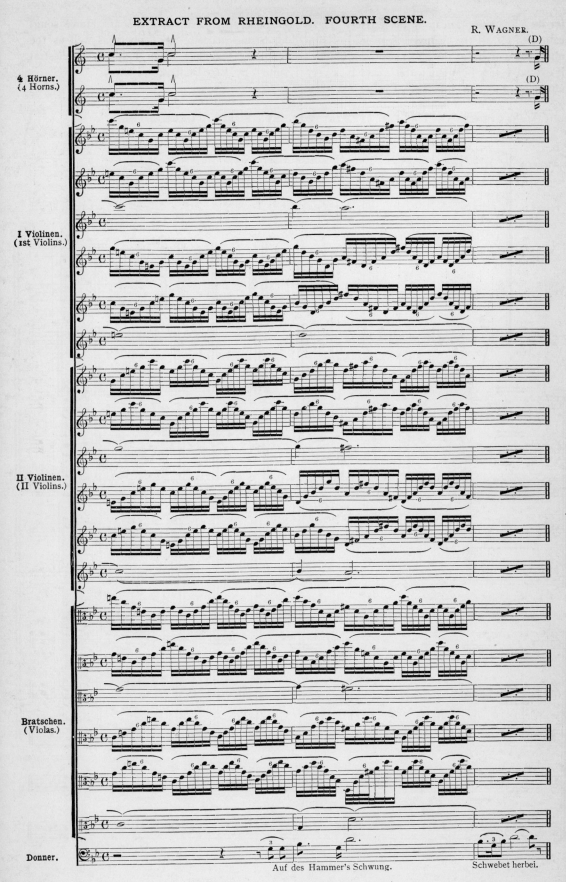

Auf des Hammer's Schwung. Schwebet herbei.

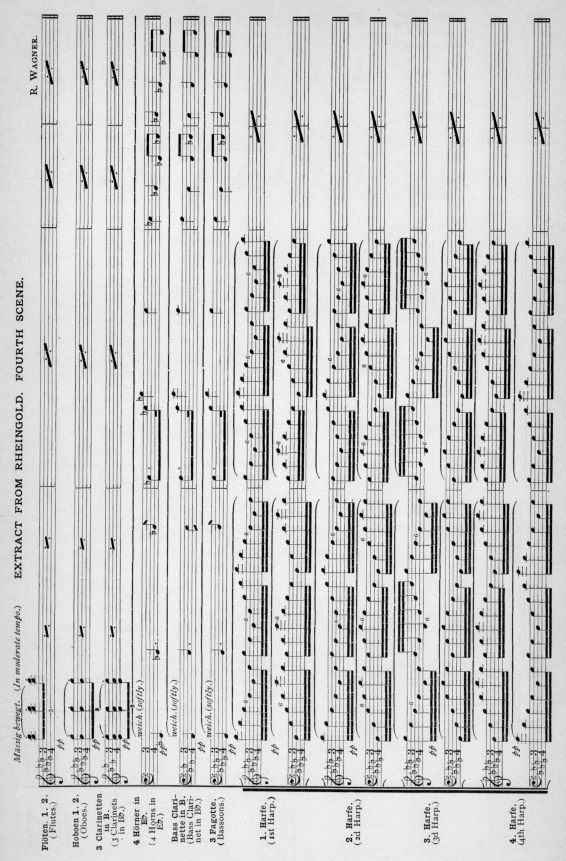

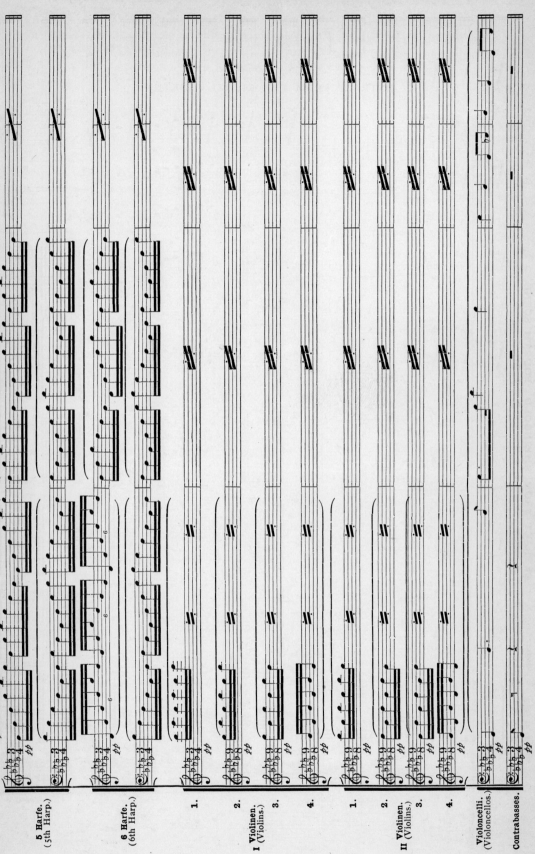

5 Harfe. (5th Harp.)   **6 Harfe.** (6th Harp.)   **1.**   **2.** I **Violinen.** (Violins.)   **3.**   **4.**   **1.**   **2.** II **Violinen.** (Violins.)   **3.**   **4.**   **Violoncelli.** (Violoncellos.)   **Contrabasses.**

The church organ can be excellently imitated by the Stringed Instruments by means of strong drawn or vigorously sustained notes. R. Wagner produced a surprising effect with the *Unisono'* passages of the Violins and Violas in his "Rienzi" overture, as shown below:

EXTRACT FROM THE RIENZI OVERTURE.

RICHARD WAGNER.

If the bow is applied near the bridge with extra pressure (*sul ponticello*) a rough and somewhat unsympathetic tone is produced; nevertheless this effect can be used to good advantage in dramatic scenes descriptive of terror and fear. If the strings are struck with the stick of the bow instead of the hair, a very dry but noisy and unmusical tone is produced. Boïeldieu, Adam and Meyerbeer (the latter in " L'Africaine ") have used it, but the effect is very disagreeable.

Arpeggios for all the Stringed Instruments would create an extraordinary and extremely grand effect if used in the appropriate place; according to my knowledge the possibilities of such arpeggios have not been made use of to their fullest extent, by any composer. An important example of the Arpeggio as employed in modern orchestral scoring may be found in the love-song of Siegmund in R. Wagner's "Walküre " (Arpeggios of the Violas); and in the arpeggio passages for Violins and Violas as employed by R. Wagner in the 4th scene of his "Rheingold." See Score example on page 31.

With the exception of Berlioz (as shown in the following extract from his " Romeo and Juliet ") and R. Wagner, only a few composers have tried to make use of Harmonics for the entire String-quintette, and wherever they have been made use of, they have been written chiefly for the 1st Violins and sometimes for the Violoncellos.

EXTRACT FROM ROMEO ET JULIETTE.

HECTOR BERLIOZ.

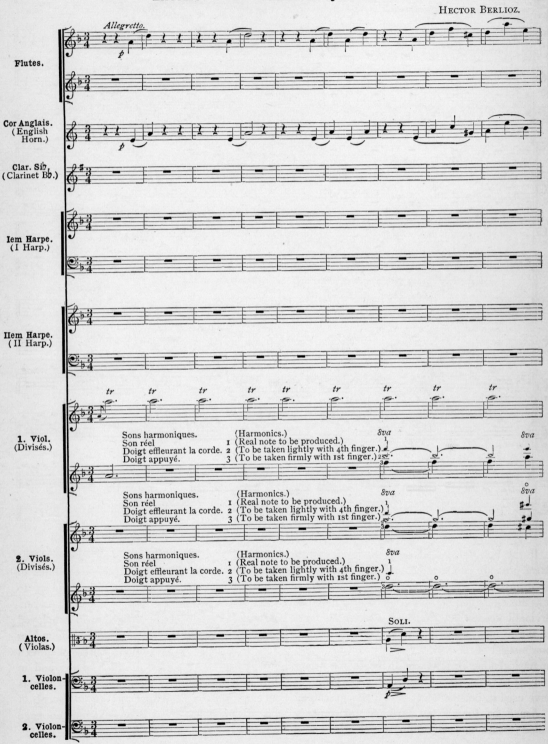

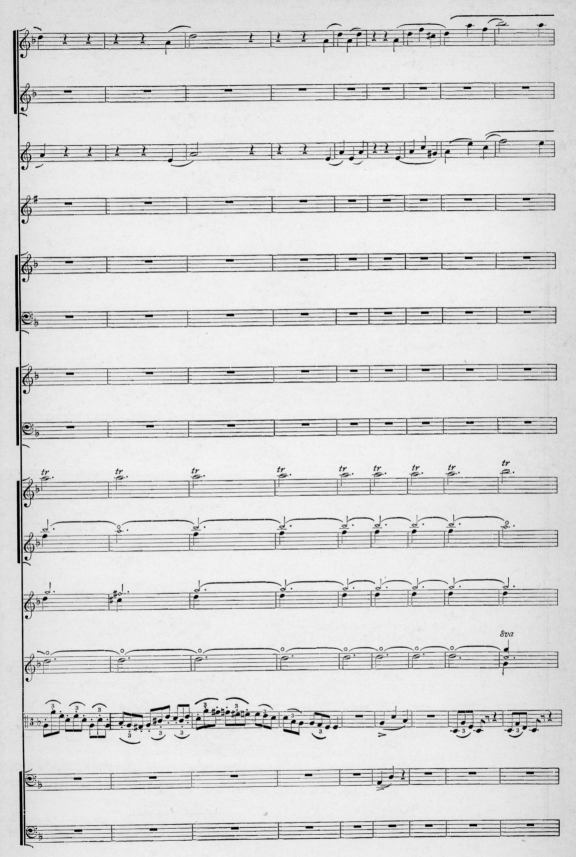

This particular branch, which has been entirely neglected till now, should be thoroughly studied and mastered by every composer, as in my estimation a variety of effects will be obtained and produced by means of this material in the future, which are entirely unknown at the present time of writing. In the following example I have added a little movement of my own composition written entirely in Harmonics for all the Stringed Instruments.

HEAVENLY DREAM.
For Stringed Instruments.

H. KLING.

Still other effects are possible, brought about by the combination of the Viola d'Amour with muted String-quartette or Viola d'Amour in connection with Flutes, Clarinets and Horns, admirably descriptive of love-scenes as well as for picturing the beauty and serenity of a moon-lit summer's eve, etc.

Division and sub-division of the Violin parts must be well understood and correctly applied. The student's attention is especially directed to the works of R. Wagner, in which abundant material for studying this particular branch can be found; for instance, the wonderful Introduction (Vorspiel) to "Lohengrin," the overture to "Tannhäuser," etc. The Tremolo adapts itself exceedingly well to all kinds of situations, but should not be used to excess. A fine example of this kind is found in the 1st Act of "Lohengrin," where in one particular instance the tremolo of the strings together with the Harp, the Flutes, Oboes, English Horn, Bass Clarinet and Trumpets produces a beautifully clear effect. Another variety of tremolo, the effect of which is even more striking than in the above named example, will be found in the 3d Act of "Tristan and Isolde," as well as in the overture to "Tannhäuser" by R. Wagner.

EXTRACT FROM THE "TANNHÄUSER OVERTURE."

R. WAGNER.

A grand and magnificent effect is produced if the entire String-quintette plays a *unisono* passage with strong and weighty bowings while the other instruments and the chorus execute the melody and accompaniment. An imposing ensemble of this kind is offered in the first Act of "Lohengrin," as well as in the celebrated "Tannhäuser" March. To be convinced of the great diversity possible in the treatment of Stringed Instruments a look must be taken at the Grand Duett in the 2nd Act of "Tristan and Isolde." In this wonderful creation R. Wagner has displayed and unfolded every conceivable grade of tonal-coloring and delicate shading possible in the Art of Instrumentation.

DIRECTIONS AS TO SCORING FOR STRINGED INSTRUMENTS.

The most highly developed tonal-body of the orchestra is formed by the Stringed Instruments; their capacity for tonal-shading is unlimited, and no other instruments can be compared with them in this particular respect. They lead and control the entire orchestra, their influence manifesting itself everywhere. It is therefore especially necessary for the student who wishes to score correctly, to begin by acquainting himself with the treatment of the Stringed Instruments. The best proceeding with which to acquire the knowledge necessary therefor is probably the one I used in my own case, and which consisted in taking the separate parts of a String-quartette by either Mozart, Haydn, Beethoven or Mendelssohn and scoring them. By entering each part separately in this manner, the student will identify himself with the ideas of the composer; following the thematic development and manifold transformations of the theme will prove interesting, besides showing the methods employed by the author in bringing them about and the manner in which he distributes his ideas among the four instruments, awakening scores of different sensations in the souls of his listeners.

Besides this it is necessary to make a practice of arranging piano sonaten by Mozart and Beethoven for String-quartette and having the arrangements played by several good players. As it is highly necessary for the student to hear his own efforts in the course of studying the art of instrumentation, frequent performances of this kind will present the opportunity of judging his work from a practical standpoint, improving weak or ineffectual parts, while offering additional advantages in the shape of personal criticism and advice from the assisting players. After this a start should be made in writing Duetts for 2 Violins or Violin and Viola, Violin and Violoncello, Violoncello and Double-bass, etc. Following this Trios for 2 Violins and Viola; Violin, Viola and Violoncello; Viola, Violoncello and Double-bass, etc., should be taken up. The writing of Duetts for Piano and any one of the Stringed Instruments, as well as Trios for Piano and two Stringed Instruments, should also be taken up and practised. After this Quartettes, Quintettes, Sextettes, Septettes, Octettes, etc., for Stringed Instruments alone or with Piano, should be taken up.

Haydn, Mozart, Beethoven, Mendelssohn, Schubert, Schumann, Brahms, Spohr, Veit, Rubinstein, Volkmann and many others have provided us with immortal works of this class, and it is very advisable to consult them as often as possible. In the following example I desire to offer some advice in regard to arranging Piano Sonaten for Stringed Instruments; industrious practice in arrangements of this kind is indispensable.

SONATE.

ARRANGEMENT OF THE FOREGOING ANDANTE AND FIRST VARIATION FOR STRING QUINTET.

[For complete arrangement see Addenda, page 315.]

The student should continue arranging the remaining Variations of the above sonata in the manner as indicated, taking care to maintain the independent development of each part together with a well-calculated, good-sounding and effective ensemble. After this the arrangement of other Sonaten by Mozart, Beethoven and Haydn should be taken up.

The String-Quintette as used in Dance-music.

Dance-music is usually arranged in such a manner, that it can be effectively performed by the smallest combination of instruments. It is therefore necessary to write both the melody and complete accompaniment for the String Quintette.

In scoring for this class of music it is necessary to write the Cello part in such a manner as to be readily omitted, this instrument in most cases being only included in larger and better equipped orchestras. This applies especially to such works intended for general and popular use, as shown in the following example:

CONCERT POLKA.

E. WIEGAND.

But in scoring for better equipped or complete orchestras no restraint need be placed upon our imagination in this direction and the String-Quintette should be subordinated to such an extent as to allow the Wood-wind and Brass instruments to appear to equal advantage. See the following example:

LE MURMURE DES FEUILLES.

Waltz.

J. BLANCHERAU.

The first Violin is treated and recognized as the leader of the melody, while the second Violin and Viola execute the regular accompanying figures of the dances. As these figures constitute both the accompaniment and harmony of this class of music, the parts of these instruments must be well supplied with double stops (with frequent use of the open strings), in order that the complete harmony be contained in a combination of 5, 6 or 7 instruments or smaller orchestras in general. The middle register is most frequently used in these successive chords and oft repeated accompanying figures, necessitating only the use of the G and D string of the Violin and Viola, but at times also the A string of the former and the C string of the latter.

The Violoncello may be treated in a variety of ways: it can be employed to assist the Double-bass; it may execute an extra melody or figure of accompaniment or strengthen the principal melody; for instance, if the 1st Violin is playing in the lower register, the Violoncello-part may be written *unisono* with it, in order to give prominence to the melody. But on the other hand the Cello-part, as already mentioned, is usually written in such a manner as to be readily omitted in smaller combinations.

The part of the Double-bass consists in the execution of single fundamental notes, as guardian of the rhythm so to say; in nearly every instance it merely marks the heavy beats and is especially used to execute the first note in each bar. Nevertheless little melodic passages may be entrusted to it, as well as the melody of an entire part, chiefly in forte-passages.

B. Instruments, the Strings of Which are Plucked by the Fingers.

1. THE HARP.

(HARFE, ARPA, HARPE.)

This poetic instrument is included in nearly all modern scores. Music for it is written on two staves in the Treble and Bass clef in the same manner as for the Pianoforte.

Trills should be dispensed with as much as possible, excepting for Concert or Solo compositions, owing to their difficulty; a poorly executed trill invariably produces a bad and marring effect.

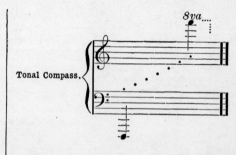

Used in the orchestra, the Harp will sound to best advantage in passage-work, arpeggios and full heavy chords.

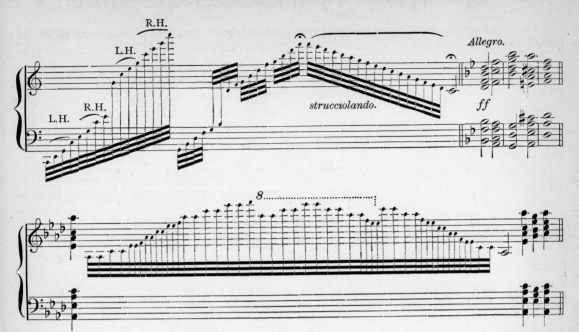

EXTRACT FROM "LA DAME BLANCHE."

BOIELDIEU.

The diatonic scale can be executed but is very difficult; the chromatic should be entirely dispensed with. Modulation upon the Harp is brought about in exactly the same manner as in compositions for the Pianoforte, but care must be taken to avoid a too frequent change of Keys, as this invariably requires an excellent Harpist, proficient in the use of both pedals and chords. As a general rule Harp-parts should not be written in too complicated a manner.

Harmonics are best applied and used in the following positions:

Scales in harmonics are seldom or hardly ever used, but successive thirds or triads are frequently employed.

Of course all Keys can be produced; the easiest playable Keys are F, B♭, E♭, A♭, D♭, C, D, G, and E major; the best sounding Keys A♭, D♭, and G♭ major.

Modern masters, like Marschner, Rossini, Meyerbeer, Halévy, Berlioz, Wagner, Gounod, Massenet, Saint-Saëns, Ambr. Thomas, Donizetti, Verdi, etc., have all produced beautiful effects with the aid of the Harp.

The effect of several Harps playing in unison or executing different parts, as shown in the following example, is very imposing.

The tone of the Harp blends very well with the French-Horn; when accompanying the human voice it sounds especially effective and beautiful.

In the Finale to the 3d act of his opera "The Prophet," Meyerbeer has produced a magnificent effect by accompanying the singing of the Prophet by 4 Harps.

EXTRACT FROM THE OPERA "THE PROPHET."

Rossini in the first act of "Tell," Richard Wagner in "Tannhäuser," Verdi in "Il Trovatore," V. Massé in "Galathée," etc., have written complete vocal numbers accompanied solely by a Harp with equal success as Meyerbeer.

The Harp adapts itself excellently to the portrayal of fantastic scenes, prayers, serenades and for poetic, ideal, elegiac and religious situations in general. The tone of the lower strings is very sonorous and they possess a well-rounded and sympathetic quality. In the higher registers the Harp-tones are very clear and fine.

Considered as a *Solo Instrument*, the Harp may be used as successfully as the Violin or Piano, either with accompaniment of a few stringed instruments, or of the entire orchestra. In the latter case the score must be arranged in such a manner as to allow the Harp to appear to best advantage and not be crushed by the mass of accompanying instruments. To form a correct idea of writing an effective solo-part for the Harp I add two fragments from the works of C. Oberthür, well-known as an excellent performer and composer:

LORELEY.
Legende.

CH. OBERTHÜR, Op. 180.

EXTRACT FROM "DIE MEISTERSINGER VON NÜRNBERG."

RICHARD WAGNER.

lag; aus ihren Au - - gen Won - ne saugen Verlan - gen einz'ger Macht in mir nur wacht.

EXTRACT FROM A CONCERTINO FOR THE HARP.

CH. OBERTHÜR Op. 175.

A very poetic effect is produced by H. Ritter, through the use of the so-called "Bisbigliando" (this term is used in connection with so-called synonymous notes or passages as shown in the following example, indicating that a rustling or whispering effect is to be produced).

EXTRACT FROM THE ANDANTE OF A CONCERTO

For Viola alta with orchestral accompaniment.

HERMANN RITTER, Op. 35.

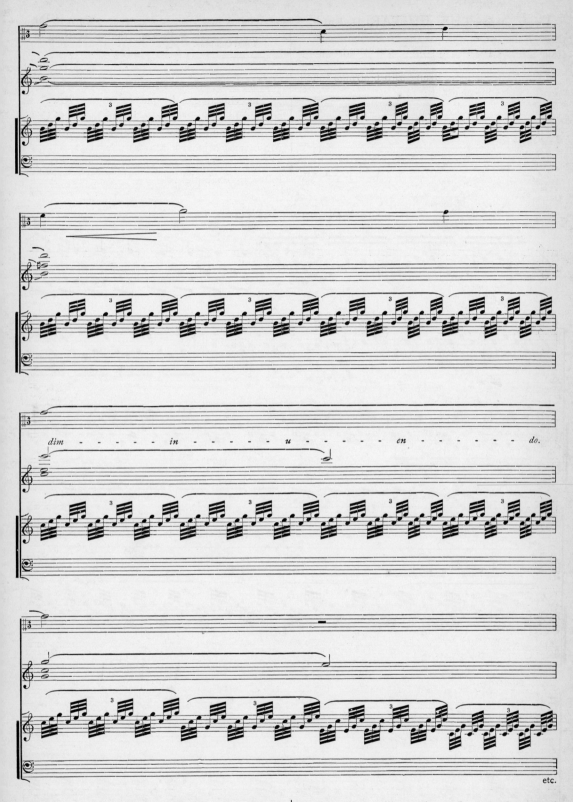

etc.

Before closing we might mention the "Steel Harp," used by Richard Wagner in his opera "The Meistersinger of Nüremberg," as a characteristic illustration of "Beckmesser." The tone of this peculiar instrument is reported as sounding very unmusical.

2. THE GUITAR.

(GUITARRE, CHITARA, GUITARE.)

This instrument is strung with 6 strings tuned in the following manner :

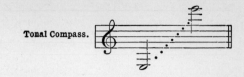

Tonal Compass.

The Guitar can be played in any Key. It sounds to best advantage in the Keys of C, G, D Major and Minor, A Major and Minor, E Major and Minor, F Major.

Easy Arpeggios and Chords are shown in the following examples :

Easy Arpeggios and Broken Chords.

etc.

Easy Chords: also playable in a broken or arpeggio-like manner.

Moderato.

In his opera " The Barber of Seville," Rossini has introduced it into the orchestra and entrusted the accompaniment of Count Almaviva's Aria to it.

EXTRACT FROM "THE BARBER OF SEVILLA."

ROSSINI.

Conradin Kreutzer, in his beautiful opera, " A Night in Granada," has used it in the same manner for accompanying the Moorish Romanza in the 2nd Act.

3. THE MANDOLIN.

(MANDOLINE, MANDOLA, MANDOLINE.)

This instrument is strung with 8 strings. They are tuned in perfect fifths in the same manner as the Violin, two of each being tuned in unison.

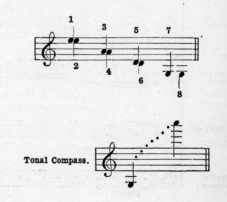

Tonal Compass.

Practical Double-stops and Arpeggios are shown in the following examples:

Double-stops with 2, 3, and 4 notes.

etc.

Arpeggios.

The best and most effective Keys are: C, G, D, A, and E Major.

The Mandolin adapts itself excellently to accompanying the voice. It is the favorite instrument for the interpretation of Serenades.

Grétry in his opera "The Two Misers," and Mozart in his "Don Juan," have written very effective solo "obligato parts" for the Mandolin. See the following example:

ROMANZA FROM "DON JUAN."

Serenade.

W. A. MOZART.

nes - tra,   o mio . . . . te so - ro!   Deh vie - ni con - so - lar   il

In modern orchestras Guitar and Mandolin parts are very often interpreted by the pizzicato of a solo Violin; but through a substitution of this kind, the principal effect intended by such composers as Grétry, Mozart and Rossini, *local-color*, so very essential for graphic dramatic portrayal, is entirely lost.

4. THE ZITHER.

(ZITHER, CYTHARE, CYTHARE.)

During the last twenty years this instrument has been gradually advanced into an entirely new sphere, brought about principally by the fixed and practical stringing agreed upon at the Musical Congresses of 1877 and 1878, transforming it into quite a perfect musical instrument.

The modern 29 Stringed Zither is tuned and its music written in the following manner:

Finger board or Melody Strings.

Accompaniment Strings.

Bass Strings.

the Accompanying and Bass strings sounding an octave lower than they are really written. Some composers write the accompaniment and bass in the Bass-clef, in accordance with their true pitch; but if we take into consideration that in the first place, the Zither is principally an instrument for amateurs, and secondly that the use of the Bass-clef would necessitate writing the notes mostly above the staff, the notation in the Violin-clef with lower sounding notes is really the most practical. (The use of the Tenor-clef would also be difficult to apply for various reasons.)

The two A strings (serving to facilitate passages in thirds in the higher positions) are made of steel, the next one (D) is made of brass or German silver, and the G and C of covered brass; the accompaniment strings are partly made of gut and partly, like all the bass strings, from covered silk.

Instead of the first finger-board string (A), some Zithers are provided with an additional E string made of steel; being very thin this string possesses a disagreeable quality of tone; again many others are supplied with several additional bass strings, placed in succession after the regular bass strings and erringly designated as Contra-bass strings.

Compositions for the Zither are written upon two staves, the upper one for the left hand (finger-board) principally for notation of the melody, the other for the right hand (notation of the accompaniment and basses).

The tonal-compass of the Zither is:

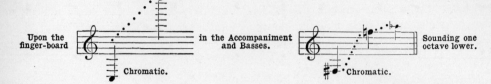

Upon the finger-board   in the Accompaniment and Basses.   Sounding one octave lower.

Chromatic.   Chromatic.

Total compass of the 40 stringed Zither, with additional so-called Contra-basses:

Real Sound.

Chromatic.

somewhat over 5 octaves. All the Contrabasses are not added together, but 3, 4, 5 or 10 *ad libitum* as indicated at the beginning of a composition, necessitating their being retuned before starting.

The strings of the finger-board are set in vibration with the thumb of the right hand, which is supplied with a plectrum for producing a better and clearer tone; the notes upon the fretted finger-board are produced with the four fingers of the left hand (beginning with the thumb) for which, as may be imagined, there are definite rules for fingering. The remaining three fingers of the right hand are employed in executing the regularly repeated major-chords of the accompaniment, the 4th finger always taking the Tonic as bass, the 3d the third, and the 2nd the fifth and higher tonic simultaneously. Both the little fingers are not used.

This style of accompaniment is most frequently used, but imparts an extremely monotonous character to the playing, besides giving rise to false or inharmonic relations.

Only lately compositions are being introduced, adopting a more unrestrained and freer style of accompaniment. Now-a-days chromatic and diatonic passages, as well as runs in thirds and movements in contrary motion, may be introduced providing the tempo be a moderate one. In the same manner the basses have gradually abandoned their former stiffness of character and every variety of progression may be employed, providing, as already mentioned, the tempo is slow enough; this latter provision is extremely important, as allowance must be made not alone for producing the following bass but also for damping or stopping the vibrations of the foregoing one, without which the most disagreeable harmonies would be produced.

But the finger-board is entirely free from any restraint of this kind; every degree of technical execution being possible and only dependent upon an agile and flexible thumb of the player. But in a classical treatment of this instrument, its peculiar idyllic-elegiac tonal character, which strictly limits its possibilities, must never be lost sight of. It is absolutely beyond the powers of the Zither to show to advantage by means of quick passages or brilliant variations; its expressive nature will not admit of any brilliant, boisterous, earnest or dramatic music; on the other hand its sympathetic tonal character is capable of every possible degree of naïve, sad, melancholy, foreboding musical expressiveness (Chorales are very effective). The original tone of the Zither can be varied in many ways by striking the strings at different points, making it possible to reproduce a variety of characteristic sounds, similar to many orchestral instruments, ranging from the sharp tone of the Oboe to the round soft tone of the Horn. The pizzicato as produced upon a Violin can also be imitated.

The Zither has been introduced into the orchestra by Lumbye ("Traumbilder fantasie") Strauss ("Stories from the Vienna Woods") and later on very frequently by Grasmann, but in connection with the orchestra it must be treated absolutely as a solo-instrument and will bear only a light, airy and muted accompaniment. How to write in a correct and artistic manner for the Zither may be learned from the older compositions of Burgstaller, Rudigier, Darr, and from the more modern ones of Kretschmar, Graeter and others. An excellent school has been written by A. Darr.

Special Remarks as to Accompaniments. The Ländler as the genuine type of Zither music possesses the characteristic accompaniment peculiar to the Zither; the bass continually consisting of tonic and dominant (very seldom the lower dominant), followed up (in a Major Key) by the middle parts executing the complete major triad, but omitting the minor third in the minor triads, being difficult to perform. See following example:

A more animated style of accompaniment is already illustrated in the next example:

as well as in the following more difficult example:

Modulations as shown in the following example are possible but quite difficult, and do not sound to advantage if executed in quick tempo.

In the following examples, a, b, and c, illustrations are given of difficult but effective compositions for the Zither :

EXTRACTS FROM "THE LORELY."

Paraphrase by F. GRAETER.

Harmonics, both natural and artistic, can all be produced upon the Zither; the latter are very difficult and are employed and used only by Virtuosi. The natural harmonics are written as they sound without the additional supporting note. For instance :

The supporting note (in the form of a half-note) is added to the artistic (chromatic) harmonics. For instance :

In order to avoid the difficulties encountered in the execution of artistic harmonics, it is advisable in compositions of an easy grade to write them in the key of F or D major (or their parallel keys) and then have the first "A" string tuned to F or F sharp, as may be necessary; the advantages of such a proceeding will be, that the natural harmonics of both the tonic and dominant will then be at the writer's disposal. An illustration is shown in the following example :

THE MONASTERY BELLS.

Especially arranged for Zither.

LEFÉBURE-WÉLY.

Different Varieties of Zithers.

1. *The Elegie* or *Basszither* has a longer body, in some cases extending to as much as 1½ times the length of the ordinary Zither. It serves both as a solo-instrument for compositions of a pathetic and elegiac nature and as an accompanying Zither to the ordinary instrument. It is tuned a fourth lower than the Prim (ordinary) Zither.

2. *The Bow-Zither.* This instrument is strung with only 4 strings, tuned either like the Violin or Viola. Similar to the Violin, its strings are set in vibration by means of a bow, but its fingerboard is fretted like a Zither's, and the instrument is played while resting upon a table, this usage probably justifying its being designated as a Zither.

A different variety of the Bow-Zither is known by the name of *Bow-melodion;* but its tone and manner of playing is identical with that of the above instrument. In some respects its tone is similar to that of the Viola d'amour minus that instrument's sweetness, and possessing a peculiar thin and nasal quality of tone.

Its music is written like that for the Violin, but its technique and execution is in no way as extended and developed as that instrument's; it is usually accompanied by 1 or 2 Zithers.

The Banjo.

The Banjo, originally a favorite instrument of the American negroes, who brought it with them from Africa, might be described as a kind of Guitar with a long neck. The sounding-body, composed of a ring, covered with a skin, is somewhat similar to a drum.

The ordinary Banjo, as used at present is usually strung with five strings and tuned in the following style:

The strings of the six-stringed Banjo are tuned in the following way:

The tonal-compass is:

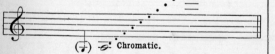

but the best-sounding position is the following:

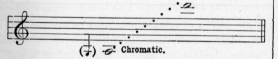

The Banjo can be played in all Keys. Those in which it sounds to best advantage are: C major, A minor, G major, E minor, D major, B minor, F major, D minor, B flat major, and G minor.

Easy Arpeggios and Chords are shown in the following examples:

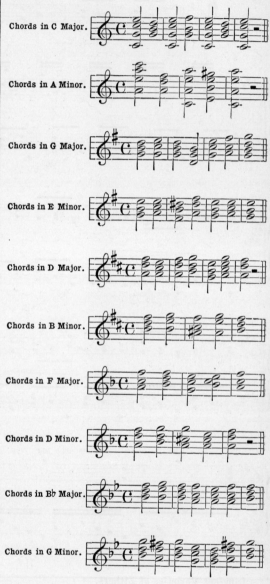

These chords can also be used and executed in arpeggio-like manner as shown in the following example:

The Banjo, possessing a soft and mild tonal-character, is especially well adapted as an accompanist to the voice, as well as for the interpretation of songs, dance-tunes, etc.

HOME, SWEET HOME.

Especially arranged for 6 stringed Banjo.

If the Banjo is to be played with accompaniment of other instruments, such accompaniment must be written very lightly and *con sordini.*

The American Banjo as played at the present time is strung with five strings and tuned in the following manner:—

C. Instruments, the Strings of Which are Struck by Means of Keys or with Hammers.

1. The Pianoforte.

(KLAVIER, PIANOFORTE, PIANO.)

Although the Pianoforte is such a well-known instrument, I believe it necessary to submit it to a detailed discussion, especially as it commands such a prominent position in musical paedagogics. The Piano is an instrument possessed of unlimited musical resources; beneath the fingers of an accomplished artist, difficulties of every conceivable variety and grade are possible; it adapts itself to every form of musical composition, blends admirably with every instrument, as well as with the human voice. Taken independently it represents a little orchestra in itself, which accounts for every variety of vocal and instrumental composition being arranged for it, and which in turn has rendered the works of the great masters accessible to all.

It takes a leading position as a Solo-instrument, and such classic masters as Mozart, Beethoven, Weber, Mendelssohn, Schumann, etc., have demonstrated in their special works for the Piano alone or with accompaniment of several String or Wind instruments or with complete orchestra, what beautiful and manifold effects may be produced upon it.

Sometimes the Piano is made use of in the orchestra as a substitute for the Harp; but the effect is anything but the same. A few composers have made use of the Piano in the orchestra, for instance, Méhul in his comic opera "Une Folie," Donizetti in his opera "The Daughter of the Regiment." As an accompaniment to a chorus of "aerial spirits" (Lelio, Mélodrame Lyrique) Berlioz has introduced two Pianos (each two-handed) for producing a harmonious rippling effect, such as can be brought about upon the Piano without any difficulty and which fittingly illustrates the sylph-like character of the composition. In the following example, an extract from the 3d Symphony in C minor by C. Saint-Saëns is presented in which this eminent composer has also made use of the Piano (four-handed) in connection with the Organ and the Stringed Instruments, producing a charming effect.

EXTRACT FROM THE THIRD SYMPHONY IN C MINOR.

CAMILLE SAINT SÄENS, Op. 78.

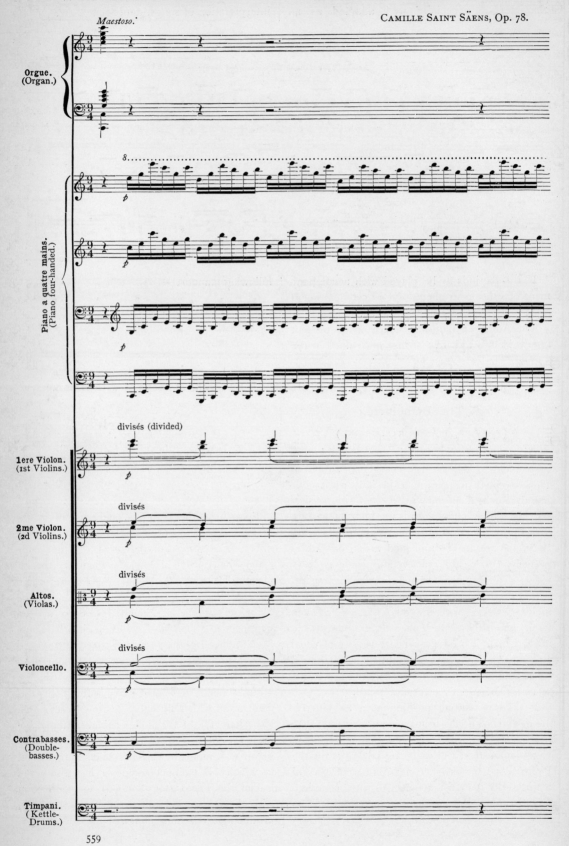

559

The correct use of the pedals is usually left to the discretion of the player, although many composers indicate its use. The following signs are employed for this purpose (Ped. — ⊕). A pedal much less in use than the Damper pedal is the so-called "Shifting pedal," usually indicated by the term "una corda" (in German, "Mit Verschiebung"). As only one tone is set in vibration, through the use of it, the entire tonal-volume of the instrument is lessened by two-thirds, a result which brings about a very noticeable difference of tonal-character. This excellent effect is specially well adapted for use in accompanying the voice or for imbueing a performance with a characteristic touch of delicacy and sincerity.

One reason why this valuable pedal is probably less frequently used than the others might be, that the appliance is not yet attached to all Pianos. As a rule it is only found with the different varieties of Grand or upon expensive Upright Pianos.

Practical Manner of Arranging an Orchestral Score for the Piano.

The idea is to convey the various effects, contained in the score, to the Piano as completely as possible, and in such a manner as to keep within the technical possibilities of the instrument.

This is brought about in the following way:

1. The *melodies* (*or melodious passages*) are usually given to the right hand; the left hand executing the accompaniment in the shape of sustained, broken, or arpeggio-like chords.

EXTRACT FROM THE SEPTETT.

BEETHOVEN.

2. If the score contains one or two voice-parts, and the accompaniment thereto is simple and not complicated, the passages of the Violins and Violas are played by the right hand and the Bass by the left.

EXTRACT FROM "DON JUAN."

Duettino.

MOZART.

3. If the score is complicated, an effort must be made to convey those effects, which can best be reproduced and played upon the **Piano**.

EXTRACT FROM "THE MAGIC FLUTE."

Overture.

MOZART.

4. Sometimes it is impossible to convey dissimilar figures or polyphonic parts simultaneously to both hands. In such cases only the most prominent parts should be selected, which are best adapted to create the most effective general impression.

QUINTETT.

5. Sustained notes, as well as differently formed or oft repeated figures, in sixteenth or thirty-second notes, are best conveyed in the shape of sustained arpeggio-like passages or through the use of the Tremolo.

EXTRACT FROM DON JUAN.

Scores can also be arranged for 4 hands, as well as for 2, 4, 6, or a greater number of Pianos,* according to the fancy or inclination of the composer.†

The achievements in this particular field of arranging orchestral works for the Piano, by such artists as Hummel, and in modern times, Liszt, is well-known. The Piano arrangements of such orchestral works as the Overtures to "Tell" by Rossini, "Egmont" by Beethoven, the Bridal Song from "Lohengrin" by F. Liszt, may be designated as master-works of this particular class.

2. THE DULCIMER.

(CIMBAL OR HACKBRETT, CIMBEL, CIMBALON, CIMBALO OR SALTERIO, TYMPANON.)

A very ancient string instrument, formerly known as the *Psalterium*, and fore runner of the modern Pianoforte.

The Dulcimer consists of a shallow, trapeze formed sounding-box, strung with 49 steel strings, which are struck with 2 hammers (one for each hand). The instrument, which possesses a bright and brilliant sound, is excellently adapted for orchestral use. It is the most indispensable requisite of every Hungarian-Gypsy orchestra.

Its tonal-compass is:

Music for this instrument, as shown in the following examples, is written either in one or two parts, upon one staff or upon two, exactly as for the Piano-forte.

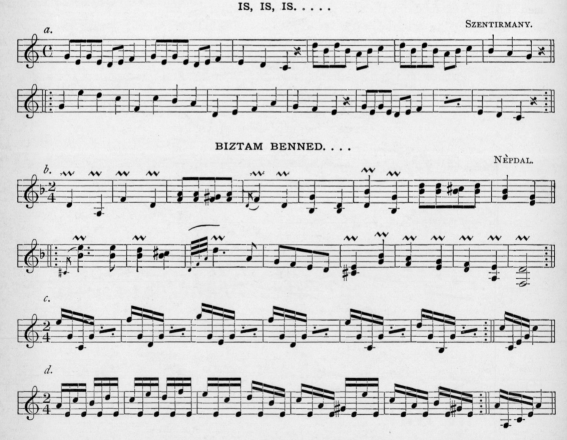

IS, IS, IS. . . . .

SZENTIRMANY.

a.

BIZTAM BENNED. . . .

NÉPDAL.

b.

c.

d.

---

* A Fantasie on the motives of "Ojos criollos," and "Ay! Pimpollo no ne mates," composed for 40 Pianos by Gottschalk, was performed for the first time at a concert given in the Tacon Theatre, Havana, April 17, 1861.

† Now-a-days the study of arranging instrumental or vocal compositions for Piano is greatly facilitated, as the majority of master works of olden and modern times have been published in Piano-score editions, offering any amount of models to the student.

SIR A KIS LÀNY. . . .

All the major and minor, as well as the chromatic scales, can be executed upon the Dulcimer. Likewise the following passages in broken chords can be executed in all Major and Minor Keys, extending over the entire compass of the instrument:

Likewise the Dominant-chords of the Seventh.

as well as chords of the Diminished Seventh, etc.

Of course all Keys are at the command of the player, the easiest and most effective ones being C major, A minor, F major, D minor, G major, E minor, D major, etc., etc.

Group II.

WIND INSTRUMENTS.

A. Wood Wind Instruments.

1. THE PICCOLO.

(KLEINE FLÖTE, PICCOLO FLÖTE, OTTAVINO, PETITE FLÛTE.)

This instrument adapts itself excellently to illustrating the elements of nature, the whistling of the winds, the lightning of the storm, as well as infernal noise. Added to this it is well adapted as an interpreter of joyous moods, martial music, ballets and other compositions with accented rhythms of a sharp, decided nature.

The Piccolo is unusually effective if used Pianissimo.

The notes of the Piccolo sound an octave higher than they are written.

Easy as well as difficult trills are shown in the following examples:

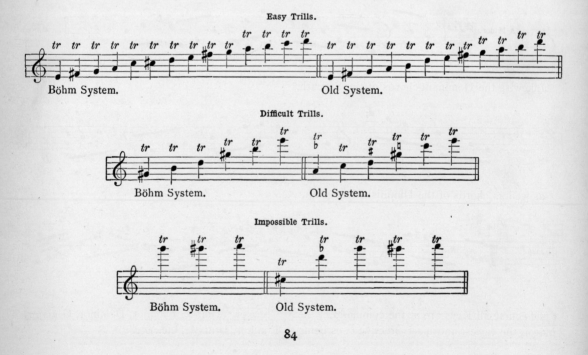

84

Upon the old system B, F sharp, D flat, and G flat major and upon the Böhm system Piccolo B major and G flat major are very difficult to play.

Difficult Passages.

As to broken chords, skips and arpeggios, the following examples should be consulted :

a. Easy Broken Intervals.

Old System, very easy.

b. Difficult Broken Intervals.

a. Easy Skips.

b. Difficult Skips.

a. Easy Arpeggios.

etc.

b. Difficult Arpeggios.

Single, double and triple tongueing as shown in the following examples is not difficult:

The most **Effective Keys** for orchestral use are C, G, D, A, E, F, B flat and E flat major.

The **Tonal-color** of the different registers of the Piccolo might be classified in the following manner:

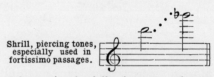

Shrill, piercing tones, especially used in fortissimo passages.

As shown in the following example two Piccolos are sometimes used; employed in this way they are excellently adapted for portraying wild and infernal joy:

Weak Tones.   Brilliant Tones.

EXTRACT FROM "DER FREISCHÜTZ."

WEBER.

In the introduction to Gluck's "Iphigenia in Tauris," the double-trills of the Piccolos create a highly dramatic effect. Meyerbeer has used this instrument to excellent advantage in his opera "Robert le Diable" (Infernal Waltz), its peculiar tonal character adding much to the general effect. In "Marcel's Song" (Act 1 of "Les Huguenots"), Meyerbeer accompanies the voice solely with the Piccolo and Cymbals, as shown in the following extract:

EXTRACT FROM "THE HUGUENOTS."

MEYERBEER.

Mozart, Beethoven, Marschner, Félicien David, Maillart etc., used the Piccolo to excellent advantage and achieved many excellent romantic effects through its employment.

Used in Dance-music the Piccolo usually interprets the melody either in unison with the Flute or an octave higher, although independent melodies or embellishments may be entrusted to it. As a *solo-instrument* the Piccolo is specially adapted to imitating the song of birds. A charming waltz by Jullien, "The Nightingale," and a polka for two Piccolos, "Die Grasmücken" (The White-Throats), by Bousquet might be mentioned as exceedingly brilliant solos.

Of course any number of dance compositions have been written in which the Piccolo is used very prominently, and it will be an easy matter for the student to acquaint himself as to writing in an effective manner for this instrument.

Finally I will add that the Piccolo should not be used too frequently; the high notes in particular prove very tiresome to the listener in a short time owing to their sharp and whistling timbre; its part should therefore be well supplied with pauses.

2. THE FLUTE.

(GROSSE FLÖTE, FLAUTO, FLÛTE.)

This instrument can best be compared to the female voice; but besides its brilliant qualities it is well adapted to express impulsive sorrow, lonely sadness, weakness and intellectual weariness.

The song of the nightingale and all birds in general can be excellently imitated upon the Flute.

Tonal-compass for orchestra and solo use:

rare

As the fingering upon the Flute is identical with that of the Piccolo, everything remarked of the latter as to trills, passages, broken chords, skips, arpeggios and tongueing, applies equally to the Flute.

The tonal-color of the Flute from :

is expressive of a religious character, which if used "piano" produces a very characteristic, ideal and elegiac effect; this register can also be used to express the dreaminess of love or situations of a mysterious, worshiping character.

The notes from :

sound soft and plaintive.

The notes from :

are bright, penetrating and brilliant, and are specially well adapted for vigorous passages.

For compositions which demand no great amount of tonal-volume, usually two and sometimes three Flutes are employed, as illustrated in the following extract from Hayden's "Creation : "

EXTRACT FROM "THE CREATION."

In several instances Meyerbeer has entrusted very important solos to the Flute; this has been especially the case in his opera, "The North-star," in which he has written a trio for voice with accompaniment of two solo Flutes, which is exceedingly effective. The Flute can successfully compete with the most accomplished coloratura singer. In the nightingale-aria of V. Massé's charming opera, "Les Noces de Jeanette," the Flute and voice are alternately employed in solo work of the most effective kind; likewise in an aria ("Grasmücken"-aria) in Grétry's opera "Zemire and Azor." In the Andante of Rossini's "William Tell" overture, the composer has written a brilliant and very effective part for the Flute. In the overture to my opera "The Flutist," I have entrusted an important solo to the Flute as shown in the following example :

EXTRACT FROM THE OVERTURE TO THE OPERA "THE FLUTIST."

H. KLING.

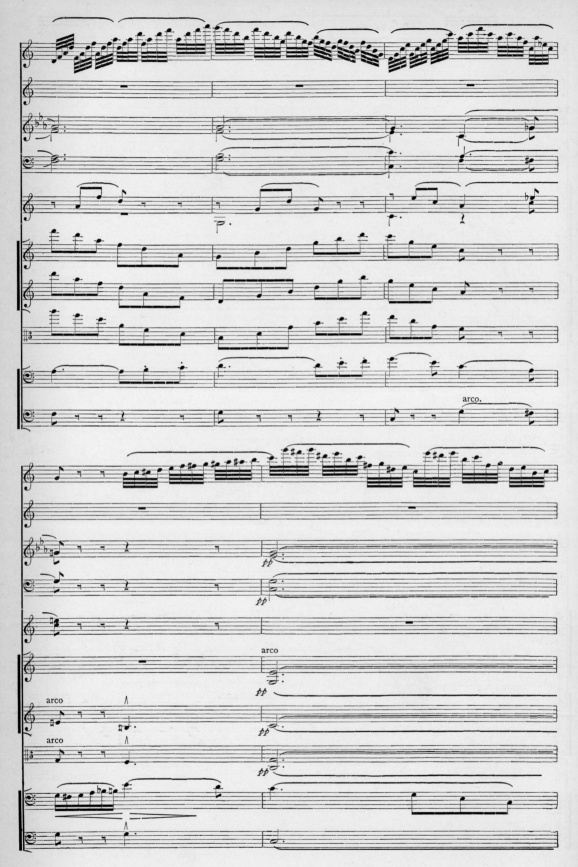

Used in Dance Music the Flute executes the melody in unison with the first Violin or an octave higher; independent melodies or brilliant embellishments can also be written for it, as may suit the imagination or intention of the composer.

and sad, and is excellently adapted to the illustration of pastoral (rural) scenes. Used in the Minor Keys it is expressive of ennui, extreme sadness and suffering.

3. THE FLUTE D'AMOUR.
See Addenda, page 317.

4. THE FLAGEOLET.
See Addenda, page 317.

5. THE OBOE.

(OBOE, OBOE, HAUTBOIS.)

The tonal-quality of this instrument is nasal

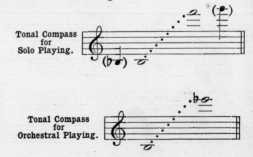

Tonal Compass for Solo Playing.

Tonal Compass for Orchestral Playing.

Trills, broken chords, skips and arpeggios as adapted to this instrument are shown in the following examples:

The intervals from:

are rough; those from:

are the best-sounding notes of the Oboe, and those from:

are sharp and cutting and not effective to any extent. In scoring, 2 Oboes are usually employed, of which the first is often used as a solo-instrument for passages expressive of a simple, graceful, rural or sad character. The

Oboe is also well adapted for joyous, droll and humorous scenes. Detached passages executed staccato are very effective at times, providing they are not used too frequently; Legato passages are more expressive of the true character of the instrument. Haydn, Mozart, Beethoven, Weber, Meyerbeer, R. Wagner, Auber, Halévy, H. Berlioz, etc., have used the Oboe extensively in all their works, and have brought about beautiful effects through its employment. In the Andante of his C major Symphony, Franz Schubert has entrusted a charming solo to the Oboe, which is exactly adapted to the character of the instrument.

6. THE OBOE D'AMORE.
See Addenda, page 317.

7. THE OBOE DI CACCIA.
See Addenda, page 317.

EXTRACT FROM THE C-MAJOR SYMPHONY.

FRANZ SCHUBERT.

In the Scherzo of his Pastoral-Symphony, Beethoven has given a theme of a very joyous, pastoral nature to the Oboe, which is wonderfully effective.

8. THE ENGLISH HORN.

(ENGLISCHES HORN, CORNO INGLESE, COR ANGLAIS.)

This instrument is admirably adapted to portray sad or painful feelings, moral suffering, as well as tragic situations in orchestral compositions. The combination of the Flute, the Clarinet and the Oboe or English Horn produces a tender, impulsive, languishing and plaintive tonal-coloring, especially in the Minor Keys. These same instruments are also excellently adapted for the expression of religious feelings or situations.

The tonal-compass of the English Horn is:

It is played in the same manner as the Oboe, that is, as far as its fingering is concerned, but its tones sound a fifth lower than they are written. Many English Horns also possess the low B flat.

Musical compositions of slow tempo and with slurred notes are best adapted for this instrument. Trills as well as quick running passages are not effective. Detached (staccato) notes create a somewhat ridiculous effect.

Sometimes two English Horns are employed, as Halévy has done in his opera "The Jewess" (in the Ritornell of Eleazar's Aria), and J. S. Bach in his St. Matthäus, "Passion music." Donizetti has also produced some very poetic effects by means of the English Horn, entrusting several beautiful solos to it in his opera "La Favorita." In his celebrated Ave Maria, Cherubini has written a concerted part for it together with the voice. Beethoven has composed a charming Trio for 2 Oboes and English Horn; and Mozart, who is ever to be relied upon for using and creating new ideas, employed 2 English Horns in several compositions, especially in a few of his delightful "Divertimentos" for Wind instruments.

The English Horn is also well adapted for illustrating rural scenes, as it can imitate the Shepherd's pipe or Alpine Horn (the favorite instruments of shepherds) excellently. With this special characteristic tonal-quality in view R. Wagner has employed the English Horn to excellent advantage in his "Tannhäuser" (see following example) and still better in his "Tristan and Isolde" Act III., in which he has written an important pastoral scene, a kind of shepherd's dance for it. (But this solo already demands an accomplished artist.)

EXTRACT FROM "TANNHÄUSER." ACT I, SCENE III.

R. WAGNER.

A young shepherd is playing upon his pipe. The chant of the elder pilgrims is heard as they are approaching the hill-path, from the direction of the Wartburg.

Hector Berlioz has written solos for the English Horn for several of his larger orchestral compositions, the effect of which may be described as simply wonderful. Rossini, in the Andante of the "William Tell" overture, and Meyerbeer in his various operas, have used this instrument to excellent advantage.

The tonal-quality from

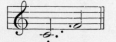

is bright and carrying; the notes from

possess a somewhat gloomy timbre and are difficult to produce, and the high notes

are quite similar to those of the Oboe, but are never absolutely in tune.

Usually in orchestras where an English Horn is missing, the first Oboeist plays its part upon an Oboe by simply transposing it a fourth higher; this not alone falls short of anything of the intended effect, but also in marring the entire tonal-quality of such a part, as the Oboe can in no way reproduce the real sound of the English Horn. It is astonishing that musical conductors will put up with any such substitution, the only possible excuse which could be offered in such a case being that an English Horn could not be procured.

In dance-music the English Horn is seldom, we might say never, used; but on the other hand, the Oboe is always used, and melodies, embellishments, sustained notes, etc., are assigned to it.

9. THE CLARINET.

(KLARINETTE, CLARINETTO, CLARINETTE.)

This beautiful instrument possesses a variety of sympathetic, dignified, and tender qualities. Added to this it possesses a religious character, can imitate the echo or resounding of bells, and is especially well adapted for pastoral scenes. For orchestral use, three varieties of Clarinets in C, B flat and A, are made use of; for dance-music sometimes the E flat and D Clarinet in addition to the above.

Manner of notation for all the differently pitched Clarinets is shown in the following table.

COMPARATIVE TABLE OF ALL THE DIFFERENT CLARINETS.

(For Extended Compass as used for Military Bands, see page 215.)

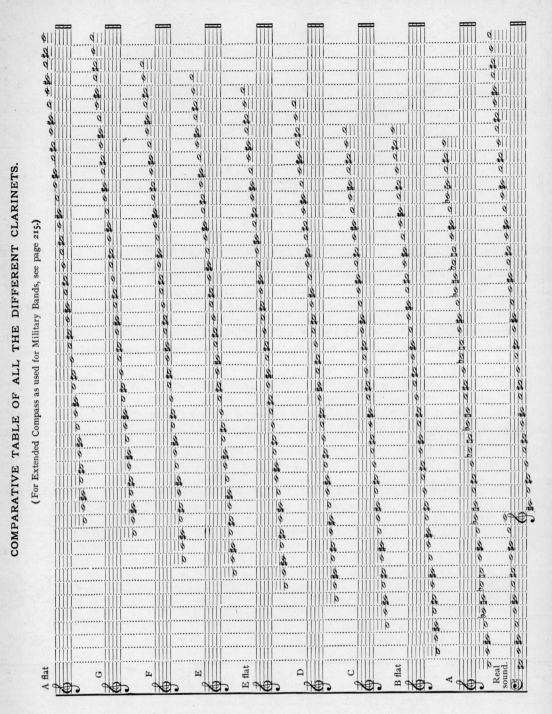

Practically the Clarinets in A flat, G, F, E, D, and C are no longer in use. Those in use at the present day are the E flat, B flat, A, and very rarely the C Clarinet.

According to differences in tonal-quality the compass of the Clarinet is divided into the fol-lowing three registers·

Religious seriousness; sadness; horror; dramatic.

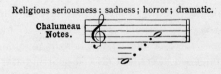

Chalumeau Notes.

Tender feelings; naive; joyful; delicacy; pastoral; lovable; impulsive.

Is little used; might be employed to illustrate a terrific stroke of lightning or for the expression of coarse or vulgar joy.

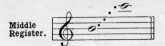

Middle Register.

Highest Register.

Trills, passages, broken chords, skips and arpeggios as adapted to this instrument are **shown in** the following examples:

a. Easy Trills.

Böhm System.

Old System.

b. Difficult Trills.

Böhm System.

Old System.

c. Impossible Trills.

Upon both Systems.

a. Easy Passages.

Upon both Systems.

b. Difficult Passages.

Böhm System.

etc.

Old System.

etc.

etc.

a. Broken Intervals, easy.

Difficult.

For the writing of easy runs and passages, the keys of C, G, F and B flat major should be selected ; E flat, A flat, D and A major can also be used, but only to better advantage in compositions of slower tempo. The most effective keys for orchestral use are C, G, D, A, E, F, B flat, E flat and A flat major ; for solo-playing, C, G, F and B flat major.

The Clarinet is capable of expressing a great variety of different feelings. While the low notes are admirable for the production of dramatic, awe-inspiring or ghostly effects, the notes of the middle register are excellently adapted for the expression of tender or impulsive feelings, whereas the higher notes possess the characteristics for illustrating coarse, vulgar and plebeian joyfulness. Mozart was the first of all composers who clearly understood how to make use of and bring to light the unlimited resources of this instrument. In consequence we find that he has entrusted solo parts to the Clarinets in his operas, which demonstrate the brilliant qualities of the instrument to the best advantage. After him, Beethoven, Weber and a great number of the modern composers have written for the Clarinet, with special preference, and have used its numberless brilliant qualities to the best of advantage and with great success.*

The tonal-quality of the smaller Clarinets in A flat, F, E flat and D, is screaming, cutting and trivial ; they are, therefore, only adapted for use in military or dance music The C-Clarinet has a hard but brilliant sound, and is excellently adapted for compositions of a joyous nature. The B-flat Clarinet is the finest of all, owing to its soft and at the same time, brilliant tone. The A-Clarinet possesses a soft, melancholy, tonal-quality and adapts itself more for the expression of pathetic, elegiac, serious and religious feelings. It need hardly be mentioned that for compositions with many flats, the B♭-Clarinet, and for such with many sharps, the A-Clarinet should be employed. In dance-music the Clarinet is used for doubling the melody of the first Violin. But independent melodies, accessory themes, as well as embellishments, arpeggios, etc., may be written for it.

Two Clarinets are always employed for orchestral scoring.

10. THE BASS-CLARINET.

(BASS KLARINETTE, CLARINETTO BASSO, CLARINETTE BASSE.)

A beautiful instrument possessing a full, round, majestic tone, excellently adapted for compositions of a religious character, whether in a major or minor key. Sadness can also be excellently expressed with it, as well as imitating the sound of a bell, which can be employed to excellent advantage in scenes of a sad, gruesome or awe-inspiring nature. Three varieties of Bass-Clarinets are in use, in C, B♭, and A, and they sound exactly an octave lower than the ordinary Clarinet.

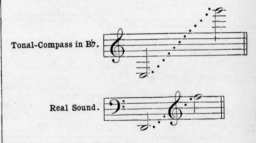

Tonal-Compass in B♭.

Real Sound.

Everything which can be played upon the ordinary Clarinet can also be executed upon the Bass-Clarinet, as the fingering for both instruments is the same. But the serious tonal-character of the instrument demands that it be entrusted with fitting cantabile passages. Meyerbeer (as shown in the following extracts) has used it to excellent advantage in the Grand Trio, 5th Act of "The Huguenots," where he has employed it in such a manner as to participate in a kind of dialogue with the voices, which combination, while producing a rather painful impression upon the listener, is entirely in accordance with the situation.

---

* In his opera "Titus," Aria of Sextus (No. 9 Parto!) Mozart has written an obligato Clarinet part to the voice. This is an exceptionally fine example of this style of writing, and is exceedingly effective. Mozart also left a beautiful Concerto in A major, and a Quintette for the Clarinet.

EXTRACTS FROM "THE HUGUENOTS."

Used in connection with the full orchestra, the Bass-Clarinet is very effective as it heightens the strength of the lower notes in general, imparts more brilliancy to other instruments, especially the Bassoons, and at the same time softening the rough tones of the lower registers. Richard Wagner, Hector Berlioz, and many others have accorded a prominent and important position to the Bass-Clarinet in their scores.

11. THE BASSET-HORN.

(BASSET-HORN, CORNO DI BASSETTO, COR DE BASSET.)

The sound of this instrument is very similar to that of the Bass-Clarinet, especially in the lower registers. It sounds a fifth lower than the C-Clarinet.

Tonal-Compass.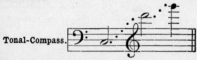

Real Sound.

Everything that can be played upon the Clarinet can also be executed upon the Basset-Horn. Sustained cantabile passages are better adapted to the character of the instrument than quick successive runs. The most effective keys are C, G, F, and B flat major or minor.

Mozart used this instrument very frequently; in his Trios for three voices, "Luci care, luci belle," and "Ecco quell fiero," he has written solo parts for three Basset-Horns. In his operas "Titus," * "The Magic Flute," and in his "Requiem," this master has employed two Basset-Horns in the most appropriate and effective manner. Now-a-days the part of the Basset-Horn is usually played upon an Alto-Clarinet in F; that is, in such orchestras for which a Basset-Horn cannot be procured.

---

* The second Aria of Vitellia ("Titus," Mozart) is written with the accompaniment of a concerted Basset-Horn. It is one of the most beautiful Arias ever conceived, imbued with an exalted, highly poetic spirit.

12. THE BASSOON.

(FAGOTT, FAGOTTO, BASSON.)

This instrument is well adapted to picture mysterious situations; in slow tempo with arpeggio-like slurred notes, it can imitate the movements of ocean waves; the snorting of hunting-dogs as well as the tramp of horses can also be fittingly expressed by it.

In writing for the Bassoon the Bass or Tenor clef is used.

Tonal-Compass for Orchestral Use.

Tonal-Compass for Solo-Playing.

Upon some instruments it is possible to produce a low "A" but as they are not in general use, it is advisable not to write this note.

Appropriate trills, runs, skips and arpeggios for the Bassoon are shown in the following examples:

a. Easy Trills.

etc.

b. Difficult Trills.

c. Impossible Trills.

etc.

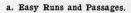
a. Easy Runs and Passages.

etc.

b. Difficult Runs and Passages.

etc.

Skips and Arpeggios.

Possible in all keys.

Skips and Arpeggios can be executed upon the Bassoon in all Keys. In moderate tempo staccato passages are very effective; on the other hand Legato presenting greater difficulties to the player. The easiest and most effective Keys for orchestral use are C, G, A and E major or minor; for solo playing C, G and A major or minor.

All Keys with many sharps or flats are difficult to play.

The notes

possess a decided humorous, comical quality.

The notes

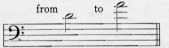

possess a quality similar to that of the human voice.

Employed in this sense in minor Keys they can be put to excellent use, in portraying pain, lamentation, fear or the like.

In orchestral scoring two Bassoons are usually employed, the first one being entrusted with a solo at intervals. Sustained and slurred notes are more adapted to the nature of the instrument, especially in the higher register, than detached (staccato) notes; the latter possess characteristics of a comical, ludicrous or humorous nature in every instance; this applies to every register of the entire compass, and especially to the intervals of the lower octave.

The following extract from "Don Juan" shows a very comical effect which Mozart has produced in the scene where Leporello admits to Elvira that Don Juan prefers very young maidens, whispering this confession secretly into her ear, while the careful steps of the lover, who is about to follow such a maiden, are betrayed in the most humorous manner by the notes of the accompanying Bassoon.

EXTRACT FROM THE OPERA "DON JUAN."

MOZART.

é la - gio - sin prin - ci - pi - an - te; non si

The notes of the middle and those of the higher register can be well combined with those of the Flutes and Clarinets. Excellent and effective scoring for the Bassoon is shown in the following extracts from Mozart's "Magic Flute" overture.

EXTRACTS FROM "THE MAGIC FLUTE" OVERTURE.

b. From the above.

Haydn, Beethoven, Meyerbeer, Mendelssohn and many others have displayed perfect mastery in the use and treatment of the Bassoon, and have entrusted many important parts of a characteristic nature to it.

Its notes blend excellently with the pizzicato of the Violoncellos and Basses, and with those of the Kettledrums. Sometimes as many as four Bassoons are employed. In dance-music the Bassoon usually doubles the Violoncello or Bass part, but embellishments, sustained notes, independent melodies or themes etc., may also be written for it.

13. THE DOUBLE BASSOON.

(KONTRA-FAGOTT, CONTRA-FAGOTTO, CONTRA-BASSON.)

This instrument has been almost entirely dispensed with, owing to its tiring effect upon the player. In view of the entire tonal-effect of the orchestra the dispensation of this instrument is to be greatly regretted.

The notes of the Double Bassoon sound an octave lower than those of the ordinary Bassoon.

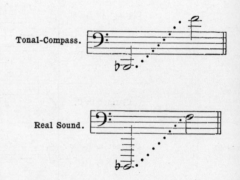

Haydn, Mozart, and Beethoven have used this instrument with great success in their works. It has been employed with special effectiveness in Mozart's beautiful Serenade for thirteen Wind Instruments, and in a very characteristic manner in Haydn's "Creation." In such orchestras where a Double Bassoon is missing, its part is usually substituted by a Double-Bass. It need hardly be added that a substitution of this kind can in no way make up for the original intentions of the composer.

In the following I present a comparative table of the tonal-compass of all the Wood-wind instruments.

COMPARATIVE TABLE OF THE TONAL-COMPASS OF ALL THE WOOD-WIND INSTRUMENTS

(For Orchestral Purposes.)

In addition to the above, a few differently pitched wood-wind instruments are yet to be mentioned; but they are never employed in String-orchestras, and are only exceptionally found in Military Bands. They will be discussed later on.

The Wood-wind Instruments as Used in Dance Music.

The Flute and Piccolo are generally used to interpret the melody, like the first Violin, but in the higher registers. The Flutes can also be employed to execute little independent melodies or accessory themes, trills and imitations of separate tonal-phrases. The Oboe is employed in strengthening the melody, also in filling the harmony by means of sustaining its lower notes. Its part is usually written in such a manner as to be readily omitted in a smaller combination of instruments. The first Clarinet as a rule doubles the melody by playing *unisono* with the first Violin, or an octave higher. The second Clarinet is used for filling up the harmony, for accompanying passages or for sustaining notes in the lower register; in addition to this, it sometimes plays the melody along in the lower octave. Both Clarinets are also well adapted for the execution of tonal-phrases or passages in thirds or sixths, and admit of being used in a great variety of ways. The Bassoon can be used in an accompanying manner and in appropriate cases as a doubler of the melody; it can also support the 2nd Clarinet by means of sustained notes. But in writing for the Bassoon or 2nd Clarinet the parts should always be arranged in such a manner as to be readily omitted in a smaller orchestra.

General Remarks. Each one of the instruments, which has been discussed in detail in the foregoing pages, can also shine to advantage as a solo-instrument upon the concert stage, either with accompaniment of the Pianoforte, a few stringed instruments, or complete orchestra. Of course the necessary accompaniment must be written in a very delicate and refined manner in order that the solo instrument will show to best advantage, and that its brilliant and beautiful qualities may be fully displayed.

Mozart, whose genius was inexhaustible, has left some charming concertos for the Flute, Oboe, Clarinet and Bassoon to the musical world.

As can be seen from "the comparative table of the tonal-compass of all the Wood-wind instruments," an entire and complete orchestra can be formed from this combination, which in itself is capable of producing the finest varieties of tonal-shadings. Mozart was well aware of the effectiveness of such a combination when he wrote his beautiful Serenade for 13 Wind instruments.

In writing for these instruments, it is necessary not to separate the different tonal-registers too far from each other; that is, the Oboes should not be allowed to climb into the highest regions while the Bassoons are exploring the lowest. As shown in the extract from the "Magic Flute" overture, on page 112, the chords should be placed in such a manner as to keep the various instruments in close contact.

Combining the Clarinets and Bassoons in their middle registers and playing "piano" produces an excellent tonal-quality, very similar to the tone of an organ. These instruments can furthermore be combined with Flutes and Horns, this combination being excellently adapted for the portrayal of solemn or religious scenes.

The Wood-wind instruments blend especially well with the Horns, and beautiful tonal-effects may be produced with this combination. Mozart and Beethoven have been exceedingly successful in their chamber-music works for combinations of this kind, written especially for 2 Clarinets, 2 Bassoons, and 2 Horns; or for 2 Clarinets, 2 Oboes, 2 Bassoons, and 2 Horns, etc.; beautiful works of art, which are neglected altogether too much now-a-days and unknown to the majority of musicians, which to a certain degree accounts for modern composers leaving this fruitful branch of musical art to lie entirely idle.*

It need hardly be mentioned that the Wood-wind Instruments can also be combined with the Stringed Instruments to the best advantage in the manner employed by Beethoven in his celebrated Septette for Violin, Viola, Violoncello, Double-Bass, Clarinet, Horn and Bassoon.

They are equally effective in a combination with the Pianoforte, and it will be of the greatest benefit to the student to consult the beautiful Quintettes by Mozart and Beethoven for Pianoforte, Oboe, Clarinet, Horn and Bassoon. Especially in Mozart's, the 5 instruments are employed in such a manner as to yield the greatest amount of tonal beauty and purity, owing to the artistic application and combination of the different instruments.

---

* Now that the chamber-music works for Wind instruments by Mozart and Beethoven have been published in so many cheap editions, both in scores and parts, I would earnestly advise the student to study them thoroughly and conscientiously.

Flute and Oboe blend very well with the Violin and the Violoncello; Clarinet and Bassoon with the Viola and Violoncello. For the production of tonal-effects, the artistic combination of the Wood-wind with the Stringed Instruments offers unlimited material to the accomplished composer.

Played "forte," the lower Clarinet and Bassoon tones possess characteristics of a devilish, brutal and awe-inspiring nature, which adapt themselves excellently to scenes of a ghostly, supernatural kind, as well as to the portrayal of demoniacal, wild or vulgar expressions. Mozart and Weber have produced the most impressive effects by means of the lower notes of the Clarinet; the former in "Don Juan," and the latter in "Freischütz."

Played "pianissimo," these instruments can imitate the sound of a bell. In the fourth Act of "The Huguenots," Meyerbeer has produced a very remarkable effect with the help of this very device as shown in the extract on page 113. He lets the Clarinets and Bassoons execute twelve successive bars, answered by the Horns and Trombones; this peculiar combination, together with the successive harmony, imitating the clock of Saint Germain l'Auxerrois striking midnight, in a wondrous manner.

EXTRACT FROM THE OVERTURE TO "THE MAGIC FLUTE."

EXTRACT FROM "THE HUGUENOTS."

Act 4.

MEYERBEER.

Directions as to Scoring Effectively for the Wood-wind Instruments.

The method which I proposed for the above purpose in connection with the Stringed Instruments can also be employed to excellent advantage with this body of instruments; that is, the separate parts of a Sextette, Septette or Octette, etc., for Wind Instruments by Mozart or Beethoven should be scored. Through this proceeding we will not alone become thoroughly imbued with the spirit of the composer, impressing the beautiful traits and tonal-combinations of these works (which could be easily overlooked by a flighty reading of the score) upon our memory step by step, but we gain the ability to score in an artistic and thorough manner for these instruments, and employing them in accordance with their individual character and tonal-qualities. After this some of the Pianoforte sonaten of Haydn, Mozart, Beethoven, Mendelssohn, etc., are to be arranged, selecting such as are specially adapted, as far as melody and harmony are concerned, for this purpose.

As an example of arrangements of this kind, I have selected the Adagio from Beethoven's "Sonate Pathétique," and have arranged it in the following manner:

ADAGIO FROM THE SONATE PATHÉTIQUE.

Arranged for 1 Flute, 1 Oboe, 2 Clarinets, 2 Basset-Horns, 2 French Horns in E flat, 1 Bass-Clarinet, 2 Bassoons and 1 Double-Bassoon, by H. KLING.

BEETHOVEN.

NOTE. I have taken up 2 French Horns in this arrangement, as the Horn, owing to its peculiar tonal-quality, blends admirably with the Wood-wind instruments besides adding color and effectiveness to the entire combination.

B. Brass Wind-Instruments.

1. THE FRENCH HORN

(WITHOUT VALVES), (WALDHORN, NATURHORN, CORNO, COR.)

This beautiful instrument possesses an exceedingly peculiar tonal-character; it revives the memories of fragrant hills and dales, the mountains and forests, and awakens the love for the hunt. Employed in its middle register it pictures the mysterious, and in short notes serves excellently for the production of mysterious calls or signals.

The *stopped notes*, if played *forte*, possess a dull, terror-awakening quality of tone, and should only be employed for scenes of special dramatic significance, requiring an appropriate effect of this kind. Added to this, these dull, but nevertheless dismal crashing sounds are well adapted to illustrate revenge, fear, distress, danger, horror, disaster, as well as fiendish, passionate, furious and impulsive characteristics; but if, on the other hand, these stopped notes are played *pianissimo* and in sustained notes, they will awaken feelings of a disagreeable, painful and oppressing nature; in other words, they are well adapted to picture such situations in which the human soul finds itself overcome and at the mercy of the conspiring powers of fate. Aside from this wealth and variety of expressiveness, the Horn can also imitate the human voice excellently; but this necessitates the entire command of a soft, round, pliable and expressive tone on the part of the player. It is due in particular to the extremely peculiar tonal-color of the Horn that these manifold and opposite effects are possible. The tone of this instrument is also possessed of characteristics of a certain romantic, poetic nature; it is therefore well-adapted for the performance of expressive, song-like passages or compositions.*

The Horn is a transposing instrument; that is, its pitch can be altered at will by means of crooks. In the following table I present a list of all the differently pitched Horns, with notation of their real sounds, tonal-compass for practical use, as well as the possible open and stopped notes which can be employed. The high pitch Horns in B flat, B and C sound exactly an octave higher than the low Horns of the same pitch; they are employed very rarely.

TABLE OF NOTATION FOR THE FRENCH HORN. (Without Valves.)

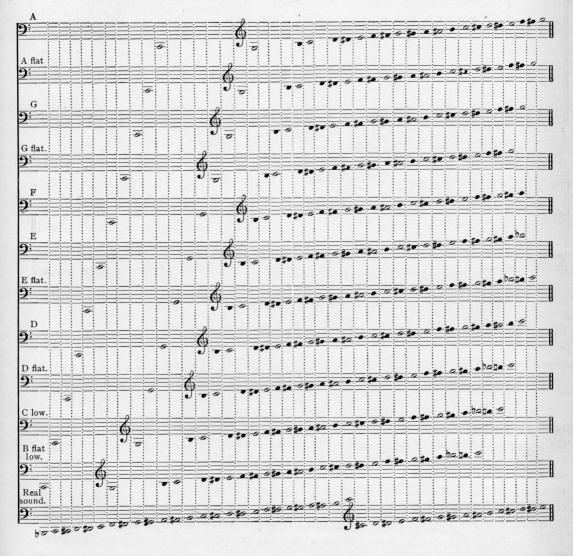

The ◯ notes in this table are the open or natural tones; those designated by ● are the stopped ones; naturally the former sound more brilliant than the latter.

---

* The Horn virtuoso Gumbert in Leipzic has invented and constructed a very bright and clear-sounding *Corno Piccolo* in F (sounding equally as high as the Trumpet); this instrument serves as an excellent Siegfried horn

Trills, Passages and Skips as adapted to this instrument are shown in the following examples:

Easy Trills.

Difficult Trills.

Impossible Trills.

Easy, Brilliant Passages, especially well adapted to the tonal-character of the Horn.

Allegro.

etc.

Easy Skips.

The notes:

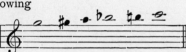

sound somewhat dull, but are excellently adapted for sustained notes.

The notes:

are the best;

the following

are very difficult to play and not very agreeable to the ear; it is therefore advisable not to write any sustained notes in this register for E flat, E or F Horn, and above all not to begin a solo with one of these notes, especially in *piano* passages.

Upon the G flat, G, A flat, A, B flat and B Horns the note

is a very difficult one and the tonal-quality in general thin and poor. For the above pitched instruments the note

should be the limit as to height.

The tonal-quality of the differently pitched Horns may be summed up in the following manner: B flat, B and C (low) have a somewhat stiff and strained, but not very bright tone; D flat and D possess a round, full tone, especially well adapted for hunting-calls; E flat, E and F are of a mild soft, glowing but nevertheless bright and brilliant tonal-quality and are excellently fitted for solo-work; the one in F is the most brilliant of these, owing to which it is generally preferred to all others by the majority of Horn-players; G flat and G possess a sharp quality, which fits them splendidly for the execution of brilliant compositions: A flat, A, B flat, B and C (high) possess a penetrating, cutting tone. The last-named ones should be used with great care and only the following open notes should be employed:

as the stopped notes are very false, especially for combinations like the following:

On the other hand, passages like the following are easy and effective in every pitch:

The keys which are best adapted and most effective for this instrument are C major and A minor; G major and E minor; F major; C minor.

THE FRENCH HORN WITH CYLINDERS, PISTONS OR VALVES.

(CHROMATISCHES OR VENTIL HORN, CORNO CROMATICO, COR À PISTONS.)

This beautiful instrument is in reality nothing more nor less than a perfected Natural or Wald Horn; it is played in the identical manner, and everything possible upon its forerunner can also be executed with ease upon this instrument. Therefore how is it possible that some of our best composers and conductors are in many cases unjustly prejudiced against this instrument? The reason of this disfavor is not caused by the instrument itself, but must rather be attributed to the Horn-players, the majority of whom do not possess the slightest idea of how to treat this noble instrument according to its true character and who blow into it as though it were a Trumpet, a Cornet or a Trombone. It is owing to this manner of tone-production that this class of players are utterly incapable of connecting and sustaining the intervals in the manner which is so essential and important in bringing to light the genuine characteristics of the Horn. The position of the hand in the bell of the instrument is of great importance; decreasing as it does the rougher and sharper elements in the quality of tone and lending more pliancy and flexibility to the entire tonal-production.

The Chromatic Horn (German designation) is of greater use to the composer than the Natural Horn, as all the intervals of the chromatic scale can be produced upon it in an equally clear and precise manner.

The tonal-compass of the Chromatic Horn is:

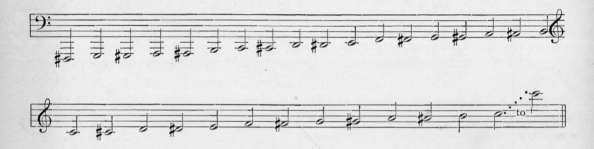

It is very easy to transpose from one Key to another upon this instrument without the aid of crooks. If the following passage, a) is played upon the F Horn in open notes the same will sound one tone lower b) by pressing down the 1st valve.

through pressure of the 2nd valve one-half tone lower;

through pressure of the 3d or of the 1st and 2nd together, a minor third lower:

through pressure of the 1st and 3d valve a fourth lower:

With the 2nd and 3d valve:

With the 1st, 2nd and 3d valve:

These notes sound like the natural tones, and create the effect as though they were being played upon the respective E flat, E, D and C Horns, etc. A similar result can also be obtained through application of all the different crooks. If the composer desires that the notes are to be stopped, he simply designates it in his score, as this effect is just as easily produced upon the Chromatic as upon the Natural Horn.

The Chromatic Horns in F, E and E♭ sound to best advantage. If employed at all, it is advisable to use only the open or natural notes of those in C, D, E, G flat, G, A, B flat, and B high, as the notes produced upon these by means of valves are never absolutely in tune.

Let us suppose that a composer wishes to score the following phrase for Horns:

The same could be undoubtedly executed upon the F, E or B flat Horn, although quite difficult; but it would sound very brilliant and to excellent advantage upon the G Horn and its execution be greatly facilitated thereby.

The majority of Horn-players as well as some orchestral conductors are of the opinion that the application of crooks upon the Valve Horns or Trumpets is unnecessary and nonsensical; that this opinion is totally wrong is proven by the great difference of tonal-quality produced by the different crooks, some affecting the instrument so as to sound thin and weak, and others as to sound bright and brilliant. In this manner Mozart, in his wonderful G Minor Symphony, has written the two Horn parts for differently pitched instruments; it must not be imagined that their employment in this manner was due to any accident or caprice, but because he wished to produce a specially bright-sounding tonal-quality. Taking a look at this master-work we find that the String Quintette is assisted merely by 1 Flute, 2 Oboes, 2 Bassoons and 2 Horns. The Horn parts are written in such an ingenious manner as to employ only natural tones, the 1st part being executed upon a high B flat and the 2nd part upon a high G Horn.

The modern Horn-player who uses nothing but the F Horn naturally fails to produce this peculiar tonal-quality which cannot possibly be produced in as bright and brilliant a manner upon this instrument as upon the originally prescribed B-flat and G Horns.

It is therefore of frequent occurrence that the following charming passage from the Minuet of the above symphony is not properly executed:

EXTRACT FROM THE MINUET OF THE G MINOR SYMPHONY.

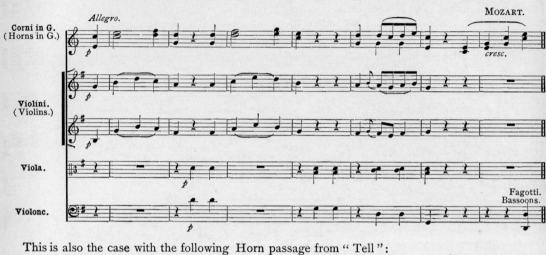

This is also the case with the following Horn passage from "Tell":

Now-a-days it is customary to score for 4 Horns: for instance, the first two parts for F and the other two for C Horn, similar to the celebrated Horn-quartette of the "Freischütz" overture, presented in the following example:

EXTRACT FROM THE FREISCHÜTZ OVERTURE.

Haydn, Mozart, Beethoven, Méhul, Meyer-beer, Weber, Halévy, Spohr, Rossini, Boieldieu, Fél. David, Kreutzer, Bellini, Donizetti, etc., and especially R. Wagner, have produced the most beautiful effects with the Horn; and the modern composers, such as Gounod, Ambr. Thomas, Massenet, Saint-Saëns, Brahms, Rubin-stein, Bruch, Dvŏrák, etc., have all been well aware of the effectiveness of the Horn, employ-ing it to excellent advantage in their orchestral works. The natural characteristics of the Horn qualify it exceedingly well for hunting-calls and woodland scenes, as illustrated in the following extract from " Tannhäuser," Act I., Scene 3.

EXTRACT FROM TANNHÄUSER.

Act I. Scene III.

R. WAGNER.

In the second act of his opera "Tristan and Isolde" Wagner has introduced an admirable Fanfare for 6 Horns, which are placed behind the scenes and their parts alternating with those of the 4 Horns in the orchestra. These Horns are all in F. *

The Horn is also excellently adapted for scenes of a pastoral or legendary nature and can furthermore imitate the human voice and execute expressive cantabile passages as shown in the following examples:

EXTRACT FROM THE MIGNON OVERTURE.

A. Thomas.

---

* At the same time I desire to call attention to the fine Fanfare for 4 Horns in the opera "William Tell" by Rossini. In the opera "Freischütz" the Horns are used and treated in the most artistic and appropriate manner, which is also the case in Beethoven's "Fidelio."

FROM THE OPERA "LA DAME BLANCHE."

BOIELDIEU.

In the Prelude (Vorspiel) to his "Rheingold," Wagner has employed 8 Horns in a very original manner and it is highly interesting to study his use of the instruments. The following extract shows the manner in which he has employed the Horns which are in E flat:

EXTRACT FROM PRELUDE TO "RHEINGOLD."

R. WAGNER.

A very good effect is produced with the Mute * although it should not be used too frequently. Through placing the mute into the bell of the instrument the pitch of the latter is lowered one-half tone. But this need not inconvenience the composer, as the Horn-players are prepared for such emergencies. Care must be taken to use only natural tones for such passages which are to be executed with the mute, whether for the Natural or Valve Horn. See following example:

Horns in F.

Echo with mute.

* A small pear-shaped object made of wood, tin or pasteboard, which is placed in the bell of the instrument.

Some composers desirous of producing more tonal-volume than these instruments are already capable of producing sometimes mark certain passages in their scores with "Turn the bell upwards" ("Stürze in die Höhe," in German). But this is in reality a senseless error which it is impossible to justify. The Horn played in this manner will sound similar to a hunting-Horn or a Trombone; and what is worse still the purity of the tones is interfered with, as through the change of position the hand is removed from the bell, causing the natural tones to sound a quarter of a tone higher. A proceeding of this kind is therefore clearly contrary to the nature and character of the instrument and such tricks should be banished to the circus, where they would probably be more appropriate. A person of taste must always remember that every exaggeration is a mistake; and it may certainly be termed an exaggeration to demand productions which are entirely contrary to the real character of the instrument.

It only remains for me to mention a few words in regard to the double- and triple-tones which can be produced upon the Horn.

At the same time, while producing a tone with the lips, a different tone can be sung by the player, no matter whether higher or lower than the blown tone. For instance, the player intones C with his lips, and at the same time sings the E one third higher; in this manner it is possible to form a chromatic chain of ascending dual-sounds:

It is also possible to sing the lower note and play the higher one upon the instrument:

If the fundamental note is intoned upon the Horn, for instance, and the sixth is sung, the fourth will become audible through the joint vibrations of the first two, and we obtain the following complete chord:

if B is sung and the low G played thereto, the D will become audible and we obtain the following chord:

Even successions of chords can be produced in this manner as shown in the following examples:

In the same manner

In this manner, the possibility of executing Duos and Trios upon a single Horn is offered to a player, providing he possess good embouchure, a skilled voice and a good ear. Effects could be produced in this manner which would certainly arouse the admiration of the public owing to the latter's lack of knowledge of this acoustic phenomenon. But the real artist will look with contempt upon productions of this kind. Taken all in all, whatever is accomplished in this direction is not entirely legitimate and the approbation of the really educated or art-connoisseurs will never be bestowed upon it. These double or triple combinations are not applicable in the orchestra.

The most effective Keys for the Chromatic Horn are: C, G, F, E flat, D, and A major; C, E, D, F, and B minor.

The tonal-quality of the differently pitched Chromatic Horns is identical with that of the Natural Horns. The low notes, whether employed in sustained or slowly moving passages, are very effective. The Horn blends excellently with every instrument as well as with the human voice. The art of writing Horn-parts in an exactly appropriate manner is very difficult, and the whole attention of the composer must be directed towards this highly important branch. To begin with a start should be made by writing duos, trios and quartettes for Horns alone, and consulting a practical and experienced Horn-player, who will certainly be able to judge correctly and offer valuable advice wherever it is necessary.

Mozart has composed several Concertos for the old style Waldhorn which are very appropriate to the character of the instrument; he also wrote an excellent Quintette for Horn, Violin, 2 Violas and Violoncello; Beethoven also wrote a brilliant Sonate for Horn and Pianoforte. Rob. Schumann has written a "Concertstück" for 4 Horns as well as an Adagio and Allegro for Piano and Horn; Weber a very charming Concertino for Horn with orchestral accompaniment. Méhul, in his opera "Phrosine," has employed the stopped notes to excellent advantage, producing an entirely appropriate tonal-coloring for the illustrated situation.

EXTRACT FROM THE OPERA "PHROSINE."

Méhul.

Tu se ras mon - ven - geur!

In the following example I show a few chords which can be easily executed in stopped notes upon either F, E, or E flat Horns; they are equally effective whether executed pp. or ff.

IV. Horns in F, E, or E flat.

The open or natural notes are marked with o.

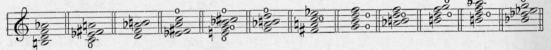

I repeat once more that the stopped notes can be played with equal ease as upon the Natural Horn; taken altogether it is one and the same instrument, only offering more advantages to the writer.

Used in dance-music the Horns are usually employed in executing sustained notes and accompanying figures; sometimes the melody or an accessory melody is written for the first Horn as shown below:

2. THE NATURAL TRUMPET.

(EINFACHE OR NATUR TROMPETE, CLARINO OR TROMBA, TROMPETTE.)

This instrument adapts itself excellently for sounding an alarm or for a challenge to combat, as well as for announcing the approach of soldiers or armor-clad men; in addition to this it can be put to excellent use in executing the signals of retreat or attack. Scenes of a riotous and murderous nature can be excellently illustrated by means of rhythmic detached figures in

dotted eighth notes, or dotted or plain sixteenth notes executed fortissimo by several Trumpets.

The Trumpet is also well adapted for the expression of joy, confidence, sincerity, sovereignty, courage, zeal and victory. It is also an admirable exponent of exalted, noble and religious feelings; it is very effective in pianissimo passages.

Tonal–Compass for Orchestral Use.

In a like manner as with Horns differently pitched Trumpets are used. The following presents a complete table of notation of all the different Trumpets together with their real sounds:

TABLE OF NOTATION FOR THE NATURAL TRUMPET.

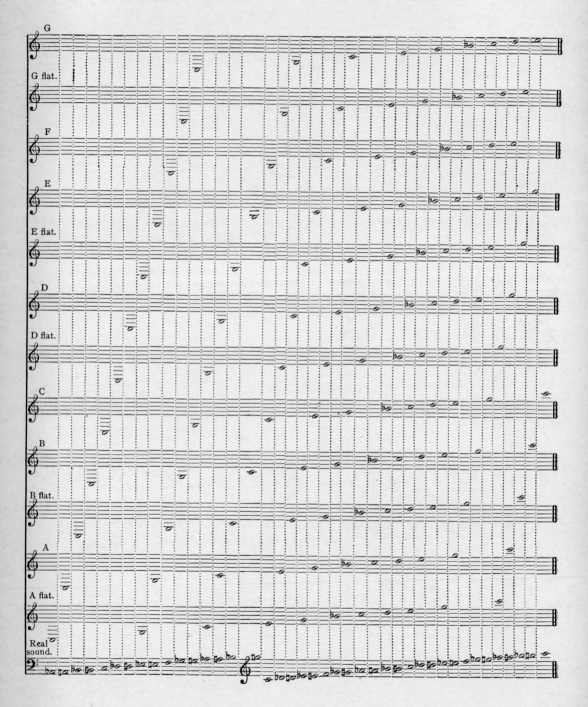

Trills, skips and broken chords, as adapted to this instrument, are shown in the following examples:

Easy Skips and Broken Chords.

In the following examples a variety of easily executed styles of single, double and triple tonguing is shown:

The Trumpets in F, G flat and G, possess a sharp, blasting quality of tone. In writing for them the following tone should never be exceeded, as this one is already difficult to produce and applicable only in fortissimo passages.

The D flat, D, E flat and E Trumpets possess a brilliant and sonorous quality of tone.

In forte-passages as high as may be written for them. The A flat, A, B flat and C Trumpets possess a soft, languishing, but nevertheless penetrating tone.

In forte-passages they can reach with ease.

THE VALVE OR CHROMATIC TRUMPET.

(VENTIL OR CHROMATISCHE TROMPETE, TROMBA-
CROMATICO, TROMPETTE À PISTONS.)

This instrument possesses the advantage that all the chromatic intervals can be produced upon it in an equally clear, true, and precise manner. It is in reality a Perfected Natural Trumpet.

Tonal-Compass. from 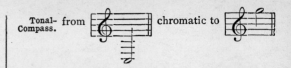 chromatic to

The Chromatic Trumpet is treated in the identical manner as the Natural Trumpet, and the difference of the instruments in regard to pitch is also exactly alike. The following examples present a list of trills applicable to this instrument.

Easy Trills.

Difficult Trills.

For orchestral writing all Keys can be employed.

The most effective Keys for solo-playing upon the Natural Trumpet in F, E, E flat and D are the keys of C, F, and G major. For the Chromatic Trumpet in B flat, and A, the keys of C, F, B flat, E flat, G and D Major or Minor are very effective.

Two Trumpets are usually employed, but a greater number can also be used to good advantage. The tone of the Trumpet blends very well with that of the Horn, the Clarinet, the Trombone and the Kettle-Drums. Combined with the Horns it produces a chivalrous quality of tone; f. i., in "Lohengrin" Act II., Scene 3, a very brilliant movement. Händel, Bach, Haydn, Mozart, Beethoven, Weber, R. Schumann, Fr. Liszt, Auber, Rossini, Meyerbeer, Halévy, Verdi, etc., have produced excellent effects through the correct and appropriate application of the Trumpet.

So-called Echo Mutes or Church Mutes can be used for the Trumpet, the latter especially in the production of Requiems or sad situations. But in employing these Muted Trumpets, special attention must be directed towards writing only sustained notes, and furthermore only natural tones, as the chromatic intervals, exactly as with Muted Horns are not true.

Andante sostenuto.

The following example if played with a mute will sound as an exact imitation of a toy Trumpet, an effect which several composers, R. Wagner, Lumbye, etc., have already employed.

With Mute.

This example is sufficient to warn the composer to be cautious with the use of the mute; otherwise he will incur the danger of having a movement, which in his imagination is to create a noble and tragic effect, bring about exactly the opposite, — a ludicrous one.

In dance-music the Trumpet can be used to execute sustained notes, rhythmical contrary passages, the melody or accessory melodies.

In addition to these so-called low Trumpets, the so-called High Trumpets, usually in B flat, and A (more seldom in C) are employed in the modern orchestra; the pitch, tonal-compass and treatment of these instruments, is identical with that of the Cornet (see " The Cornet," page 140). In his opera " Der Trompeter von Säkkingen " V. E. Nessler has written some very important solos for this instrument, several of which are shown in the following examples:

EXTRACTS FROM THE OPERA, "DER TROMPETER VON SÄKKINGEN."

For change of scene. Act I.

V. E. NESSLER.

OBLIGATO TRUMPET BEHIND THE SCENES.

Act. I. Trumpet in C.

Act II. Trumpet in C.

Act II. Trumpet in Bb.

3. THE CORNET.

(CORNET À PISTONS, PISTONE, CORNET À
PISTONS.)

The Cornet is a brilliant instrument possessing a bright penetrating quality of tone; its
popularity in America has in reality raised it to
the position of principal instrument in every
orchestra, be it large or small; owing to this,
it is advisable for the composer to study this
instrument in every detail and always to direct
his attention towards writing as effective and
thankful a part for it as possible.

The above tonal-compass of this instrument
is again divided into the following three registers:

1. The low register, somewhat dull.

Chromatic.

2. The principal or middle register, which is the best sounding.

Chromatic.

3. The high register, only possible for skilled Soloists.

Chromatic.

The open or natural notes, as well as those
obtainable with the aid of the three valves, are
shown in the following examples:

A. Natural or open Notes.

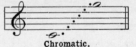

B With the 2nd Valve.

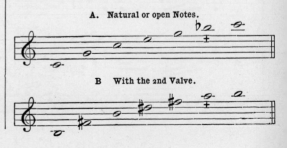

C. With the 1st Valve.

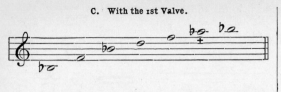

G. With combination of the 1st, 2nd and 3d Valve.

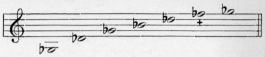

D. With combination of the 1st and 2nd, or 3d Valve alone.

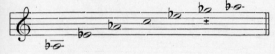

The sixth interval in each of the foregoing examples of open notes, marked with an ✛ is false and must not be employed in progressions as above.

The instrument is played exactly like a Trumpet and everything possible upon the latter instrument can be executed upon the Cornet; the difference of the instruments as regards pitch is also the same. But the Cornets most in use are those in A and B flat, owing to their clear and brilliant quality of tone as well as to their easy delivery; added to these the Cornets in C, B natural and A flat can also be employed to good advantage.

In the following I present a table of notation for all the differently pitched Cornets:

E. With combination of the 2nd and 3d Valve.

F. With combination of the 1st and 3d Valve.

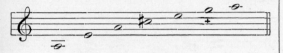

TABLE OF NOTATION FOR THE CORNET.

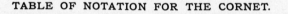
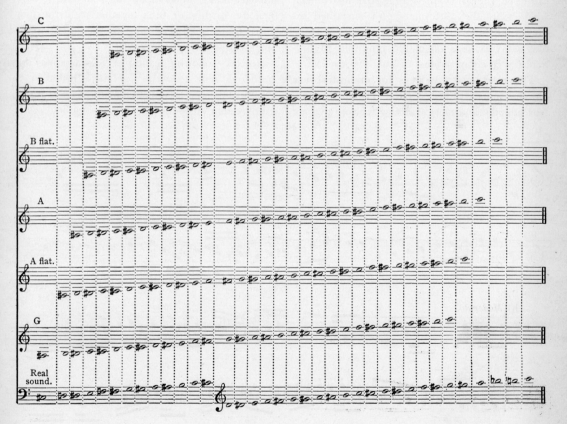

Easy trills upon any of the above varieties are shown in the following examples:

Easy Trills upon All the Differently Pitched Cornets.

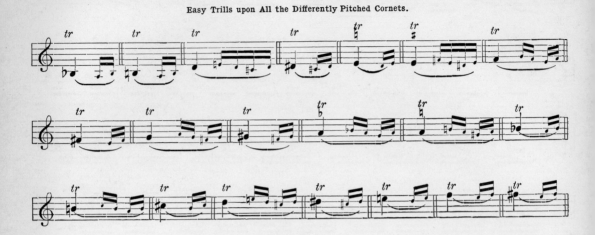

The above table as well as the trills can also be applied for: *Piccolo-Cornet, Flügel Horn, High A, B flat, B and C Trumpet, Alto and Tenor Horn.*

The tone of the Cornet possesses neither the smooth, voluminous, noble nor chivalrous qualities of the Trumpet, but nevertheless blends admirably with all the Brass instruments. It commands a leading position as a solo instrument, whether in the performance of sustained expressive cantabile passages, in double or triple tongued variations or in the rendition of brilliant dance compositions.

The most effective Keys for orchestral use are the same as those for the Trumpet; those best adapted and most effective for solo playing

are: C Major; A Minor; G Major; E Minor; F Major; D Minor; B flat Major; G Minor; E flat Major; C Minor; as a rule two and sometimes three Cornets are employed in scoring.

Used in dance-music, the melody or brilliant accompanying or ornamental figures are written for the 1st Cornet. The second executes sustained notes, accompanying passages, the melody in 3ds or 6ths together with the first Cornet, etc. All according to the intention or imagination of the composer.

In the following examples an idea may be gathered, how to write for the Cornet in a practical as well as effective manner and for the employment of double and triple tonguing:

DUETT FOR 2 CORNETS.

MENDELSSOHN.

As Trumpets and Horns are missing in most orchestras or smaller combinations (especially in America), it falls to the Cornet in nearly every instance to interpret one or the other of their parts. From a practical standpoint therefore these parts must be transposed, placed or written in such registers as to make their execution upon the Cornet possible.

In the following I present a table of the most usual transpositions of Trumpet-parts for the Cornet:

TABLE OF THE MOST USUAL TRANSPOSITIONS OF TRUMPET PARTS FOR THE CORNET.

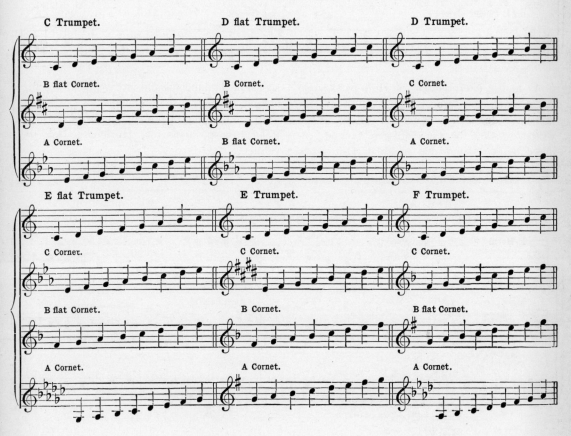

As to the interpretation of Horn-parts upon the Cornet, this proceeding involves greater difficulties due to the difference in pitch. If not written too low the 1st Horn-part can be rendered by the Cornet; but the other Horn-parts must be assigned to either the Clarinets, Bassoons, or Trombones, and in case these are also missing to the Violas or Violoncellos.

In the following I present a table of the most usual transpositions of Horn-parts for the Cornet:

TABLE OF THE MOST USUAL TRANSPOSITIONS OF HORN PARTS FOR THE CORNET.

At any rate it is always advisable for the composer, especially if the work, is intended for popular or selling purposes, to write or arrange his score in such a manner as to be equally effective for either large, small, or for String orchestra alone. I have illustrated an arrangement of this kind in the following example:

LA PASTOURELLA DELL' ALPI.

Transcription by H. Kling.

Specially arranged to be equally effective for either large, small or String orchestra.

ROSSINI.

Finally I will add that if the Cornet is used as a Solo-instrument, the accompaniment thereto must not be written in too prominent a manner. The mute is used in the identical manner and creates the same effect as in connection with the Trumpet.

4. THE SLIDE TROMBONE.

(ZUGPOSAUNE, TROMBONE, TROMBONE.)

The tone of this fine instrument possesses qualities which may be described as both noble, heroic, emotional and majestic. Employed "fortissimo" in its middle and lower registers, it can be used to advantage in expressing energy and brutality; in sustained cantabile passages performed "piano," it is expressive of earnest religious feelings. It is also well-adapted for dramatic scenes or situations demanding expressions of a dismal, demoniacal or terror-awakening nature.

In accordance to their tonal-compass we distinguish three kinds of Trombones : a) the Alto, b) the Tenor, and c) the Bass Trombone.

Tonal-compass of the three Trombones for orchestral use :

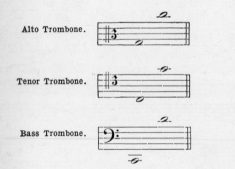

The Alto and Bass Trombones have become almost obsolete in modern times, which is to be greatly regretted, especially as far as the Bass Trombone is concerned ; it is owing to this that the following little passage from the "Freischütz" overture, is invariably played an octave higher ; this reproduces the original intention in no way, and the effectiveness of the passage is almost entirely destroyed.

At any rate, the modern composer in nearly every instance, writes only for 3 Tenor Trombones.

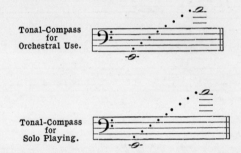

and in addition to this, the so-called Pedal-tones possible with good embouchure :

Berlioz in his famous "Requiem" employed these low tones in a very ingenious manner as shown on page 151.

The notes of the different positions are shown in the following examples :

The Different Positions.

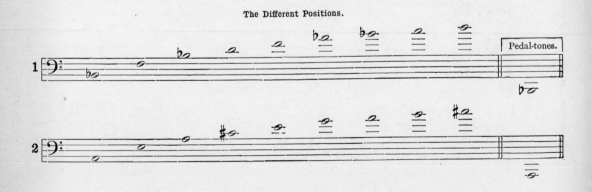

REQUIEM.

HECTOR BERLIOZ.

The notes of the Flutes at such a great distance from those of the Trombones sound like the harmonic vibrations of these low pedal-tones which are employed at such a low range and in slow tempo, with the special object of heightening the impressiveness of the pauses of the Choral voices and which create a surprising and well-sounding effect.

There are no easy trills and all lip-trills are even more difficult.

All trills below the following note are impossible; the trill executed by means of the slide is unmusical.

Some difficult passages are shown in the following:

All runs, whether diatonic or chromatic, in which the note of the seventh position occurs, are difficult.

Employed in broad and sustained chords the Trombones possess characteristics of a grand, overpowering and elevating nature, which are especially well adapted for serious and religious situations; Mozart has used them to excellent advantage in his opera "The Magic Flute." Played "fortissimo" the 3 Trombones can produce the most overwhelming and tremendous effects. The force of these instruments lies in their triple combination, the power of the simple triad.

The most effective Keys for orchestral or solo use are the flat-keys.

The Trombone is a very effective solo-instrument. Mozart employed it to great advantage and very effectively in his " Don Juan," " Magic Flute," Requiem, and in several of his masses. Notwithstanding it has become customary in modern times to correct his scores, employing Trombones where this greatest of masters did not wish them, and on the other hand allowing the beautiful solo in the " Tuba mirum " of his Requiem, which was specially written for a Trombone, to be played almost invariably upon a . . . . Bassoon. It is needless to add that this instrument cannot replace nor does it possess

the voluminous, majestic tone of the Trombone in any way.

R. Wagner, Meyerbeer, Halévy, and A. Thomas have entrusted very important passages to the Trombones in their score. A. Thomas has introduced a very effective solo for the first Trombone in his opera " Hamlet."

Usually only one Trombone is employed for dance-music, serving as a strengthener of the bass, but also for the execution of accessory melodies in appropriate places. When employing three Trombones the first two can execute accompanying figures, while the third strengthens the bass, as shown in the following example :

Sometimes sustained chords are written in the following manner :

The 3 Trombones can execute a melody or accessory melody unisono, which will always prove exceedingly effective :

The Valve-Trombone has the same tonal-compass and is treated exactly like the Slide-Trombone. The Valves or Pistons are the substitutes of the slide.

5. THE SAXOPHONE.

(SAXOPHON, SAXOPHONO, SAXOPHONE.)

This instrument, belonging to the family of Clarinets, possesses a soft and noble tone; it is an excellent substitute for the Alto and Bass Clarinets, as well as for the Bassethorn, and if need be, even for the Bassoon.

Differently pitched Saxophones are in use, and a list of the different varieties, with their tonal-compass, etc., is shown in the table on page 154.

Usually the following combination is employed : B flat Soprano, E flat Alto, B flat Tenor, and E flat Baritone. This simple quartet is entirely sufficient for the production of the most excellent effects. Sustained or cantabile passages are better suited to this instrument than quick runs; skips from lower to higher intervals or the reverse, as well as detached passages, are to be avoided. See following examples :

TABLE OF NOTATION FOR ALL THE DIFFERENT SAXOPHONES.

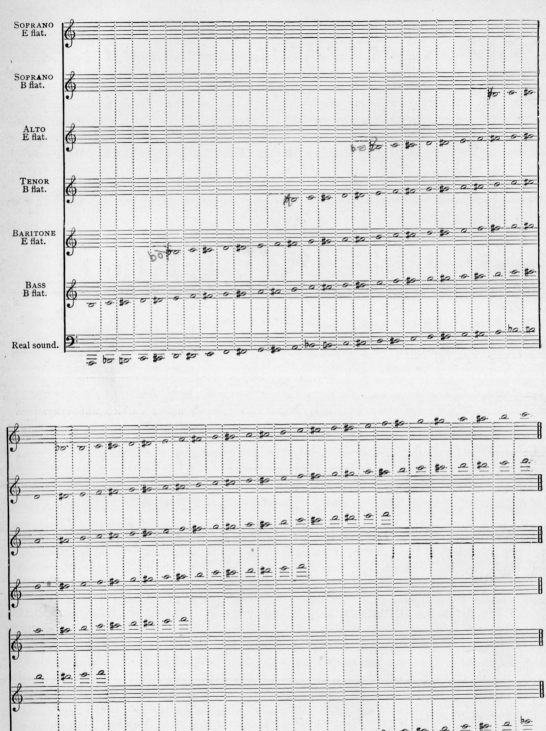

Music of a serious, religious character is best adapted for these instruments, and sustained intervals, as contained in the following example, are especially effective:

AVE VERUM.

MOZART.

The tonal-quality of the different Saxophones might be described in the following manner : Soprano B flat, shrill, especially if employed "forte." Alto E flat, soft and brilliant, excellently adapted for solo-playing. Tenor B flat, expressive and melancholy, making it well adapted for use in sentimental, cantabile passages. Baritone E flat, somewhat hollow and harsh, especially in the lower notes, but which could be used to excellent advantage in sad or funeral music.

So far, only few composers have added this instrument to their scores,* which is to be regretted, as the soft but nevertheless penetrating tonal-qualities of this instrument is excellently adapted for a great variety of tonal-combinations. With its use more variety could be produced, both through combination with the Wood-wind instruments, which would gain considerably in volume and smoothness, as well as with the Brass, especially the Trombones, the blaring and cutting quality of which would be considerably subdued in "forte" passages. Therefore in adding the Saxophones to our present orchestral forces, a greater variety of tonal-quality and character, and a much greater degree of volume and perfection, as far as the harmony is concerned, would become possible, stamping such an addition as a valuable and decided improvement.

* Hugo von Senger, in his military " Funeral March" for orchestra, has employed a single, and J. Massenet in his " Marche héroique de Szabody " a double quartet in a very effective manner.

In the following extract from A. Thomas's opera "Hamlet" a very effective solo for the Alto Saxophone in E flat is presented.

EXTRACT FROM THE OPERA "HAMLET."

A. THOMAS.

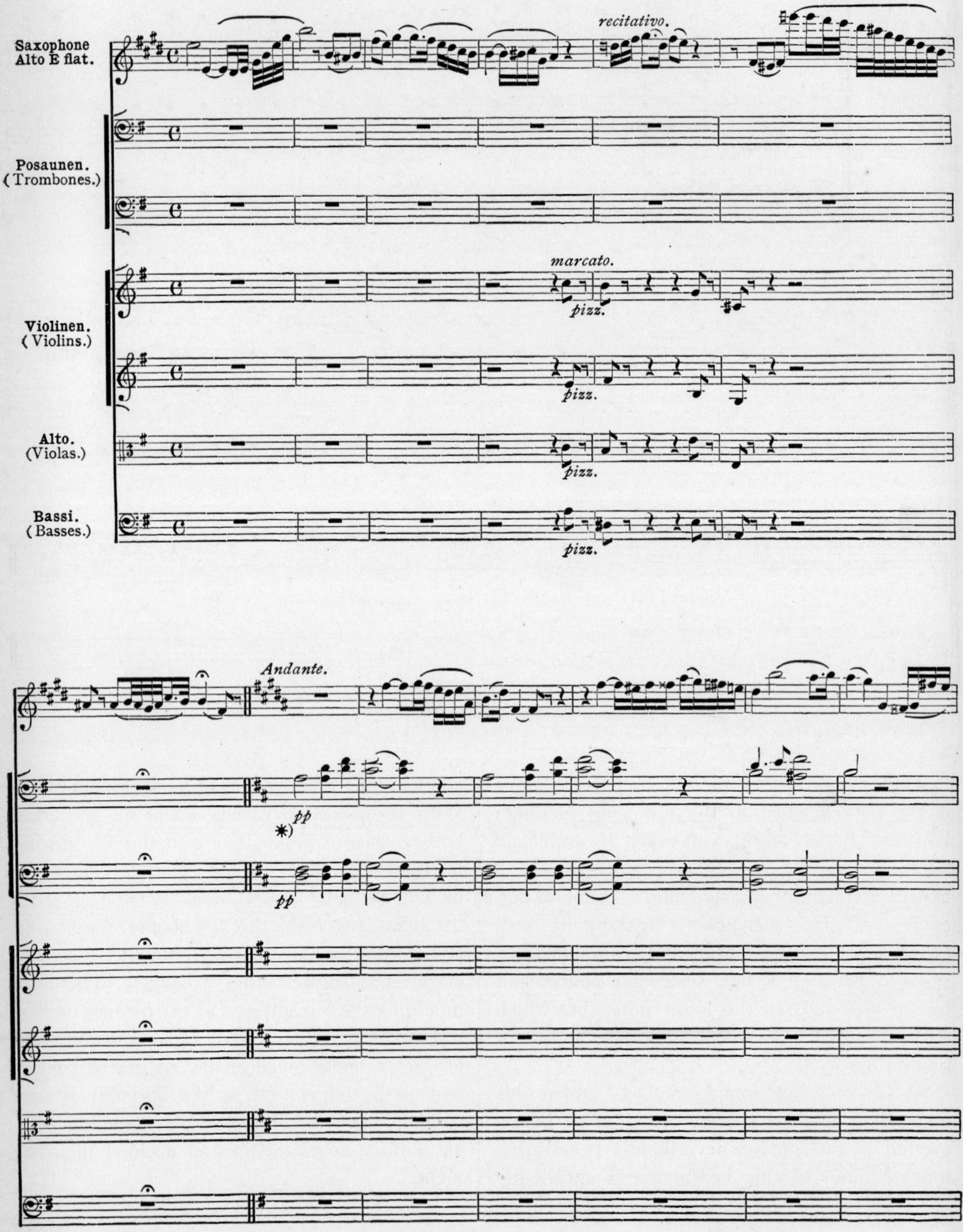
Saxophone Alto E flat.
Posaunen. (Trombones.)
Violinen. (Violins.)
Alto. (Violas.)
Bassi. (Basses.)
recitativo.
marcato.
pizz.
Andante.
pp
*)

* This soft Trombone accompaniment is exceedingly effective, and sets off the Saxophone solo in the most prominent manner.

In the French Military Bands the four Saxophones have been introduced since many years with great success. We will refer to this point again later on. The peculiar tonal-quality of the Saxophone does not fit it for use in dance-music; but in case it is employed in a complete orchestra, the melody, sustained notes, accompanying figures or accessory melodies may be written for it.

6. THE OPHICLEIDE.

(OPHICLEIDE, OPHICLEIDE, OPHYCLEIDE.)

This instrument was formerly much in vogue. But it has gradually and justly been put aside, as its croaking, unmusical and false tones are, to say the least, quite disagreeable. Employed in the orchestra it may answer as a substitute for the Bass-Trombone, but as a solo instrument it would be simply disgusting. Ophicleides in B-flat and C are in use.

Mendelssohn, Berlioz, Auber, Halévy, Meyerbeer, etc., have made use of this instrument in their scores. Practical manner of writing for it is illustrated in the following examples:

7. THE BASS-TUBA.

(BASS TUBA OR BOMBARDON, PELLITONI CONTRE-
BASSE.)

This colossal instrument has replaced the
Ophicleide excellently ; it possesses a serious,
penetrating, but rough quality of tone, which is
of excellent effect in the orchestra, forming an
excellent and appropriate Bass for the Trumpets, Cornets and Trombones.

Tonal-
Compass,
for Orches-
tral Use.

Meyerbeer, in his " Prophet," and especially
R. Wagner in his later scores, have raised this
instrument to a very high and important position. It is equally effective if employed "pianissimo." It stands to reason that for an instrument of such dimensions and of such low range
no quick passages or skips should be written,
excepting for the production of comical effects,
although I am no admirer of putting the instrument to any such use, by any means. The examples given for the Ophicleide, on the preceding page, may also serve as an illustration of
how to write for this instrument, according to its
tonal-character.

Combined with the Trombones, the Bass-
Tuba can produce the grandest and most impressive effects, as shown in the following extract from R. Wagner's " Tannhäuser," and as
is further demonstrated in the 1st Act of his
" Lohengrin."

EXTRACT FROM " TANNHÄUSER."

Act 3. Scene 2.

R. WAGNER.

The beautiful Introduction to the 3d Act of "Lohengrin" must also be mentioned. A tremendous unisono of 4 Horns, 3 Trombones, Bass-Tuba, Violoncellos and Double-Basses tearing along, while the remaining instruments execute the accompaniment in triplets. Following this enormous outburst, the diminuendo losing itself in a gradual pianissimo, is very effective.

For dance-music the Bass-Tuba * is employed to strengthen the Bass parts; but it is rarely used.

General Remarks. If interesting and effective tonal-combinations are to be produced, it is advisable to be as sparing and economical in the use and distribution of Brass instruments as possible. Of late years it has become customary to overcrowd the String Orchestra with Brass instruments of every description to such an extent that even the simplest Romance or Chansonette is sometimes accompanied by 2 Trumpets or Cornets and 3 Trombones, without counting the Stringed and Wood-wind instruments. There can be no doubt that instrumentation of this kind produces a very monotonous effect, as no tonal-shading is possible. It is deplorable that so many composers are not capable of employing the Wind instruments with taste and according to the individual characteristics of the different instruments. This excessive, indiscreet and inappropriate use of the

Brass is certainly one of the reasons that modern productions of this class are so quickly doomed to oblivion, even if possessed of originality as far as melodic and harmonic invention is concerned. But if employed with moderation and skill the grandest and most impressive effects are possible with the use of the Brass instruments. They are, therefore, only to be used where the gradual climax or burst of expression demands their co-operation; as in a crescendo ending in forte or in the expression of various feelings demanding a great exhibition of tonal-volume and strength.

Special attention must be directed towards writing Trumpet, Cornet and Horn parts in as natural a manner as possible; that is, that the natural or open notes are brought into prominence either singly, in thirds, fifths or octaves. If soft, expressive passages are to be entrusted to the Wind instruments they should be written in their middle register, and not in their higher ones. In consideration of the player, this point demands careful attention, as in performing such high passages he (the player) runs chances of over-blowing certain tones or that his embouchure will give way entirely, and in consequence ruin the desired effect.†

Passages in the following tonal-registers are therefore to be avoided:

The tonal character and type of the differently pitched instruments must be studied very conscientiously and with great care, and special attention must be directed towards becoming

thoroughly acquainted with their individual and normal tonal key.

Effective and successful scoring is only possible after this has been accomplished.

* The Tenor-Tuba in E flat and Bass-Tuba in B flat, which R. Wagner has employed in his "Götterdämmerung," are in reality nothing else but Tenor-horns in E flat and Baritone in B flat, which are in general use in Military Bands, and which will be discussed later on.

† I am always reminded of this when listening to the entrance of the Brass instruments in the Adagio of the "Oberon" overture. This particular part, which according to directions is to be played "pianissimo," is so difficult for the Trumpets and Trombones that its clear and faultless execution and delivery are very rare, the notes either breaking or as is generally the case, refusing to speak.

The Brass Instruments as Employed in Dance-music. The Horns are employed to strengthen either the harmony or the accompanying figures of the second Violin and Viola. But sustained notes are also written for them, which, if introduced appropriately, will always prove very effective; sometimes solos and melodic passages are also entrusted to the 1st Horn. The Trumpets are used in a great variety of ways in dance-music. The 1st Trumpet is often employed as the leader of the melody, and the 2nd as an accompanying instrument for filling or strengthening the harmony. If a melody moves entirely or partly in passages of thirds or sixths, and the 1st Trumpet is entrusted with its execution, it is natural that the 2nd Trumpet can take part by joining the 1st Trumpet in thirds or sixths. In "forte" passages both are often used unisono, especially if they are leading the melody.

The Cornet is an indispensable instrument for dance-music, especially in France and America. the first is always employed as a leader of the melody, and oft-times alone for solo work; the 2nd Cornet is used and treated like the 2nd Trumpet. The Trombone furnishes the bass for the other Brass instruments, Horns, Trumpets, and Cornets, although solos and accessory melodies are also assigned to it. When scoring for 3 Trombones as many sustained chords as possible should be assigned to them, as they are very effective and sound especially well. In addition to the usual complement of Brass instruments, larger orchestras are provided with an additional Bass-Tuba, which forms an excellent aid for strengthening the tonal volume of the Double-Basses, and lending a degree of firmness and sonority to the entire ensemble, which this admirable instrument alone is capable of.

C. Instruments with Keys.

1. THE ORGAN.

(ORGEL, ORGANO, ORGUE.)

Most Organs possess two key-boards, the one being played by the hand (*manus*), the other with the foot (*pes.*); consequently the names Manual and Pedal. An Organ without Pedals is called Positive. Organs are made with 2, 3, 4 and 5 Manuals, which are placed terrace-like above each other. Upon Organs with only 2 Manuals, the lower one is usually the Principal and the upper one the Choir Manual. With three Manuals the Principal one is placed in the middle, the highest or third following, according to volume, and with four Manuals the successive order of construction is 2, 1, 3, 4. Some larger Organs are supplied with two sets of Pedals, of which the lower is the Principal.

The Manual consists of 54 Keys in chromatic succession from:

the Pedals as a rule only about half, from C to d̄:

Every Organ-stop influencing a certain number of pipes of uninterrupted tonal progression and identical construction, whether large or small, is designated as a Register. This same term is also applied to the different stops, placed at both sides of the key-board, serving to open or shut the valves of the different organ-pipes by being pulled out or in. Upon the knob of these stops, by means of which the stop-levers are manipulated, the name of the different Registers together with their tonal volume (indicated by the term *foot*) is written, f. i.: Principal 8 foot, Gedackt 4 foot, Spitzflöte 2 foot, Rohrflöte 1 foot, etc. Added to the real Register-stops, every Organ possesses a smaller or larger number of additional so-called *accessory register-stops* which are sometimes attached to the instrument in such a manner that they can be managed either by the feet or knees. Among these *accessory register stops* the following must be specially mentioned: a) *The Couplers*, which connect the interior key-action or either the Manuals (manual-coupler) or that of the Pedals (pedal-coupler) with each other in such a way that when the keys of the Principal Manual or Pedal are pressed down the respective keys of the accessory stops will be brought into play, and consequently the entire keys of two or rather all the Manuals will be brought into simultaneous action.

The contrivance which brings about the simultaneous action of the Bass octave of the Principal Manual and the interior key-action of the

Pedals is also named Pedal-coupler. This latter contrivance is very important, as only low and not enough stops for the Pedals are at command, as a rule; but through combination with the brighter stops of the Manuals, the lower ones of the Pedals gain in quicker action, strength and decision, volume and brilliancy, and only then can the Bass supply and form the basis necessary for a strong and complete organ-work. Smaller works, as a rule, possess only 16-foot stops, and cannot be manipulated without the Pedal-coupler. b.) *The Composition-stops* which bring about the simultaneous sounding or stopping of a number of stops. They are also attached to the instrument in the form of Pedals, directly above the regulation Pedals, and are called *Combination*-pedals. c.) *The Crescendo or Decrescendo stop*, which can be found in larger works and which serves to diminish the stiffness and inflexibility peculiar to the tone of the Organ. d.) *The Tremulant*, which should only be employed in weaker registration.

The Pipe-work consists of: 1) Flue-pipes or Flute-work and 2) of Reed-work. The former have derived their name from one of their component parts (Labien-languets), and owing to their Flute-like tonal-quality, and the latter from their similarity of tonal-quality to various reed instruments like the Bassoon, Clarinet, Oboe, etc.

The tonal quality of the Flue-stops is designated as: sharp, bright, brilliant, breezy, lean, thin, hard, voluminous, thick, round, dark, soft, tender.

The tonal-character of the Reed-work is dependent upon the size and kind of tubes. *Beating reeds* produce a hard, blaring quality; *free reeds*, a more pleasing, bright and brilliant tone. In addition to these a variety of shadings is possible, brought about by the partial beating of the reeds. Two equally high-sounding reeds of different size possess different qualities; the larger producing a more voluminous and the smaller a finer, sharper tone.

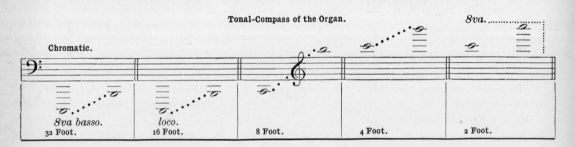

Tonal-Compass of the Organ.

The Organ-stops are divided into Plain- and Mixture-stops. With the Plain only one tone is produced with each stop. If this is the same tone designated by the Key, the fundamental tone of the respective Key becoming audible at the same time, the stop is called Foundation or Principal stop. All 32, 16, 8, 4 and 2 foot Registers are included in this, whether contained in the Manual or Pedals; or in other words the entire Principals, together with their dependent Octaves and Superoctaves, the Gambe Salicet, etc., furthermore all the Registers designated chiefly with the term "Flöte" (Flute) f. i., Doppelflöte, Rohrflöte, etc., and lastly all the Reed stops like Trombone, Trumpet, Oboe, etc. The most important and appropriate *Fundamental stops* for the Manual are the 8 foot, as they are in unison with the human voice and specially adapted for accompanying it, but for the Pedals the 16 foot are the most appropriate;

they constitute the Bass for the 8 foot. A different species are the *Mutation stops*. These do not allow the tone of the respective Keys to be heard, producing an entirely different effect; if a Quintstop is in use the Key C will produce the tone g; if a Terzstop the C will produce f. Height and Depth in this case are also dependent upon the size of the respective registers. All registers bearing the name of Quint or Terz, whether in the Manual or Pedals, are included in this department. The Quint and Terz registers cannot be used independently, but serve only for imparting more volume to the entire work and especially to fill the gap, which would be created by their absence, between the Fundamental and Mixture stops; they also aid in subduing the peculiar and disagreeable squeakiness of some of the mixtures, especially those composed of small pipes, and therefore serve as a strengthener to them, justly deserving their name of "Fillstops." Furthermore we have the mixed stops (Mixtures). This species of Register has several pipes to every Key which are tuned in the Octave, perfect Fifth and Major Third, making it possible to produce a more or less complete major triad upon every Key, according to the dimensions of the instrument. As the intervals of a triad are not adequate for the diversified composition of a mixture, some of them are doubled. Therefore as these registers possess several pipes of different pitch for every tone, they are collectively called mixed stops or mixtures to distinguish them from the Fundamental and Choir stops, designated as Plain stops. These are again divided into various kinds and designated by special names, the pipes allotted to each register differing in their construction as far as size and pitch are concerned. The following stops — Cornet, Cymbel, Rauschquinte, Scharf, Sesquialtera, Tertian, etc., — belong to this department. Like the Accessory stops the Mixtures cannot be used independently, serving only to give strength to the entire work, and impart sparkle and life and a certain silver-like quality to the tone of the Organ. The false- or miss-tones produced through these applications are lost in the harmonic mass of the instrument. See following examples:

The Organ registers can therefore be divided into the following Choirs:

a.) **The Principal choir** ("Prästant" is the old designation of Principal). The Principals, 32, 16, 4 and 2 foot; the largest is also named Sub-Principal. In such cases where the 4 foot occurs in connection with the Principal 8′ it is frequently designated by Oktave 4′; the 2 foot are usually designated by Oktave 2′ and Super-oktave. In the Manual the Principals occur 16 to 2′, in the Pedals 32 to 4′, consequently 32′ only in the Pedals, 2′ only in the Manual, but 16 to 4′ in both Manual and Pedals. The Principal choir also includes the open Quinten and Terzen of Accessory stops, as well as the Mixture-stops.

b.) **The String-Choir** contains only such stops possessing a strong or weak, stroke-like, sharp or moderate cutting, also singing or lisping quality of tone. The Geigenprincipal occurs 8 and 16 foot, and possesses a very pleasing cutting quality of tone. The Viola da Gamba, 8 foot, is very effective as a solo register, especially for the performance of sustained cantabile compositions. The Viole d'amour, 8 foot, charming and pleasing. Fugaro 8′ or 4′ with a sharp penetrating tone. Violon 16′, Violoncello 8′- a, fine Pedal solo stop; likewise the Gamben bass 8′, etc.

c.) **The Flute-tone,** consisting of: Flauto traverso 8′, Flauto dolce, also named Flauto amabile (charming Flute), 8 and 4 foot, well adapted for the performance of expressive Adagios, owing to its soft, sweet and charming quality of tone. Hohlflöte 8 and 4 foot. Flautino, Flauto minor and major; Bourdonal-flöte, Dolcissimo 4 and 8 foot. The Spitzflöte 8 and 4 foot. When 2 foot the Spitzflöte is called Piccolo. Flachflöte, Salicional, also called Salicet, 8 and 4′. Large works are also provided with a Salicet bass 16′, Gemshorn. The tone of the 8 foot Gemshorn sounds soft and horn-like, that of the 4 foot penetrating and Gamba-like. The Pedal-stops are named Gemshornbass and Gemshornquinte or Gross-Nasat; the smaller, Manual-stops: Oktavengemshorn (4′), Klein-Oktaven or Supergemshorn (2′), Gemshornquinte and Nasat.

d.) **The Gedacktchoir,** Gedackt 8′, also named *Starkgedackt* to distinguish it from *Still* or *Lieblichgedackt,* 8 and 16 foot. Kleingedackt mostly 4 foot. Doppelflöte 8', also in the Pedals as Doppelflötenbass 8'. Bourdon or Grobgedackt, a 16 foot Manual stop with a heavy tone excellent for filling the harmony. Sometimes 32 foot Bourdons are met with, Sub-bass 16', of uncertain weak quality of tone, Untersatz 32', also called Major bass, Gross-Subbass, Cross-Untersatz, and Suboktave, a 32 foot subbass, which provides the remaining Pedal-stops with an excellent foundation. Added to these the Flötenbass, an 8 foot Pedal-stop, as well as Rohrflöte 16', 8' and 4', are included in the Gedackt choir. After the Fundamental stops already named two Accessory stops must finally be mentioned, namely: the Rohrquinte and Quintatön 16', and 4', also known as Quintgetön, Quintadena, and Hohlschelle, and named Quintatönbass in the Pedals. The 16 foot Pedal-stop fills exceedingly well.

e.) **The Reed-choir,** containing only Fundamental stops: The Posaune (Trombone) 16', the best-known Pedal-stop Posaune 32.' The Trompete (Tromba) usually 8', but also adapted to 16' and 4', is also designated in the 4 foot Register as Clarin (Clarion), it occurs both in the Manual and Pedals. The Hoboe (Hobo, Oboe, Hautbois) an 8 foot Manual stop the tone of which is delicate and bright. The Clarinet, an 8 foot Manual, possesses a much stronger tone than the Oboe. The Fagott (Bassoon) 16' as a rule only occurs in the Pedals. Dulcian 16' similar to the Fagott but weaker in volume. Aeoline 16' and 8' with soft and delicate tone. Physharmonika or Harmonium, 16' and 8', is very similar in tone to the instruments whose name they bear. Vox humana, 8', which imitates the quality of the human voice.

Vox angelica (Voix celeste), a splendid 8' Solo-stop.

It would be entirely impossible to mention all the different Organs which have been erected or to explain their separate Registers in detail,

as every church possesses a different work, planned and finished by different Organ-builders, according to individual ideas and principles. Every Organ-builder directs his energies and talents towards furnishing a work which, in his estimation, will make it possible for the player to display and produce the greatest number of effective and beautiful tonal combinations.

The Thunder-stop or Thunder Effect

Is especially adapted for use in storm-scenes; this effect can be produced upon every Organ possessed of the following Fundamental stops: Sous-Basse 16', Bourdon 16', Principal 16', etc., to which several 8' Fundamental stops like Bourdon 8' and Flöte 8', etc., are added. The effect is produced by playing the lowest notes upon the Manual and Pedals in Chromatic succession, sustaining them in steps, but never overreaching the lower octave. See following example:

The pitch of the Pedals is an octave lower than that of the Manual. Care must be exercised in the use of the Basses of the Organ, as they speak much slower than the tones of the Manual, and therefore adapt themselves only to slow progressions. The Pedal-basses are expressive of an earnest, lofty, mighty, impressive and mysterious tonal character; employed with such characteristics in view, the Pedals can be put to the most artistic uses. Usually the Pedals are employed singly, but two-part Pedal-playing is not infrequent, calling into action both feet of the organist; two-part Pedal-playing should be rarely employed, and as a rule only for the doubling of the Bass in the Octave, as shown in the following example:

Adagio.

The best compositions for this wonderful instrument have been left to us by J. S. Bach, Händel, Mozart, Mendelssohn, Rinck, Buxtehude, Van Eyken, Saint-Saëns, Gade, Richter, Ritter, Schumann, Liszt, Rheinberger, Piutti, Volkmar, etc.

In order to gather an idea of the appropriate manner of writing for this instrument, the organ compositions of J. S. Bach, the greatest organist of all times, should be studied and consulted.

Registration.

The art of registration is analogous to that of instrumentation. The organist must be capable of deciding and combining the appropriate tonal-colors, which naturally necessitates a great amount of taste and imagination. It is advisable for the composer to indicate the registration himself, in this way offering a guide to the organist; in doing this the composer should remember that he must treat the Organ like an orchestra, and bring the rich and beautiful effects of modern instrumentation into play.

Classification of the Characteristic Properties of all the Registers of the Organ.

Tonal - Volume. Brilliancy.

All Flutes; Bourdon; Quintatön; Spitzflöte; Cymbel; with Pedals Sub-Basse 16′, Principal 8′.

Tonal-Strength. Brilliancy.

Prinzipal, Prestant with Pedals Prinzipal 16′; 8′.

Tonal-Color. Solo Performances.

Every 8 foot Register can be employed separately; the following are especially adapted for Solo-stops: Viola di Gamba; Salicional; Physharmonika; Klarinette; Dulciana; Krummhorn or Cromhorn; Violoncelle; Vox humana; Oboe; Gedackt; Geigenprinzipal; with Pedals Violoncelle 8′, Flöte 8′.

Tonal-Brilliancy. Complete Work.

Oboe; Trompete; Scharf; Cornett; Fagott; Doublette, etc., with Pedals, Posaune 8′, 16′, 32′, Bombard 16′. The above-mentioned registers sound best and clearest in the 8′ and 4 foot sizes, especially in their middle positions; the finest, best shaded and most varied tonal-combinations can be produced with the help of these stops. The smaller or larger Organ-stops are not possessed of such decided tonal-character.

As can be gathered from the foregoing, this mighty instrument is capable of placing an unlimited amount of beautiful tonal combinations of every description at the disposal of the accomplished Organist.

Upon entering the church our thoughts and feelings are completely concentrated upon the greatness, majesty and eternity of God. In accordance with these holy impressions the organist ought only perform sterling compositions of the great masters for the devout listeners; as everything great and beautiful in music can serve to heighten the glorification, dignity and sanctity of the divine service. Especially during the singing of the Choir, which in reality should strengthen and help the Organ to greater prominence, the organist should refrain from any unnecessary embellishments or ornaments.

The Organ is also employed to excellent advantage in theatres and concert-performances, and was principally used by our old classic masters for their religious compositions (Masses, Oratorios, etc.), in connection with the orchestra; the organ-parts which these tonal heroes wrote for their respective scores are indicated by the term Organo, and are sketched only in figured basses, which of course confronts the organist with the responsibility of executing and developing them in an artistic and appropriate manner.

In modern times the Organ has also been employed for operatic purposes by such composers as Spohr, Halévy, Auber, Meyerbeer, R Wagner, Hérold, Gounod, etc. In the following example an extract from a very fine and exceedingly effective Organ part, which Meyerbeer has introduced in the 4th Act of his opera "The Prophet," is shown:

EXTRACT FROM THE OPERA, "THE PROPHET."

G. MEYERBEER.

The French composer C. Saint-Saëns has also employed the Organ in a grand and effective manner in his 3d Symphony in C minor, illustrated by the following extract:

EXTRACT FROM THE THIRD SYMPHONY IN C MINOR.

CAMILLE SAINT-SAËNS, Op. 78.

Practical Remarks as to the Employment of the Registers.

Certain registers of the Organ can be used separately as well as in connection with other similar ones; these are known as the Principal or Fundamental stops; others again, which can be employed neither separately nor collectively without being combined with the Fundamental stops; these are known as the Accessory or Fill stops and Mixed stops or Mixtures. The last species serve only to strengthen and bring into prominence the Fundamental stops, and are dependent upon these in regard to size, measurement and intonation. The most useful and appropriate Manual-stops for use in connection with the Choir are generally those which blend best and are in unison with the human voices;

they include all the 8 ft. stops without exception, as well as all the 16 ft. registers of the Pedals, which form the bass to the 8 ft. of the Manual. If the tone of the Organ is to be strengthened, or if it is to appear more prominently, the 4 ft. in the Manual and the 8 ft. Fundamental stops in the Pedals are added. In addition to the above-mentioned stops, the Accessory or Fill-stops are also employed for medium-strong registration; but these latter must never participate as the highest or smallest stop in any combination of registers, as they bring only the Quinte or Terz of the respective Key into action, and never produce the Fundamental tone; they must therefore be covered invariably by the higher-lying Superoktave stops which usually occur in the Manual in 2 ft. and in the Pedals in 4 ft. Finally, if the greatest penetrating qualities are to be imparted to the tone of the Organ the entire mixed stops or mixtures are brought into play. From the above-said we therefore derive four different principal varieties, according to which an Organ may be registered, namely :

a.) *For Moderate (weak) Registration.*

In the Manual all 8, in the Pedals all 16 foot stops. (N. B. — In speaking of strong or weak registration, naturally a great deal depends upon the number of stops possessed by an Organ. For a small instrument the registration of probably three 8 ft. in the Manual and one or two 16 ft. stops in the Pedals might be strong enough, while in a larger Organ the application of five or seven 8 ft. in the Manual and three or four 16 ft. Pedal stops might be considered weak.)

b.) *For Strengthened Registration.*

In addition to the stops mentioned under *a*) the following are brought into action: in the Manual all 4, in the Pedals all 8 ft. stops. (With larger Organs the 16 ft. registers of the Manual and the 32 ft. of the registers may be employed, according to the inclination of the player.)

c.) *For Medium Strong Registration.*

In addition to the stops mentioned under *a*) and *b*), in the Manual, all accessory or fill-stops, together with the 2 and if possible the 1 ft. registers; in the Pedals all Accessory stops in connection with all 4 ft. and if possible all 2 and 1 ft. registers; although the latter are to be found only in the larger Organs of former years. (Even if provided, the 1 ft. registers of the Manual and the 2 and 1 ft. of the Pedals can be omitted at will and only used when employing the full work.)

d.) *For Strong Registration or for the Full Work.*

In addition to the stops mentioned under *a*), *b*) and *c*): — all Mixed stops or Mixtures (both in the Manuals and Pedals).

From the above four principal combinations of the Registers two important rules are derived, (1) For proper Registration attention must be paid that the stops aid each other amongst themselves, the heavy and low ones being brought into prominence and relieved by the lighter and more penetrating ones; a combination of this kind imparting decision and clearness to the former, while the latter are covered in turn by the heavier ones and their screaming, screeching quality of tone subdued at the same time; (2) that no space or gap will occur in the progression of the Registers. It would consequently be faulty to combine say one or more 8 ft. with one or more 2 ft. stops in the Manual, as in this case the connecting 4 ft. (as well as the Quinte $2\frac{2}{3}$ ft. in strengthened Registration) would be missing; a combination of the 16 and 4 ft. stops in the Pedals would be equally faulty, as the 8 ft. Registers (and according to circumstances the $5\frac{1}{3}$ ft. Quinte) would be missed. But even if these rules are carefully observed, similar errors will surely occur, if the nature of the different organ stops is not taken into consideration. In this way the combination of several 8 ft. together with several stopped 4 ft. and one open 2 ft. stop would be faulty, owing to an open 4 ft. (Oktave) stop, and with stronger Registration the Quinte $2\frac{2}{3}$ ft. belonging to it would be missed. Faulty registration of a similar nature would be the combination of a stopped 8 ft. with an open 4 ft. stop, etc. As a rule for proper registration we will add that the number of Pedal registers employed must always be governed by the number of Manual registers in use. 1, 2, and 3 Pedal stops can always be counted as necessary for 3, 4, and 5 Manual stops; but the construction and nature of the various Registers, whether open or stopped, must always be taken into careful consideration.

2. THE HARMONIUM.

The Key-board of the Harmonium is similar to that of the Piano-forte but extending only over a range of 5 octaves. Pedals are attached below the Key-board, which, while being set in motion by the player, furnish the air to the bellows in the inner part of the instrument, necessary for the production of the sounds.

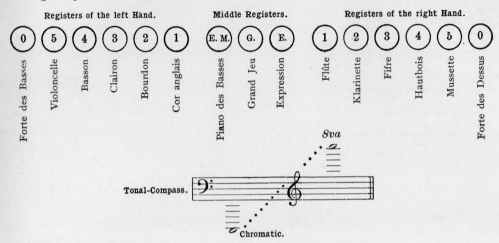

Characteristic Effects of the Different Registers.

The ① of the left hand is for the accompaniment; the ① of the right hand is adapted for light and smooth passages.

The ② is very well adapted for earnest religious and lofty cantabile playing.

The ③ is rarely employed alone, but is very effective if combined with other registers.

The ④ is an excellent imitation of the respective instrument; it is well adapted for solos, rural scenes, etc.

The ⑤ is the octave of ②, and is well adapted for expressive pastoral scenes.

The ⓪ or Forte imparts more tonal volume to the registers ③ and ④.

The Ⓖ serves to bring all the registers into play simultaneously; through which the tonal-brilliancy of the church-organ can be imitated.

The Ⓔ imparts more expressiveness to the different registers, offering the possibility of performing musical compositions with great feeling.

ⒺⓂ possesses no independent quality of tone, only serving to weaken the tones of the Bass, which as a rule always sound much stronger than the tones of the registers of the right side. If the use of a special register is to be discontinued it is indicated with a little line through the figure ④ ② etc.

A table of notation for the Harmonium is presented in the following example.

TABLE OF NOTATION FOR THE HARMONIUM.

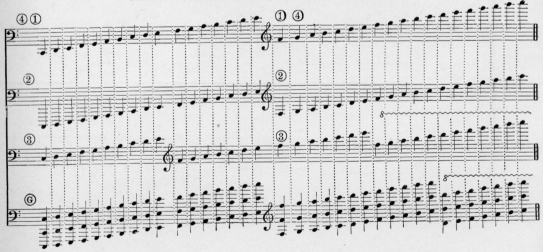

Combined with each other these various registers can produce the following effects : —

For strong voluminous playing.

All Registers or Ⓖ and Ⓞ.

For moderately strong playing.

④③① ①③④
or
③① ①③
or
③① ①②④
or
④②① ①②④

For soft, smooth playing.

① ①
or

④① ①④
or
④② ②④

For Solo or Recitative.

① ①②
or
④ ①③
or
④① ①②④.

Many more combinations are possible ; here only the principal ones have been mentioned.

Compositions of slow tempo and religious character are best adapted for the Harmonium, illustrations of which are shown in the following examples : —

"THOU SHEPHERD ISRAEL'S."

D. S. Bortniansky.

E. Feska.

dich   der Chor - ge - sang   Im fei - er - li - chen Gang   Hörst

EXTRACT FROM "LOHENGRIN."

Especially arranged for Harmonium with 2 Key-boards.

RICHARD WAGNER.

Harmonium.

a.) For larger instruments with two key-boards (Manuals) the registration is as follows: — I K. B. ① ⑤ on both sides II K. B. left ④ right ④ ⑥ b.) Ⓜ — Manual coupler.

Purely secular music, like dance compositions, is in no way adapted to either the Organ or the Harmonium. Very often the Harmonium takes the place of the Organ, but cannot replace the rich and manifold qualities of the latter in any way. In combination with various other instruments — Piano, Violin, etc., as well as with the human voice, — sustained chords may be written for it, which are exceedingly effective. A few composers have also employed the Harmonium very successfully in the orchestra.

THE CONCERT-HARMONIUM.

An instrument constructed by Schiedmayer in Stuttgart according to the directions of Hlavatsch. It possesses a compass of 6 Octaves. This Harmonium, while no larger than the usual instrument, offers a surprising amount of tonal-volume in its 29 Registers ranging from Pianissimo to Fortissimo, and in which the tonal-qualities of the Flute, Oboe, Clarinet, Bassoon, and Horn are imitated in a masterly manner. This instrument possesses 2 Key-boards (manuals) each of 6 octaves, which can be extended to 8 vibrating octaves, by means of extreme registers, offering opportunity for the production of countless and surprising registral combinations.

THE ORGUE-HARMONIUM.*

An instrument manufactured by the firm of Conty and Richard (in France) possessing 2 Key-boards with the following 34 Registers; with them a variety of the finest and most beautiful tonal and registral combinations may be brought about.

Régistres du 1er clavier (jeux sur sommier horizontal).

Basse: 1. Cor anglais. 2. Bourdon. 3. Clairon. 4. Basson. 5. Bombarde. 6. Sourdine. 7. Trémolo. 8. Expression.

Dessus: 9. Flûte. 10. Clarinette. 11. Fifre. 12. Hautbois. 13. Musette. 14. Voix céleste. 15. Harp éolienne. 16. Trémolo.

Régistres du 2e clavier (Expressif, jeux sur sommier vertical).

Basse: 17. Gambe. 18. Bourdon. 19. Clairon. 20. Basson. 21. Trompette. 22. Saxophone. 23. Trémolo.

Dessus: 24. Flûte. 25. Clarabella. 26. Larigot. 27. Hautbois de récit. 28. Hautbois de 16. 29. Voix angélique. 30. Salicional. 31. Trémolo. 32. Copula (basse). 33. Copula (dessus). 34. Grand jeu.

* There are still a few more varieties of organs, such as the " Diapason Organ," the " Orgue enchanté," the Hand or Barrel Organ, an instrument called " Pyrophon," all of which, however, it will be unnecessary to explain in detail, as they are of no value for orchestral purposes.

Group III.

INSTRUMENTS OF PERCUSSION.

1. THE KETTLE-DRUMS.

(PAUKEN, TIMPANI, TIMBALES.)

Their character expresses itself in their power of concussion, which can express itself from the faintest Pianissimo to the most tremendous and enormous Fortissimo. The Kettle-Drums adapt themselves to every variety of musical composition, but especially for storm-scenes and funeral marches. They can be excellently employed to illustrate the uneasy beating of the heart in dramatic scenes, and can add much towards the characterization of impressive situations. For instance, "Lohengrin" Act 3, and Funeral March from R. Wagner's "Götterdämmerung" an extract of which is presented in the following example.

EXTRACT FROM "THE FUNERAL MARCH" FROM "GÖTTERDÄMMERUNG."

Haydn, Mozart, Weber, etc., have produced beautiful effects with these instruments. Beethoven has used them in a very peculiar and unique manner in the Scherzo of his 9th, in the Adagio of his B flat Major, and in his C minor Symphony.

Two Kettle-Drums are as a rule employed in the orchestra with the following tonal-compass:—

The Kettle-Drums can be tuned according to the intention or imagination of the composer either in thirds, fourths, fifths, sixths, sevenths, or octaves. Every conceivable variety of tonal-shading is possible upon these instruments ranging from the softest " pianissimo " to the strongest " fortissimo " or the reverse. The following examples illustrate how these Drums are to be employed in a practical manner.

In modern times as many as from 3 to 16 Kettle-Drums have been employed in the orchestra ;† Berlioz, f. i., in the Tuba Mirum of his " Requiem " employs 8 pairs of differently tuned Kettle-Drums manipulated by ten players, as shown in the following extract :

---

* Rossini has made use of this high G in the introduction of his " Stabat Mater."

† Mozart has also employed 4 Kettle-Drums in his " 10 Compositions " (Köchel Catalogue, No. 187) as well as in one of his " Divertimentos " (Köchel Catalogue, No. 188).

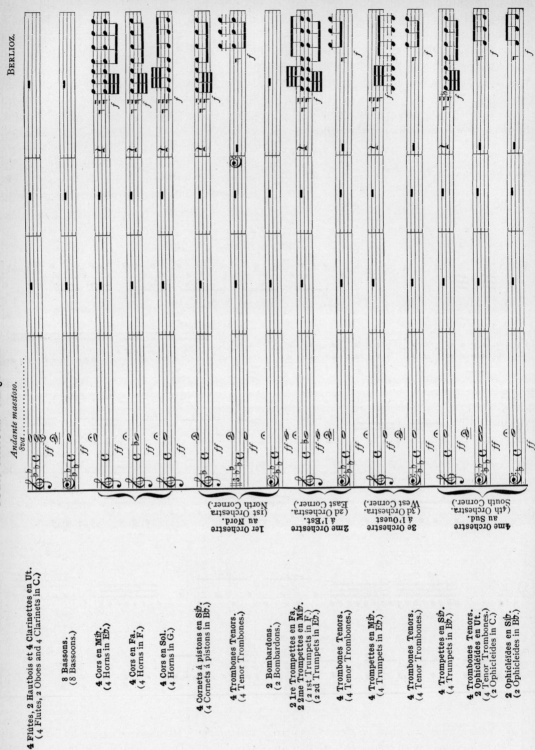

TUBA MIRUM. REQUIEM.

BERLIOZ.

Andante maestoso.

1er Orchestre au Nord.
(1st Orchestra North Corner.)

2me Orchestre à l'Est.
(2d Orchestra East Corner.)

3e Orchestre à l'Ouest.
(3d Orchestra West Corner.)

4me Orchestre au Sud.
(4th Orchestra South Corner.)

4 Flûtes, 2 Hautbois et 4 Clarinettes en Ut.
(4 Flutes, 2 Oboes and 4 Clarinets in C.)

8 Bassons.
(8 Bassoons.)

4 Cors en Mib.
(4 Horns in Eb.)

4 Cors en Fa.
(4 Horns in F.)

4 Cors en Sol.
(4 Horns in G.)

4 Cornets á pistons en Sib.
(4 Cornets á pistons in Bb.)

4 Trombones Tenors.
(4 Tenor Trombones.)

2 Bombardons.
(2 Bombardons.)

2 1re Trompettes en Fa.
2 2me Trompettes en Mib.
(2 1st Trumpets in F.)
(2 2d Trumpets in Eb.)

4 Trombones Tenors.
(4 Tenor Trombones.)

4 Trompettes en Mib.
(4 Trumpets in Eb.)

4 Trombones Tenors.
(4 Tenor Trombones.)

4 Trompettes en Sib.
(4 Trumpets in Bb.)

4 Trombones Tenors.
2 Ophicléïdes en Ut.
(4 Tenor Trombones.)
(2 Ophicleides in C.)

2 Ophicléïdes en Sib.
(2 Ophicleides in Bb.)

Ces quatre petits Orchestres d'instruments de cuivre doivent être placés isolément, aux quatre angles de la grande masse chorale et instrumentale. Les Cors seuls restant au milieu du grand orchestre.
These 4 small orchestras of brass instruments should be placed apart, at the four corners of the great choral and instrumental body. The horns alone remain in the middle of the large orchestra.

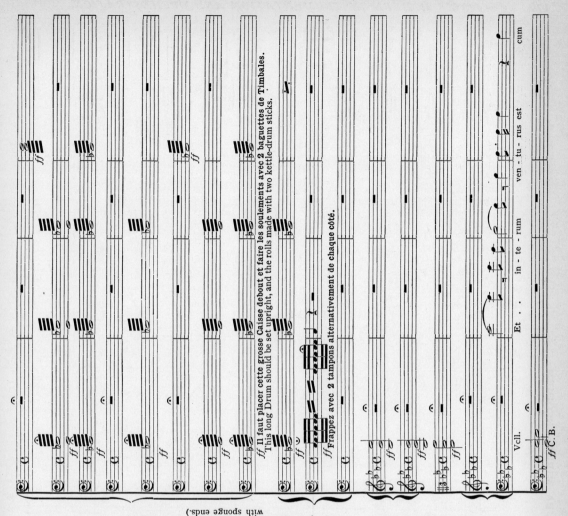

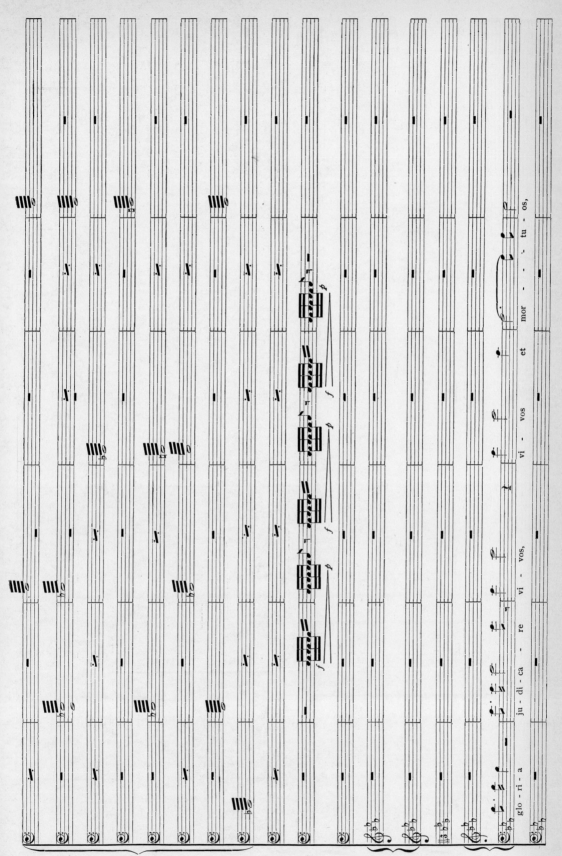

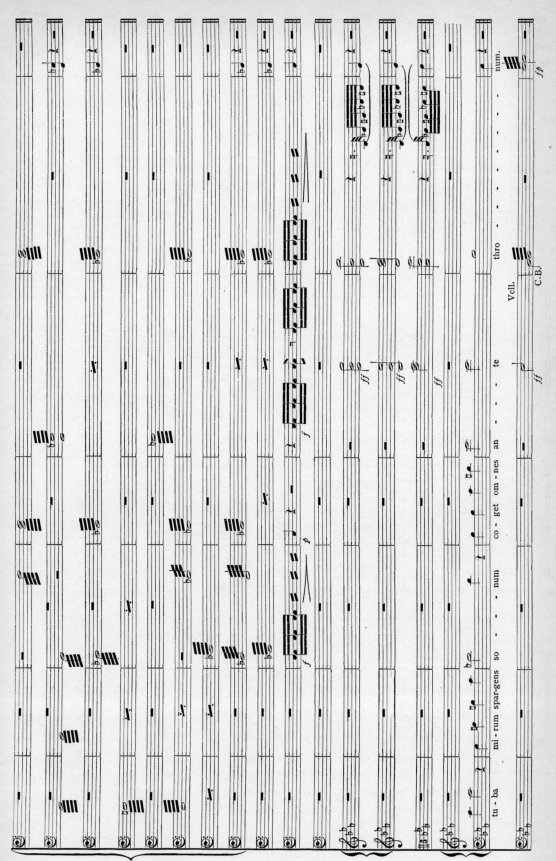

In a like manner he employs 4 Kettle-Drums in a very artistic manner in his "Symphonie fantastique," as shown below.

EXTRACT FROM THE "SYMPHONIE FANTASTIQUE."

Scene aux champs.

HECTOR BERLIOZ.

Two kinds of Drum-sticks are used; one kind with knobs of sponge are excellent for the performance of light " piano " passages, the other with knobs of wood or felt excellent for " forte " passages.   Muffled or covered Drums are very effective in Requiems or sad scenes or situations in general.   Their use is indicated by the term " covered Drums " (in German " bedeckte

Pauken "), and if the effect is to be discontinued by "uncovered Drums" (in German, "unbedeckte Pauken "). As shown in the following example, two Kettle-Drums can also be struck simultaneously, which is always very effective.

2. THE SMALL OR SIDE-DRUM.

(WIRBELTROMMEL, TAMBURO, TAMBOUR OU CAISSE CLAIRE.)

This instrument in reality should be classed as belonging to the Military Band; on this account its employment in the orchestra should be restricted to compositions of a military or martial character. It is also excellently adapted for use in dance-music.

Manner of writing for the Small or Side Drum is illustrated in the following examples :—

In dance-music the Kettle-Drums are used both for marking the rhythm and for the production of noise.

In his "Fra Diavolo" overture Auber lets the Drum execute 8 bars entirely alone ; Halévy, Donizetti, Meyerbeer, Rossini, etc., have employed it very frequently in their scores. As upon the Kettle-Drums every conceivable grade of tonal-shading is possible. Muffled Drums are employed in Funeral Marches.

A few additional varieties of Drums are mentioned in the following : —

1. **The old Turkish Drum, also called Bass Drum,** a large instrument in the form of our present Drum; is still in use upon the operatic stage, especially in modern works like R. Wagner's "Rienzi." The tone of this Drum is dull, but nevertheless possesses good carrying qualities.

2. **The Tambourin,** always mistaken for the **Tambourine** (Tambour de basque), is a long drum with no timbre, and a tone somewhat similar to that of the Kettle-Drum ; is also used upon the stage, especially for the accompaniment of Spanish or Moorish Marches and Dances.

In his opera "Lohengrin" (Act 3) Wagner designates the Tambourin (in French : Caisse roulante) with the term "Wirbeltrommel," and has entrusted a very effective part to it. The rolling of a wagon can also be imitated very well upon a muffled small Drum.

3. THE BASS–DRUM.

(GROSSE TROMMEL, GRAN CASSA, GROSSE CAISSE.)

This instrument can imitate a cannon-shot, as well as the subsequent thunder, very well; this is produced in the following manner : —

The Bass-Drum can also be played on both sides with two sticks; when it is to be played in this manner, it is designated as follows : —

This instrument is also very effective if played "piano."

It is an important and prominent instrument in the dance-music orchestras of the present day.

Spontini has employed the Bass-Drum very effectively in his operas "Vestalin" and "Ferdinand Cortez."

4. THE CYMBALS.

(BECKEN, CINELLI, CYMBALES.)

They are usually employed in connection with the Bass-Drum; but certain fantastic effects can be produced with them alone, providing the composer understands where to introduce them at the right time, and how to treat them in accordance with their own peculiar characteristics. For instance, the ingenious beat of the Cymbals in R. Wagner's Lohengrin. If a strong metallic or screaming tone or a kind of roll is to be produced, it is indicated by "Swinging Cymbals struck with a stick."

In this manner Tam-Tam like effects are produced; but they should only be employed in special and appropriate dramatic scenes where they can be exceedingly effective. They can also be employed "piano" in the above manner with equal success. If this effect is to be discontinued it is indicated by: "Use Cymbals in the ordinary way."

If, as is usually the case, the parts of the Bass-Drum and Cymbals are written together on one line, and one of these instruments should play alone, it is designated in the following manner : —

They are very effectively employed in Gluck's opera, "Iphigenie in Tauris." The modern writers and arrangers of dance-music, as a rule, employ the Bass-Drum and Cymbals unceasingly.

These instruments have been employed in most of the comic operas of Flotow, Auber, Hérold, Offenbach, Lecocq, etc., and at times in dramatic situations requiring no such effects, being introduced without any special reason and seemingly only for the production of noise and bustle. In the scores of Rossini, Verdi, and Mercadante these noisy instruments are employed very frequently.

There is still another variety, " Steel Cymbals," possessing a clear and penetrating tone, excellently adapted for bacchanalian scenes, and in addition to these the very tiny little ancient Grecian Cymbals, tuned to *high B flat* and *high F*, which Berlioz has used in a very ingenious manner in his dramatic symphony " Romeo and Juliet." The exact manner in which Berlioz has employed them is shown in the following extract : —

EXTRACT FROM "ROMEO AND JULIET" DRAMATIC SYMPHONY.

Queen Mab Scherzo.

HECTOR BERLIOZ.

5. THE TRIANGLE.

(TRIANGEL, TRIANGULO, TRIANGLE.)

If employed with taste the effect of the Tri-angle is very graceful. Weber has employed it very effectively in the gipsy choruses of "Preciosa." Notation for this instrument is shown in the following examples:—

A great variety of tonal-shadings like *p*, *pp*, *mf*, *f*, *ff*, *cresc.*, and *decresc.*, etc., can be produced upon this instrument.

The Gong-Triangle, invented by V. F. Čerčený, an instrument constructed of very strong steel in the shape of an A, brings forth a tremendous and long-sustained gong-like tone, if struck with a felt-covered wooden mallet — or sounds like a very strong Triangle, if struck with a little steel rod. It is very popular in the Military Bands of Austria and Germany, but principally so in Russia, where the greatest preference is shown for it as an instrument for special effects. It is also used very frequently in dance-music.

6. THE TAMBOURINE.

(SCHELLENTROMMEL, TAMBOUR DE BASQUE.)

Very effective in ballet music or in fantastic compositions, Gipsy scenes, etc. It is a favorite instrument of the Sicilians, Spaniards, and inhabitants of Southern France, who use it principally for their characteristic dances.

Manner of notation is shown in the following examples:—

Weber in his "Preciosa," Donizetti in the serenade of "Don Pasquale," and F. David in the "Desert" have written very fine and effective parts for this instrument. Bizet has also employed it very effectively in his opera "Carmen" and in the "Farandole" of his L'Arlésienne music, Suite II.

7. THE TAM-TAM.

Struck with force this instrument possesses a screaming, ear-splitting tone, which can be used to advantage for the characterization of scenes of murder, wild choruses, or terrible situations in general. Struck "piano or pianissimo," a mysterious, evil-boding tone is produced.

The Tam-Tam should be employed very rarely and only for appropriate situations, f. i., in the manner in which it was employed by Bellini in "Norma," Meyerbeer in "Robert le Diable," Spontini in "Cortez" and "Vestalin," etc. In his C minor Requiem, Cherubini has pictured the terrors of the last day by the strokes of a Tam-Tam.

EXTRACT FROM THE C MINOR REQUIEM (DIES IRAE).

CHERUBINI.

8. THE GLOCKENSPIEL.

(GLOCKENSPIEL, CAMPANETTA, CARILLON.)

Has become celebrated through the very interesting and characteristic use Mozart has put it to in his opera, "The Magic Flute." Adam has also employed it in his opera, "If I were King."

9. THE STEEL XYLOPHONE.

(LYRE) STAHLHARMONIKA, (LYRA) JEU DE CLOCHES DE TIMBRES.)

This instrument has entirely replaced the Glockenspiel; it is constructed in three different manners: (1) Lyre-shaped with a number of loosely suspended steel bars, tuned to the tones of the scale and struck with two little hammers; this kind is in general use in military bands.

(2) Steel bars placed in rows upon a wooden structure (similar to the Wood-Xylophone) or in a box, and also played with little hammers; this kind is always used in the orchestra. (3) the same as explained in (2), but supplied with a key-board; this latter kind, although easier to play, is rarely used. It is not frequently met with in higher class music, although Meyerbeer has used it in "L'Africaine" and Wagner in "Die Walküre."

Tonal-Compass. Chromatic.

Its tone is clear and strong, and can be heard to excellent advantage above a large and complete orchestra. I have employed it in my "Symphonie pittoresque," an extract of which is presented in the following example:—

EXTRACT FROM "LE SALÈVE," SYMPHONIE PITTORESQUE.

H. KLING.

10. THE GLOCKEN–ACCORDION.

(FOR USE IN VESTRY ROOMS.)

This instrument, invented by V. F. Çervený, consists of a console in Gothic style, made of plain or cast iron, upon which 5, 7 or 8 gongs or large bells are fastened in pyramid-form and tuned perfectly for artistic combination. If the rod, suspended from the hammer-mechanism, is pulled, all the Bells will sound simultaneously, producing a mild, long-sustained chord. The Glocken-Accordion for use at the altar is similarly constructed. The bells are attached upon a wooden handle in pyramid-form and are rung like the usual little bells, and which also bring forth a very pleasing and harmonious sound. The instruments are excellently adapted for religious music, but can also be used for secular purposes to equal advantage.

11. LARGE BELLS.

(GROSSE GLOCKEN, CAMPANA, CLOCHES.)

Separate Bells of various sizes and pitch, as well as a number of them, chromatically tuned, may be employed.

The Bells adapt themselves excellently for religious situations as well as for pastoral scenes. Meyerbeer in his "Huguenots," Rossini in "William Tell," Verdi in "Trovatore," Massé, Auber, Weckerlin, Massenet, Grisar, Thadewaldt, etc., have used Bells and employed them in an exemplary manner. The following example shows a wonderful effect which R. Wagner has produced with the large Bells in "Parsifal."

EXTRACT FROM "PARSIFAL."

RICHARD WAGNER.

A variety of Cow, Goat, and Glass Bells are also in use, employed for the illustration of rural shepherd-scenes.

Notation for Cow and Goat Bells.

etc.

I have used the above in my Pastoral-Fantasie "Shepherd Life in the Alps." The characteristic execution of these parts is left to the discretion and imagination of the player.

The principal object, in the use of Bells, such as the above, is, to re-produce local color, and their effectiveness depends entirely upon the appropriate employment to which they are put.

12. THE XYLOPHONE.

(XYLOPHON, STICCATO, XYLOPHONE.)

An instrument constructed of wood and straw and played with two little wooden hammers.

Usual Tonal-Compass.

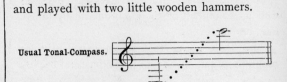

Saint-Saëns has written a very appropriate and prominent part for this instrument in his "Danse Macabre," the dry, rattling sounds of the Xylophone being excellently adapted to picture the rattling of the bones of the dancing skeletons.

Practical manner of writing for this instrument is shown in the following examples:—

Practical Examples for use of the Xylophone.

Easy Passages.

The best-sounding notes are from : —

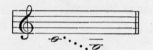

Chromatic.

as the wood sounds very poor or not at all, for the higher notes and the lower notes

hardly ever keep in tune.

The easiest keys are C, G, and F Major. Sustained notes are not applicable.

The Xylophone is also used in dance-music where all kinds of droll variations are assigned to it, especially in polkas. Lately similar instruments have been made of marble stones, which possess a bright and bell-like quality of tone.

13. THE CASTAGNETS.

(KASTAGNETTEN, CASTAGNETTA, CASTAGNETTES.)

The Spanish national instrument without which no Bolero, Fandango or Cachuca is danced.

The Castagnets are principally used in ballet-music or in musical compositions, demanding Spanish local-color. Notation for them is shown in the following examples : —

Practical Examples for use of the Castagnets.

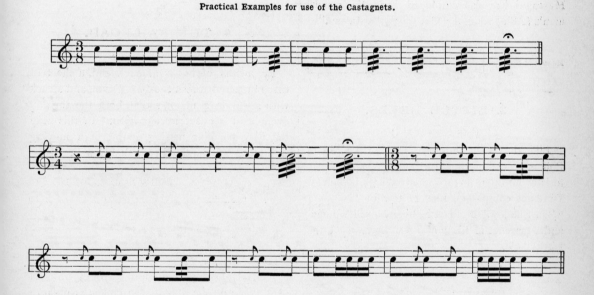

Group IV.

DIFFERENT SMALLER INSTRUMENTS

which are employed in the production of Comical Scenes, Dance-Music, Fantastic Compositions, Toy Symphonies or Potpourris of a popular character, etc

---

1. THE WHIP.

(DIE PEITSCHE.)

Is employed for Postillion-Polkas or Galops in the manner that Adam made use of it in his comic opera "The Postillion of Lonjumeau." Mascagni has also employed it in the coachman's (Alfio) song of "Cavalleria Rusticana."

Manner of Notation.

2. LITTLE BELLS.

(DIE SCHELLEN.)

Like the Whip, these are used for Postillion-Polkas or Galops, and furthermore as a characteristic addition to so-called sleighing-dances. Different composers, like Flotow in his opera "The Shadow," Maillart in his "Hermit's Bell," and Massenet in his "Manon," have used the Little Bells.

Notation.

3. THE THUNDER.

(DER DONNER.)

Consists of a machine, which in being turned produces a thunder-like noise, and serves in a very characteristic manner in the production of storm-scenes. R. Wagner employed one of these "Thunder-Machines" in his Nibelungen-Trilogy. In the orchestra a large sheet of tin is usually employed for imitating thunder. Individual strokes can be produced by striking the suspended sheet with a Bass-drumstick or with a hammer.

Notation.

4. THE RAILROAD.

(DIE EISENBAHN.)

By means of hooks at each end, a sheet of tin is fastened across the Bass-Drum, and struck with a rod in a manner that both the tin and drum-head are set in vibration. In this way the very peculiar hissing sound of a moving train of cars is imitated remarkably well.

Notation.

The departure and approach of a train of cars can also be imitated excellently upon a small Drum.

5. THE WALDTEUFEL.

(THE WOOD-DEMON.)

Large and small instruments of this kind are in use, constructed either out of pasteboard or tin. This instrument is employed for droll and comical effects, f. i., in the comic potpourri by Conradi, "A Trip through Europe," where it is used to imitate the sighing and whistling of the wind; Millöcker has used it for the same purpose in his operetta, "Apajune the Water-carrier."

Notation.  or

6. THE NIGHTINGALE WHISTLE.

(DIE NACHTIGALLPFEIFE.)

A tin whistle partly filled with water, which is used in Nightingale-Polkas or for the imitation of similar birds' voices.

Notation.

7. THE QUAIL WHISTLE.

(DIE WACHTELPFEIFE.)

Consists of a small machine or a small wooden or tin whistle, which is manipulated by the hand or blown; it is employed in comical dance-music, and forms a very characteristic and appropriate addition thereto.

Notation.

The voice of the Quail can also be imitated very well by means of two clear-sounding pebbles, struck against each other in the above rhythmical manner.

8. THE CRICKET WHISTLE.

(DIE GRILLENPFEIFE.)

Is used in the exact manner as the Nightingale and Quail whistle.

Notation.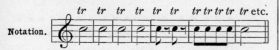

9. THE CUCKOO WHISTLE.

(DIE KUCKUCKPFEIFE.)

A wooden whistle, upon which only two intervals, those of a minor third, can be produced. It can be tuned in different keys, and is generally employed in woodland scenes.

Notation.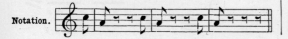

10. THE RAILROAD WHISTLE.

(DIE EISENBAHNPFEIFE.)

Is employed in compositions where a Locomotive or a Steamboat is to be imitated.

Notation.

11. THE CONDUCTOR'S WHISTLE.

(SCHRILL OR TRILLERPFEIFE.)

Used as the above, also for railroad Polkas and Galops.

Policemen's, Nightwatchmen's, and other signals can also be executed upon this whistle, which in turn can also be employed in Polkas, Galops, etc.

12. THE LOCOMOTIVE OR ENGINE WHISTLE.

(DIE LOKOMOTIVPFEIFE.)

Is generally employed in connection with the above-mentioned whistles, and answers their call somewhat in the following manner:—

13. THE PAPAGENO WHISTLE.

(DIE PAPAGENOPFEIFE.)

Also known as the Syrinx, seven-tubed pipe, Shepherd-pipe, or Pandean-pipes; became very popular through its use in Mozart's "Magic Flute," where it is employed in the 1st Act (Papageno Aria) in the following manner:—

is Pa - pa - ge - no's tone,

14. THE FIFE.

(DIE TROMMELFLÖTE; ALSO KNOWN AS TROM-
MELPFEIFE.)

This instrument is employed in every regiment or battalion of soldiers, in connection with the Drums; it serves to impart more strength and color to the march-rhythm as well as to enliven the monotonous beat of the Drums.

Tonal-Compass.

Chromatic.

15. THE TIN FLUTE.

(DIE BLECHFLÖTE.)

This instrument is sometimes employed in potpourris or comical compositions.

16. THE SPURS.

(DIE SPOREN.)

A steel machine, with which the clink of spurs, especially in Hungarian dances, is imitated.

Notation.

etc.

17. THE RATTLE AND TOY TRUMPET.

(DIE RATSCHE UND KINDERTROMPETE.)

Rattles are made in a great variety of sizes, ranging from the little child's rattle to a machine which imitates the discharge of musketry.

The latter has been employed by Beethoven in his Battle symphony "Wellington's Victory."

The little Rattle as well as the Toy Trumpet is employed in comical compositions. (Toy Symphonies by Haydn, Romberg, etc.)

Notation for the Rattles.

etc.

Notation for the Toy Trumpet.

In C.

18. THE STORM.

(DER STURM.)

This effect is produced by shaking or swinging a sheet of tin to and fro.

Vibrato.

Notation.

etc.

19. THE FIRE-BRIGADE HORN.

(FEUERWEHRHUPPE, FEUERWEHR, TURNER,

WÄCHTERHORN.)

A little Trumpet without a mouth-piece, upon which a change of intervals is brought about by means of a valve.

It serves excellently for the signals of the fire-brigade, and is employed in Polkas, Galops, Quadrilles, and marches for characteristic effects.

A different kind of Signal-horn without valves, is used in a like manner for Marches and Dances. But only the following natural notes can be produced upon it:—

20. THE POST-HORN.

(DAS POSTHORN.)

This instrument is constructed in a circular manner, and possesses the same natural intervals as the above-mentioned Signal-horn.

Beethoven has used this instrument admirably in the No. 12 of his German dances. It is generally in the pitch of C or B flat.

21. THE POST-TRUMPET.

(DIE POSTTROMPETE.)

The ordinary, simple Post-trumpet is generally pitched in G or F. In addition to these, another variety is pitched in F, and provided with a hole, which, if closed up, will cause the instrument to sound a fourth higher, as illustrated in the following example:—

Hole open.

Stopped.

Tonal-Compass in G or F.

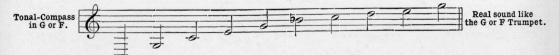

Real sound like the G or F Trumpet.

Manner of writing for this instrument is shown in the following example:—

The sign ᴧᴧ above the notes indicates that the respective note is to be executed in a vibrating manner. The instrument is used for announcing the arrival or departure of the old-time mail-coaches, and can be employed in this sense for musical compositions in a very characteristic manner. The tonal-quality of a Post-trumpet cannot be replaced by that of an orchestral Trumpet.

22. THE HUNTING-HORN.

(DAS JAGDHORN.)

A species of French-Horn without valves, only somewhat larger, and usually pitched in D or E flat.

Admirable effects are to be attained with these instruments, providing they are used as shown in the following examples:—

Tonal-Compass.   Real sound like a French-Horn
                                                                                  in D or E flat.

It is excellently adapted for hunting signals, woodland scenes, etc., owing to its somewhat rough but bright-sounding quality of tone.

The following examples, as well as the hunting-fanfare for 3 Hunting-Horns, are very effective.

FANFARE FOR 3 HUNTING–HORNS.

H. KLING.

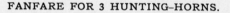

The notes marked with *tr* are not intended for trills; they are merely to be executed in a vibrating, tremulous manner, through the action of the lips.

We must not forget to mention the **Russian-Horns**: —

Peculiar instruments, a complete family of which is in existence, ranging from the smallest to the largest, and which are distinguished as follows: —

High Soprano, Soprano, Alto, Tenor, and Bass; besides these principal members, additional members are in use which include every step of the entire chromatic scale. Every Horn can produce only one tone, and the varied combinations to which these instruments can be put make it possible to reach a tonal-compass of

5 octaves; notwithstanding the very limited capabilities of these instruments, individually considered, the players become proficient to such an extent, through constant and unceasing practice, that they can perform complete compositions with precision, evenness, purity of tone and clearness, even in quick tempo.

Referring to this very subject, Fétis expressed himself as follows: "Perceptivity, the life of art, cannot be possessed by such people who in reality are nothing else but individually isolated, abstract sounding notes." As a great Russian nobleman once remarked to a stranger, "My orchestra will not be able to perform for you to-day, as my 3d Octave B flat has just received a sound thrashing."

23. THE ALPINE HORN.

(DAS ALP HORN.)

Is a trumpet-like wooden Horn, with the same compass and notes as a natural Trumpet in D or D flat, and is employed for the illustration of Alpine scenes. The following examples will illustrate the practical and characteristic manner of writing for this instrument: —

RANZ DE VACHES.
Kuhreigen.

There is also another variety known as the Swiss Alpine, or Herdsman's Horn (Kuhhirten-horn), made of ordinary Goat or Chamois (Alpine goat) horn. These possess an indescribable tone, remarkably adapted for the extensive solitude of the Alps, where the simple rural melodies are re-echoed from all sides, mingling with the thunder of the avalanche as it tears down the mountain-side, and the roar of the foaming mountain stream, as it leaps from rock to rock, and accompanied by the poetic bells of peaceful cow and goat herds. The F sharp is very characteristic upon this instrument; plain F is the note to be produced, but is invariably much too high.

The cow and goat herd calls and melodies, as illustrated above, differ in the various cantons of Switzerland, and are varied and changed according to the taste and imagination of the player.

24. THE CZAKAN.

(STOCKFLÖTE.)

A flageolet-like instrument of gentle tonal-quality; Lumbye has employed it in one of his orchestral compositions (Nebelbilder). It is generally pitched in A flat, and the compass as given below will therefore sound a sixth higher.

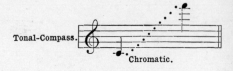

Tonal-Compass.

Chromatic.

25. THE ANVIL.

(DER AMBOS.)

Anvils of different sizes, and tuned in a variety of ways, are in use; they are struck with hammers. They are usually employed in pairs, which are tuned in thirds: —

Notation.

or   etc.

They have been used in a characteristic manner for Anvil-polkas, etc., by different composers. Verdi employed them in " Il Trovatore," and

R. Wagner in "Siegfried," while such composers as Parlow, Bléger, Beck, etc., employed them in polkas, marches, etc.

The 18 Anvils used in "Rheingold" created a great sensation at the time. They are partly

tuned to 𝄞 to 𝄢 and to 𝄢 and of course execute only rhythmic figures, while the String instruments and 4 Horns execute the so-called "Forge motive" repeatedly.

EXTRACT FROM "DAS RHEINGOLD."

R. WAGNER.

6 kleine Ambosse. (6 little Anvils.)

6 grössere Ambosse. (6 larger Anvils.)

6 ganz grosse Ambosse. (6 very large Anvils.)

Fagotti. (Bassoons.)

Violinen. (Violins.)

Cellos.

26. THE WIND MACHINE.

(DIE WINDMASCHINE.)

Special machines constructed to imitate the rush of wind or a hurricane. In case such a machine cannot be procured, the wind can also be imitated by rubbing an ordinary clothes-brush across the head of a Kettle-Drum.

Notation.

pp

27. THE RAIN MACHINE.

(DIE REGENMASCHINE.)

A round machine filled with peas, which is slowly turned. In order to imitate *hail*, the peas are replaced by little pebbles.

Notation.

28. THE POP-GUN.

(DIE KNALLBÜCHSE.)

For use in Champagne Galops in the manner as Lumbye and Métra employed it in this kind of composition.

Notation.

etc.

The Artillery Cannon was used in connection with musical productions as early as 1785, when Sarti employed it in the production of his *Te Deum*, in St. Petersburg, in commemoration of the taking of Ockakon. Rossini also employed this effect in a composition for the World's Exposition in 1867.

29. THE GUN AND PISTOL.

The former is met with in the funeral march from Tristia by H. Berlioz; and the latter I have employed in my Cat-Fantasie, "The Interrupted Rendezvous."

30. THE MOUTH HARMONICA.

(DIE MUNDHARMONIKA.)

This instrument can be used in connection with the orchestra, where the joys of childhood (Christmas, fairs or Schützenfest) are to be expressed. The sounds of the Mouth Harmonica are always grouped in chords, and by blowing into the instrument the fundamental chord, and by drawing out the breath, the chords of the second, fourth, sixth, and seventh steps of the scale, will be produced.

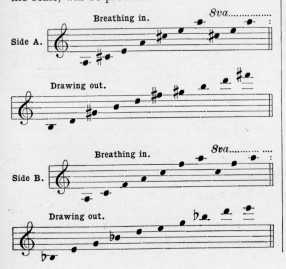

31. THE JEW'S HARP.

(MAULTROMMEL OR BRUMMEISEN.)

This is a little instrument made of steel, in the shape of a horseshoe, its size admitting that it can easily be placed and held between the teeth. Within the ends of the instrument a steel tongue is fastened, which when set in vibration, and together with the voice of the player (who sings or hums through the instrument), produces a peculiar tonal-effect.

At one time this nonsensical instrument was so popular that it was used for solo performances in concerts. The Aeolian Harp, the strings of which are set in vibration by the passing wind, has a similar tone.

32. THE VERROPHONE.

(VERROPHON, GLAS—EUPHONIUM.)

This instrument, consisting of a number of tuned glasses, adapts itself excellently for the accompaniment of a Zither, owing to its delicate tonal-quality. The following is its usual compass :—

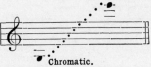

Chromatic.

But some possess a compass of only two octaves from to . Its tone is very similar to the harmonics of a Zither, and if treated skilfully can be easily produced, in all tonal-shadings, from the most delicate "pianissimo" to a moderate "forte." It is very effective as a solo instrument, with the accompaniment of a muted string quartette. Only sustained songs and melodious passages are adapted for this instrument.

33. THE TERROPHONE.

(TERROPHON.)

An instrument consisting of 44 chromatically tuned clay pots, invented by Maerky, in Caronge, near Geneva.

Tonal-Compass.

Chromatic.

Its tones possess a bell-like quality, and the instrument is in reality a large Glockenspiel (Carillon), which can be played either by one or more persons. Lively airs, especially in dance-rhythm, can be performed to best advantage upon this original instrument. A Carillon of this kind can also be put together from glass bottles.

Perfectly tuned clay pots can also be used as substitutes for metal bells in the orchestra.

34. THE BULL'S HORN.

(DAS STIERHORN.)

R. Wagner has used an instrument of this kind in his opera "Die Walküre," Act 2 : Scene 5. It is blown upon the stage, and behind the scenes; and he has written its part in the following manner : —

In addition to these instruments, with which we have gradually become acquainted, others are in use which owe their existence to the lively imagination of certain composers of dance music.

Musard, and especially Julien, were very prolific in the invention of instruments designed to imitate the lowing of calves, the braying of an ass, the demolition of houses, and the hissing of flames (as in the well-known " Fire-brigade Quadrille " by Musard). For a polka entitled : "*Human Frailties,*" Julien has invented little machines which imitate the various noises of sneezing, blowing of the nose, expectorating, coughing, lamenting, sleeping, snoring, etc., in an excellent manner. These musical jokes were exaggerated to such an extent that chairs were smashed in order to impart more firmness to the rhythm of a Quadrille ; in the Kiss polka of Musard the orchestral musicians were expected to smack their lips, in imitation of kissing. In order to complete the list I will add, that other composers have introduced the idea of letting the orchestral musicians alternate in playing and singing a polka or galop, as Fahrbach

has done in his polka " All for Joy ; " and others again have imitated the pounding of street-pavers, straw-thrashers, or the clapper of the mill. In order to picture a family quarrel, such devices as the smashing of whole quantities of dishes were introduced.

The following effects are also employed : *a.*) *Lightning :* pulverized rosin blown through a burning flame of light. *b.*) *Noise of dancing :* brought about by shuffling the feet upon a sand-strewn floor. *c.*) *The rustle of dresses during dancing :* with the aid of a heavy paper laid across the Bass-Drum and rubbed with a stiff brush. *d.*) *Stamping of the feet, etc. :* by striking a wooden floor with a stick ; by striking the rim of a Drum with the Drum-sticks ; by striking two wooden shoes against each other. *e.*) *Ghosts or other spiritual or unearthly apparitions :* throwing bags of broken and cracked glass and crockery heavily upon the floor. *f.*) *Snow falling through an opening of the ceiling* in the form of finely cut silk paper. *g.*) *The roaring of water :* brought about by a ball of strong paper rubbed along the floor or upon a paper-covered wall. *h.*) *House-bell :* the ringing of an ordinary bell. Singing, either unisono or in the form of a Duo, Trio, Quartette, and also Chorus, has been introduced in several orchestral compositions, f. i., in the Night-watchman's Song and Frog-Quartette of my Katzen (cat) Fantasia. A similar Frog-Quartette is also contained in Milloecker's operetta " Apajune the Water-Carrier."

In my " Jagd-Fantasia " (Hunting Fantasia) I have also employed the voices and cries of the following birds : Turkey, Duck, Cock's crow, Pheasant cry, Owl, Partridge, Snipe, Black-bird, etc.

In my " Concert in the Kitchen " I have made use of the following kitchen-utensils : funnel, plates, milk-pots, glasses, bottles, fire-tongs, tin covers, and stew-pans.

It need hardly be mentioned that if such effects as the above are to be employed, they should only be introduced in compositions of either a descriptive or humorous character, as they will bring about anything but a desirable effect if they should be made use of in inappropriate places.

More detailed information about such instruments can be found in my book " The Orchestral Instruments of Percussion in their entirety."

35. THE COMPLETE ORCHESTRA.

(a) THE SCORE.

Now that we have become acquainted with the peculiarities and characteristic properties of the different individual orchestral instruments, we will proceed towards combining them in such a manner as to form a complete and well-rounded body, known in its outward written appearance as an orchestral score.

No decided rules are laid down as to the order or planning of an orchestral score. The object is to facilitate the reading of such a score as much as possible for the conductor. It is advisable to place the Wind instruments in such a manner that they will stand forth in prominent groups, beginning at the top with the Wood-wind, then the Brass, followed by the Instruments of Percussion, and finally the String Quintette. This grouping of the instruments is the most practical.

In throwing a glance at the following compilations under the headings of Haydn, Mozart, Beethoven, R. Wagner, and H. Berlioz, the student may select such grouping as may be best adapted and fitted to his individual imagination, intentions, and artistic intellect.

Haydn.	Mozart.	Beethoven.	R. Wagner. (*Lohengrin.*)	H. Berlioz. (*Tuba mirum. Requiem.*)
Kettle-Drums.	Violins, I.	Bass-Drum.	3 Flutes.	4 Flutes.
Trumpets.	Violins, II.	Triangle and Cymbals.	Piccolo.	2 Oboes.
Trombones.	Violas.	Piccolo.	3 Oboes.	4 Clarinets.
Clarinets.	Flutes.	Flutes.	1 English Horn.	8 Bassoons.
Horns.	Oboes.	Oboes.	3 Clarinets.	12 Horns.
Oboes.	Clarinets.	Clarinets.	1 Bass-Clarinet.	{ 4 Cornets.
Flutes.	Bassoons.	Bassoons.	2 Bassoons.	{ 4 Tenor Trombones.
Bassoons.	Horns.	Horns.	4 Horns.	{ 2 Bombardons.
Violins, I.	Trumpets.	Trumpets.	3 Horns (on stage).	{ 4 Trumpets.
Violins, II.	Trombones.	Kettle-Drums.	3 Trumpets.	{ 4 Tenor Trombones.
Violas.	Kettle-Drums.	Trombones.	4 Trumpets (on stage).	{ 4 Trumpets.
Voices.	Voices.	Violins, I.	3 Trombones.	{ 4 Tenor Trombones.
Violoncellos.	Violoncellos.	Violins, II.	3 Trombones (on stage).	{ 4 Trumpets.
Organ.	Organ.	Violas.	1 Bass-Tuba.	{ 4 Tenor Trombones.
Double-Basses.	Double-Basses.	Voices.	Kettle Drums (in the orchestra).	16 Kettle-Drums.
		Violoncellos.	Kettle-Drums (on stage).	1 Long Drum.
Exceptionally.	*Exceptionally.*	Organ.	Cymbals.	1 Bass-Drum with 2 Sticks.
Baritone.	Piccolo.	Double-Basses.	Drum.	Tam-Tam and Cymbals (3 pairs).
Lyra.	English Horn.		Violins Divisi.	50 Violins.
English Horn.	Basset Horn.	*Exceptionally.*	Violas.	20 Violas.
	Double-Bassoon.	Double-Bassoon.	Organ.	70 Sopranos)
	Harp.	English Horn.	Voice Parts.	60 Tenors } Chorus.
	Glockenspiel.	Posthorn.	Harp.	70 Basses)
	Bass-Drum.		Violoncellos.	18 Violoncellos.
	Cymbals and Triangle.		Double-Basses.	18 Double-Basses.
	Small Drum.			
	Mandoline.			

(b) RULES TO BE OBSERVED IN WRITING A SCORE.

Every instrument and every voice-part must be placed upon a separate staff, and the clef, signature, and time indicated at the beginning of the score. If one or the other voice or instrument is to pause for any length of time, the staff may be omitted, in order to save space. But in such cases it is necessary to mention the names of the co-operative instruments even if only in abbreviated form like Fl., Ob., Cl., Tr., etc., at the beginning of each page. Two instruments belonging together, like 2 Flutes, 2 Oboes, 2 Clarinets, 2 Bassoons, 2 Horns, 2 Trumpets, can also be written upon one staff, and sometimes even as many as three similar parts, like 3 Sopranos, 3 Trombones, or the like. The tempo is written at the head of the staves, and sometimes again at the bottom, for clearness' sake. The marks of expression f., mf., p. pp., cresc., dim., etc., must be added to every part.

If two parts are placed upon one staff, they are written in the following manner : —

If both parts consist of identical whole notes they are written : —

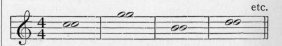

If two parts proceed unisono for several bars the terms unisono, or "à 2" or "a due" can be employed, instead of writing the notes with double stems.

a due.

If one instrument of the two is to pause, it is indicated in the following manner : —

If one of the instruments pauses entirely, the pauses may be omitted, but the part must be marked with 1mo or 2do in order to indicate which instrument is to play.   In order to mark a specially important entrance of any instrument the word " Solo " is added in the particular place.   If different instruments proceed in unison, or in octaves, or if one or the other part is to be transposed into another key, it can be indicated in the following manner : —

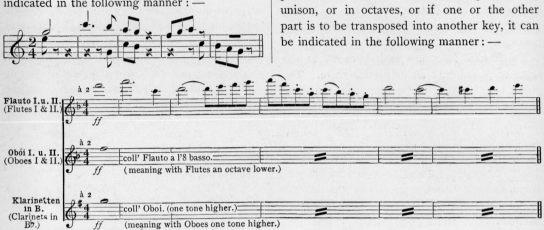

If a lengthy part or passage is to be repeated in a composition, the repetition is usually only carried out in the upper part and in the Bass, and the following is written diagonally across the remaining parts : —

come sopra   A to B oder C to D etc.,

which can be interpreted as meaning : " as before (or " like above "), including the bars from letters A to B, etc."   Numerals like 1, 2, 3, 4, 5, etc., written above the bars which are to be repeated later on, are also sufficient; simply adding " here follow bars 1 to 16," in the place where the repetition is to take place.   The latter way of abbreviating is usually employed in dance music.

(c) THE EMPLOYMENT OF THE DIFFERENT ORCHESTRAL EFFECTS.

Piano and pianissimo, or soft, suave passages in general are very effective for complete orchestra, but can be employed to even better advantage for separate groups of instruments, f. i., the Wood-wind or Brass instruments either alone or combined; the String Quintette alone or in connection with several Wood or Brass instruments.   Forte or Fortissimo is produced

by letting all the Wood, Brass, and String instruments as well as the instruments of Percussion, play simultaneously and equally strong.

Between these two grades we distinguish the Mezzo-Forte.   These different gradations can be produced and executed by individual instruments, in groups or by the entire orchestra.

Opposite effects are produced by leading the different instrumental groups against each other, and this in turn creates contrasts, which can again be classed in the following manner : —

1) From Piano suddenly to Forte and the reverse ; 2) individual instruments play Forte while others play Piano, or various groups of instruments play every note, Fp., while the other groups glide quietly along ; 3) if the Wood-wind instruments or the String quintette follow upon the Brass instruments or the opposite ; 4) the Crescendo, if individual instruments or several in groups enter in succession, or all instruments begin at once, enlarging and strengthening their tonal-volume by degrees till a tremendous Forte is produced ; 5) the Decrescendo in the opposite manner as the Crescendo. One of the finest examples of this kind is the oft-quoted beautiful Introduction to Lohengrin which I have mentioned so frequently; the Unisono of individual instruments, instrumental groups, or of the entire orchestral body, is very effective whether in piano, mezzo-forte or forte.

(d) DIRECTIONS FOR SCORING EFFECTIVELY FOR THE ORCHESTRA.

In order to become proficient in the art of instrumentation, it is not sufficient to hear many standard musical works or study quantities of scores ; we must set to work ourselves, that is, follow the directions which I have already laid down in the course of this work for the artistic treatment of individual instrumental groups, and which can be applied with equal success to the complete orchestra, namely : *the copying of numerous scores with pen and ink.*

The biographies of Haydn, Mozart, Beethoven, etc., offer convincing proof of this assertion. From their earliest childhood these masters were accustomed not alone to hearing orchestral and choral works, but also to compose and produce original compositions both for individual instruments as well as for the entire orchestra and chorus. Through this they acquired great independence in the practical employment of the forces at their command, and by gradually broadening, enlarging, and organizing the orchestra in every direction, they finally developed each group of Stringed and Wind Instruments to such an extent as to allow them to act in a thoroughly independent and form-creating manner, in accordance with their individual tonal and vibratory qualities. This accounts for the enormous wealth and variety of new forms, which have procured everlasting youthfulness to the works of these masters. Therefore, the work of copying a number of symphonic scores of Haydn, Mozart, and Beethoven, as well as of modern masters, must not be shunned ; in this manner we obtain the clearest insight into the intellectual interpretation of the compositions, and an entirely different opinion of the real worth of the works, than would be otherwise possible ; this is of special consequence, when considering the manner in which the classic symphonies are performed at the present day, every conductor interpreting according to his own ideas and routine, without paying much attention to the style of the author ; the majority evidently imagining that Haydn and Mozart, just because they are termed as " classic," must be rasped through by the orchestra without fire, sentiment, or geniality, just as though these masters had not been impressed and touched by music ; as to the latter point, we might be justified in asserting that it was evidently the case to a much greater degree and extent than we can be impressed and touched with in our own time !

The score examples as offered in this work will be amply sufficient for the study of the above-explained orchestral effects.

It will prove of great advantage to the student if he will arrange the following Piano-forte works for large orchestra, grouping the various instruments in an artistic manner, and endeavoring to blend the tonal-quality of the one with the tonal-character of the other, thereby offering a pleasing and harmonious combination to the ear.

Beethoven :

Sonate pathétique, C minor.
Marcia funébre sulla morte d'un eroe. Sonate in A flat Major.
Sonate " quasi una fantasia " C sharp minor.
Sonate E flat major (Adieux, Absence, Return).
Adagio from the Sonate in A Major (dedicated to Haydn).
Adagio from the Sonate in C Major (dedicated to Haydn).

Mozart :

Fantasie, C Minor.	Sonate D Major.
Sonate B flat Major.	Sonate C Major.
	Sonate F Major.

(e) THE ORCHESTRA AS USED FOR DANCE-MUSIC.

An accomplished composer, who makes a practice of writing dance-music for the orchestra, must spare no pains in inventing and introducing new instrumental effects for this class of music. A finely scored waltz, polka , mazurka, galop, quadrille or lancers is not to be despised, and in this very field Johann Strauss might be mentioned as a consummate master ; his dance-compositions as far as ideas, style, development, and orchestration are concerned, are perfect. The dance compositions of Lanner, Gungl, Labitzky, Faust, Métra, etc., are also very worthy of recommendation. The greatest composers of ancient and modern times have not disdained composing charming dance-music whether for Ballet or Ball, and have proven themselves masters in the creation of these more trifling musical forms. In addition to the old dance-forms, as Gavotte, Sarabande, Chaconne, Gigue, Bourée, Pavane, Passepied, Menuetto, etc., which Händel, Bach, Scarlatti, Rameau, Lulli, Gluck, etc., have perpetuated in their different works, we would recall the Allemande, Minuetto, Contredanse (our modern Quadrille), etc., which Mozart and Beethoven furnished for the Imperial Balls.

As to ballet-music, it can be found in abundance in the majority of the best operatic scores.

On pages 206, 207, 208, I present an extract from a waltz by Johann Strauss as an appropriate illustration of the treatment of the dance orchestra.

(f) THE ARRANGEMENT OF GRAND ORCHESTRAL AND OPERATIC COMPOSITIONS, VOCAL ARIAS, SONGS, ETC., FOR LARGE AND SMALL ORCHESTRAS.

Arranging is one of the indispensable necessities of music; in- and out-door concerts would soon become an impossibility if the orchestras and bands were mainly dependent upon offering only overtures and dances to the public, a large part of which are very fond of listening to operatic extracts. In this manner favorite arias or complete numbers like Duos, Trios, Quartettes, Finales, etc., from well-known and popular dramatic works, are arranged and played for the music-loving public. It is also very usual that the most popular melodies of a well-known opera, operetta, etc., are strung together in an artistic and effective manner, generally known as a Potpourri or Fantasie, and which are especial favorites with concert or theatre audiences. Of course arrangements of this kind are greatly dependent upon the artistic taste of the arranger especially in the distribution of the different effects as well as the use to which he will put the different instruments at his command. If he is to arrange for a well-equipped orchestra his task is comparatively simple and easy, while effective arrangements are more complicated for smaller orchestras, especially if there is a lack of accomplished musicians. The instruments usually employed for interpreting the human voice are the Flute, the Clarinet, the Horn, the valve Trumpet, or the Cornet, the Trombone, and sometimes the Violin or the Violoncello, the selection of any of these being dependent upon the tonal-character

of the song to be arranged. Attention must be paid that the melody will always appear in a prominent manner, that the meagre string quintette is not crushed by the Wind instruments, as is so often the case in smaller orchestras, and furthermore that the Percussive instruments will not appear too prominently, at the cost of the whole orchestra and completely drown every instrument by their unmerciful beats.

The above-said applies equally to the dances. In the arrangement of any composition, the melody and harmony of the original must be retained under all circumstances ; to begin with, the melody and bass must be written and the necessary accompaniment be added in the best possible manner. It is to be remembered above all that the style and instrumentation of the original must also be retained as much as possible.

In addition to these, a great variety of different arrangements are possible ; but these properly belong to another class, known as Transpositions, Transcriptions, Variations, Caprices, Phantasiestücke, Paraphrases, etc., and which are arranged for various solo-instruments, with or without the accompaniment of the Pianoforte in the form of Duetts, Trios, Quartettes, Quintettes, Septettes, Octettes, and Nonettes. Of course arrangements of this kind are greatly dependent upon the musical knowledge, talent, and natural skill of the arranger.

(g) HOW AN ORCHESTRAL SCORE IS TO BE WRITTEN.

No definite rules for the above can be given, every composer proceeding in such a manner as may best fit his individual ideas or intentions. The respective orchestral instruments are mentioned at the beginning of every staff. Distinctness and clearness in regard to quick comprehension are the prime requisites of a score, and this is best achieved by the grouping of instruments which produce equal effects. We must therefore aim at grouping the Solo-instruments, the Accompanying or Filling instruments, the Wind instruments (Wood and Brass) — the Stringed instruments, Voice-parts, and Percussive instruments according to their classing and write them in such order that, if possible, the higher will always be placed above the lower-sounding instruments — that the accompanying instruments will be placed in the center, every group receiving its bass if possible, and the principal bass part placed below all as a fundamental part. Proceeding in this manner the instruments would be grouped something like the following:

1. Piccolo.	11.	Soprano.
2. Flutes.	12.	Alto.
3. Oboes.	13.	Tenor.
4. Clarinets.	14.	Bass.
5. Bassoons.	15. Violin I.	
6. Horns.	16. Violin II.	
7. Trumpets (or Cornets).	17. Viola.	
8. Trombones.	18. Violoncello.	
9. Kettle-drums.	19. Double-bass.	
10. Instruments of Percussion.		

(11–14 bracketed as "Voice Parts.")

Now the question presents itself which part should be entered first, the Melody, the Bass or the Accompaniment?

To transfer every musical idea to paper in such a way that a player can perform it at once with the exact conception and delivery as we felt and heard it with our inner ear, is no small matter. To begin with, we must observe our musical orthography, as any carelessness — especially from a rhythmic and harmonic standpoint — can cause mistakes or misunderstandings exactly as in any language. As a rule the musician is not taught to note his ideas down according to definite principles, but his abilities in this direction are usually acquired simply through practice and routine. He will either execute his ideas upon some instrument and then convey them to paper, or he possesses such a lively imagination that he can develop them mentally and transfer them to paper without the aid of any instrument; this latter process of course is the best and most valuable. There is no accounting of why we sketched or wrote it down in this way and not the other. The notes have been conveyed to paper as they appeared to our imagination, and the division and arrangement of the bars was a matter of calculation.

As to the sketching (arrangement and finishing) of a score, we will suppose that we wish to write a Choral. To begin with, we note down the voice part containing the melody and the bass, figure the latter in order not to forget the appropriate harmony, and then fill out and finish the remaining parts.

We can proceed in a like manner with the sketch of other compositions for various instruments (even without figuring the bass), we mark only the entrance of all the principal instruments (that is, those to which the melody is entrusted), and we fill out the remaining parts of the score later on. But if we have not figured the Bass, the harmony must be remembered, and wherever special effects are intended, which might be forgotten, extra memorandums must be made.

But all the abovesaid is only intended as a hint for very inexperienced writers, and is in no way to be taken as a fixed rule which we are bound to observe; everyone is at liberty to follow his own inclinations in this respect, the main point being that the composition is written correctly and sounds well; at any rate the creation of a musical composition is dependent upon the imagination, feeling and disposition of the writer; he reproduces in notes what has sounded in the innermost recesses of his heart and soul.

Mozart always conveyed his musical ideas to paper in sketches, at first, and used 1, 2, and 3 staffs for this purpose; from this outline he scored.

Beethoven proceeded in the same manner; a book entitled "Beethoveniana," by Gustav Nottebohn, reveals to us the exact manner in which Beethoven pursued his studies and work, judging especially from the sketches which were found after his death; and I wish to call the attention of the student to this book which cannot fail but offer the most interesting material for study. It is quite probable that other composers proceed in the same manner.

Those instruments best adapted to interpret and lead the melody are: the Violin, 'Cello, Piccolo, and Flute, Clarinet, Oboe; expressive and sustained melodies are also excellently adapted for the French Horn; the Trumpet or Cornet is also excellently adapted to lead the melody, especially in dance-music. The Trombone may also be entrusted with a broad, stately melody at times.

Only the extensive and conscientious study of scores of Masses, Oratorios, Cantatas, Symphonies, Overtures, Concertos, and Operas of our great masters will lead the student safely towards mastery in conception and execution of his own scores.

EXTRACT FROM "THE MORNING JOURNALS" WALTZ.

(Morgenblätter.)

(See " The Orchestra as used for Dance Music," p. 203.)

J. STRAUSS.

GROUP V.

INSTRUMENTS EMPLOYED IN MILITARY BANDS.

With few exceptions all the instruments belonging to this group have already been sufficiently discussed in detail in Group II. It would therefore be useless to describe them again individually; and if I have accorded a separate grouping to the instruments of the Military Band, I have done so for the special reason that the treatment of the instruments, especially in view of their correlative tonal-character, is very different from that accorded to them in connection with the orchestra. The difference to which I refer is principally evident when considering that the Wood and Brass instruments of the orchestra demand excellent players to begin with, who have thoroughly studied the resources of their instrument, possess fine technical execution, and who have made a special study of producing a fine expressive and voluminous tone. This refinement of execution is not necessary to such a degree for the Military Band, because their performances mostly take place in the open air, which principally necessitates brilliant and bright qualities of sound,

in order that its effectiveness will not be lost at a distance.

From this will be seen that the Military Band, not alone as far as tonal-volume is concerned, but also in regard to the finer execution of a composition, cannot be compared with an orchestra.

A treatise on instrumentation like the present would certainly not be complete should I neglect this important branch of instrumental music, with which Beethoven, Meyerbeer, Spontini, Halévy, Berlioz, Wieprecht, etc., have achieved such extraordinary dramatic and symphonic effects, and which has been one of the most important factors in the musical development of our country.

1. THE PICCOLO.

The D flat Piccolo sounding a half-tone higher than the ordinary Piccolo in C, is still used quite frequently, although by degrees it is being displaced by the latter.

The Piccolo is employed much more frequently in the Military Band than in the orchestra, as through its aid the military character of the former can be expressed and emphasized in the most appropriate manner. Therefore it is used almost exclusively in marches, etc., the melody being written for it either in

unison or the octave, together with the E flat Clarinet. If two Piccolos are employed, the second can execute the thirds or sixths or play in unison with the first.

Here and there the Piccolo in E flat is met with, which is pitched a tenth higher than the Flute.

This last-named Piccolo is employed and treated in the exact manner as the D flat and C Piccolos.

As a solo-instrument for Military Band, the Piccolo is a special favorite, and its effectiveness and resources may best be learned from the study of some of the many Solo-compositions written for it with accompaniment of the full band.

2. THE FLUTE.

Here we distinguish three different kinds: —

The C Flute sounding exactly as written; the D flat Flute sounding ½ tone, and the Terz or E flat Flute a minor third or one and one-half tones higher than their notation.

Tonal-compass, manner of playing and use of these three varieties are exactly alike.

Owing to its fine, voluminous and penetrating tone, the C Flute has gradually succeeded in taking the place of all its rivals; and in arranging and writing for the Military Band it is advisable to employ it exclusively, as it is highly improbable that the differently pitched instruments (as explained above) will be met with in the general run of bands.

For Concert compositions two Flutes are usually employed, the first one executing the principal part, while the second part, in works of a mild, subdued character, is executed by a second Flute, or in compositions of a livelier nature by a Piccolo; these instruments are employed and treated exactly as in an orchestra.

In the following a complete table of all the differently pitched Flutes and Piccolos is presented: —

TABLE OF NOTATION AND TONAL-COMPASS OF ALL THE DIFFERENTLY PITCHED FLUTES AND PICCOLOS.

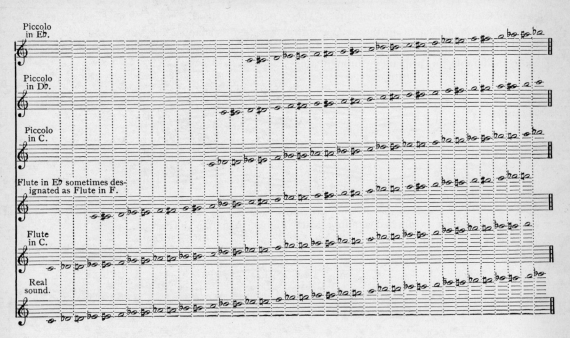

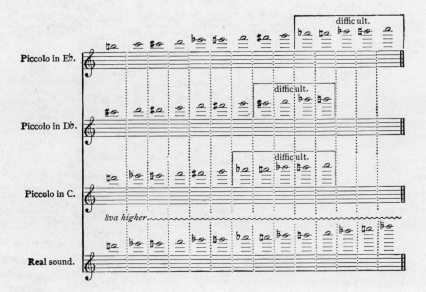

3. THE CLARINETS.

These instruments constitute the most important instrumental group of the Military Band. They are for the latter what the Violins and Violas are for the orchestra, and produce that peculiar soft tonal-quality which distinguishes the Military from the Brass Band.

The following variety of Clarinets are in use :—

1. The E flat Clarinet, an indispensable principal instrument for the Military Band, possessing an exceedingly brilliant tonal-quality. The melody (either in unison or in the octave with the first B flat Clarinet) is written for it, and gains considerably in brilliancy through this combination. Thirds, Sixths, etc., are written for the second part or it plays in unison or the octave of the first part. The E flat Clarinet is excellently adapted for solo-playing. Its tones sound a minor third higher than they are written : —

2. The A♭ Clarinet is pitched a minor sixth higher than the C Clarinet.

It possesses a sharp penetrating quality of tone, and serves principally for strengthening the melody, being written either in unison or the octave with the Piccolo.

3. The F Clarinet is pitched a fourth higher than the C Clarinet.

It is advisable not to make use of the A♭ and F Clarinets, as they are gradually being dispensed with.

4. The C Clarinet is unfortunately employed as rarely as the A flat and F Clarinets. Its sharp, screaming tone would impart a very penetrating quality to the higher passage work.

5. The B♭ Clarinet. The most important of the above-mentioned varieties of Clarinets; its fine, round, sonorous, and soft tone imparts a wealth of beautiful and brilliant qualities to the entire combination of instruments. The B flat Clarinets are divided so as to execute one, two, three and even four different parts; each part representing either the Violins, Violas or Violoncellos of the orchestra. The first part doubles the melody of the Cornet or Flügelhorn, either in unison or the octave, or moves in unison or the octave with the Flutes and the E flat Clarinet. The second, third and fourth Clarinet parts execute the accompaniment or, according to circumstances, also strengthen the melody.

A Solo Clarinet is found in most prominent bands, to which are allotted the principal and counter-melodies, variations, and smooth running passages, and in fact everything requiring an accomplished artist.

The number of B flat Clarinets necessary for

a Military Band cannot be decided, the more the better; this in a way is dependent upon the ideas of the bandmaster and principally upon the necessary funds being available for the engagement of the players.

6. The Alto-Clarinet in F sounds a fifth lower than the ordinary Clarinet in C; an octave lower than the Clarinet in F.

7. The Alto-Clarinet in E♭ sounds an octave lower than the ordinary Clarinet in E flat; a sixth lower than the Clarinet in C.

8. The Bass-Clarinet in B♭ sounds an octave lower than the ordinary Clarinet in B flat.

The beauty, uniformity, and great pliancy of tonal character possessed by both the Alto-Clarinets in F and E flat and the Bass-Clarinet subdues the tonal volume of the higher Wood and especially the Brass instruments to such an extent as to impart an even and euphonious tonal-quality to the entire instrumental masses of the Military Band, and I cannot understand why they are not included in every band; it is certainly to be regretted that they are not brought into more general use, as a very important part of the different tonal-types, necessary for the artistic blending of the wind-instruments, is lost thereby.

Apart from the advantage (brought about by the perfected mechanism of these instruments) of producing transcriptions and arrangements of symphonic works of both classic and modern masters for Military Band in their complete harmonic and instrumental entirety, in such a manner as to render the technical difficulties contained therein possible for both the conductor and his men after conscientious and repeated study, a wealth of tonal-shadings could be produced, which is entirely unknown at the present time, and which would approach considerably near to the character and tonal-quality of orchestral music.

The following presents a table of the tonal-compass of all the differently pitched small and large Clarinets:—

TABLE OF NOTATION AND TONAL-COMPASS OF ALL THE DIFFERENTLY PITCHED CLARINETS.

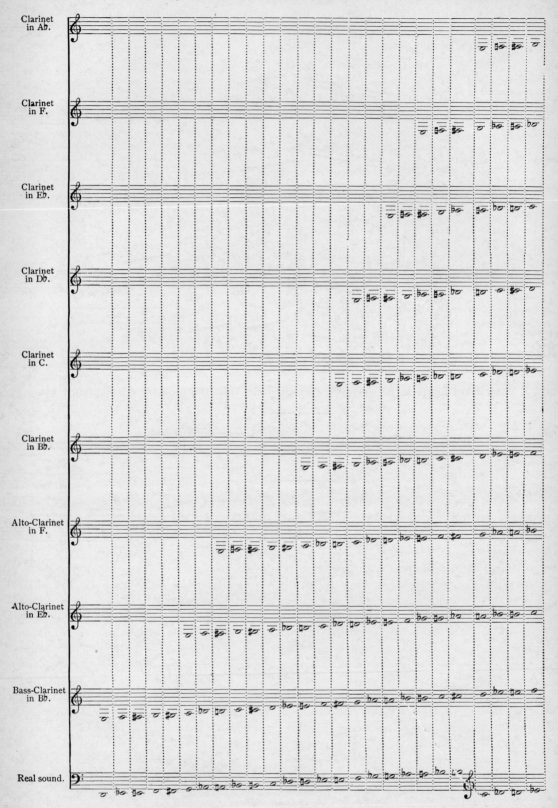

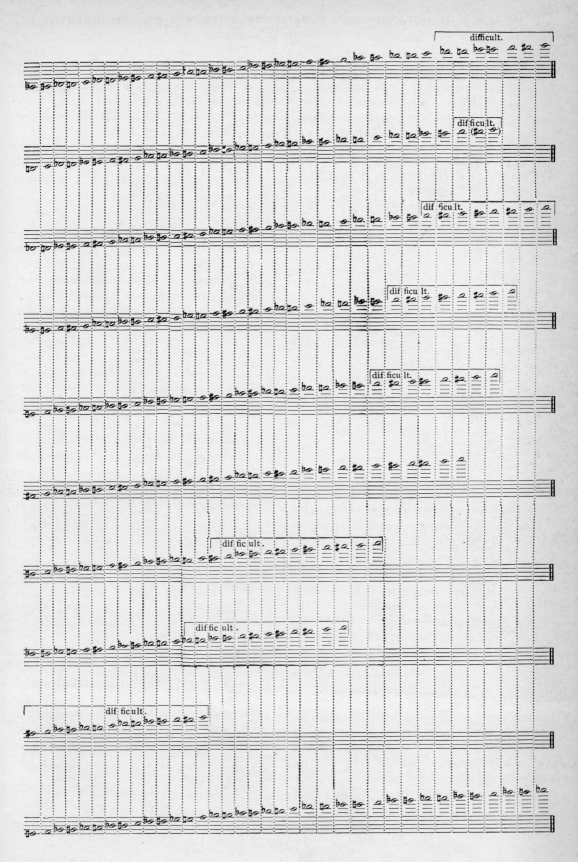

4. THE OBOE.

Is used and treated in the exact manner as in the orchestra, and attention is once more directed to the detailed explanation of this instrument on page 92. An Oboe in B flat sounding one tone lower than the ordinary one in C is sometimes met with, but is very rarely employed.

5. THE ALT-OBOE or ENGLISH HORN.

Build and manner of playing of this instrument is nearly identical with that of the ordinary Oboe. It is used in the Russian Military Bands, and is pitched in F, a fifth lower than the Oboe.

Tonal-Compass.

Sounds.

6. THE BASSOON.

This instrument is treated and employed in the identical manner as in connection with the orchestra. Usually two Bassoons are employed, but in order to strengthen the Basses or when using them to execute the parts of the Viola or Violoncello a greater number may be used. This of course is entirely dependent upon the number of musicians at the disposal of the Bandmaster. The Bassoon is indispensable to every well-equipped Military Band, and a great mistake is made in trying to drop this instrument from its ranks. Some musicians are of the opinion that as the tonal-quality of the Bassoon is not a blaring or crashing one, it cannot make itself sufficiently heard in the mass of instruments. But this is a mistake, as we must not forget, that the greater the variety of tonal-types which we combine, the greater will be the wealth and beauty of tonal-shadings. We also have Bassoons pitched in B flat, and which sound a note lower than the ordinary Bassoon in C, but they are very rarely used.

7. THE DOUBLE-BASSOON.

This instrument is only met with in very large and well-equipped Military Bands. It is treated in the identical manner as explained in the respective article for the orchestra (page 109). Its notes sound an octave lower than they are written. The lower notes:

employed in slow passages or sustained notes, sound very beautiful and are similar to the tones of an organ.

The **Tritonicon** or **Metal Double Bassoon** invented by Çervený is used extensively in the Military Bands of Austria, Holland, Russia, etc. Its tonal-compass is : —

The **Sub-Double Bassoon** in B flat, a continuation of the E flat Double Bassoon, can easily produce the Sub-contra B flat, and in consequence possesses a lower range than the Organ. Its tonal-compass extends chromatically from

The strength and volume of its tone are tremendous.

8. THE FRENCH HORN.

Both the natural and chromatic French Horns are counted among the most important factors of military music; as employed in the latter their principal usefulness presents itself in the execution of rhythmical accompaniments as well as sustained notes. At intervals the first part may be entrusted with a solo, but in doing this the ability and accomplishment of the player must always be carefully considered.

Usually two or four Horns are employed; Horns pitched in F or E flat are best adapted for the Military Band, but if certain effects or varied tonal-shadings are sought after, the other varieties of differently pitched Horns can also be employed to excellent advantage.

The Cornon (in F, E, E flat, D and also Tenor C, B♭), invented by Çervený in 1844, is substituted in some European Military organizations, for the French Horn.

The tonal-compass of this instrument is : —

The Primhorn, also invented by Çervený, is pitched exactly an octave higher than the ordinary French Horn in F or E flat; the middle register of this instrument being identical with the high register of the ordinary French Horn.

Its tonal-compass is :—

The Primhorn adapts itself excellently for the performance of songs.

9. THE TRUMPET.

Only chromatic Trumpets are employed in Military Bands. From one to four different parts are written; the first one executing solo-passages, counter melodies, and fanfaren, or for strengthening the melody as well as for accompaniments. With the exception of counter melodies, used to strengthen the first part, the second part chiefly executes accompaniments. The third and fourth part complete the accompanying harmony in connection with the Altos and French Horns. Therefore, in connection with these latter instruments, E flat Trumpets are usually taken, owing to their more voluminous tone, while the first and second parts are often written for B flat Trumpets (especially in Brass Bands). The third and fourth parts should always be written in such a manner as to allow of their ready omission in smaller combinations.

The Bass Trumpet, in B flat, is still in use in a few European countries (Bavaria, Austria, Spain, etc.), taking the place of Tenor Horns.

Its music is written in the violin clef, but an octave lower than the Tenor Horn, and serves principally for accompaniments, or for the strengthening of the melody or of bass figures. Its tone sounds an octave lower than that of the ordinary Trumpet.

10. THE PICCOLO CORNET.

(VALVE) IN E FLAT.

In the music for Brass Bands this instrument takes the place of the Piccolo used in Military Bands. It possesses a bright, penetrating tone, and is pitched a fourth higher than the ordinary Cornet and Flügelhorn in B flat, and in consequence perfects the highest register of these instruments. The intervals sound a minor third higher than they are written.

It is advisable not to crowd the part of this instrument with too many notes, and to avoid writing in too difficult a manner for it. Melodies, counter-melodies, or light and agile passages can be easily executed upon this instrument.

The Piccolo Cornet in A flat is pitched a perfect fourth higher than the E flat Piccolo, and is employed in some bands for unusually high passages, which are beyond the range of the E flat Piccolo Cornet.

For example : —

For E flat Piccolo. Difficult.

For A flat Piccolo. Easy.

Sounds.

11. THE CORNET AND FLÜGEL-HORN.

(SOPRANO—CORNET.)

The Cornet commands a leading position in French and American Military Bands, the most prominent solos, arias, cavatinas, variations with double and triple tonguing, etc., being entrusted to it. Together with the Flügelhorn it predominates as the principal leader of the melody in Brass bands. It is customary to write for two instruments. Owing to its high and bright sounding tonal-qualities the B flat Cornet is preferable, and is therefore used most frequently.

The Flügelhorn is of somewhat larger build than the Cornet, and in consequence its tone is rounder and more voluminous. Its tonal-quality is very sympathetic, soft, and glowing, and adapts itself excellently for the performance of sustained, languishing, serious, and religious melodies. The embouchure upon this instrument is more difficult than upon the Cornet, and it is therefore advisable not to write in too complicated a manner for it. Flügelhorns in B flat are mostly employed.

Tonal-Compass.   Chromatic. Difficult.

Two or three parts are written for the Flügelhorn, the first executing the melody, together or alternately with the solo Trumpet or Cornet. Accompaniments are given to the second or third part, or melodious passages in thirds, sixths, or octaves in connection with the first part.

Flügelhorns or Cornets in B♭ 1 and 2.

Sound.

In difficult passages the different parts change off in executing the melody, as illustrated in the following example : —

Flügelhorns or Cornets in B♭.

The fingering for the Cornet and Flügelhorn is identical with that of the chromatic Trumpet.

12. THE ALT-CORNET.

(ALTHORN IN E FLAT.)

In Cavalry music this instrument takes the place of the French Horns, and for the notation of its music the Violin clef is employed as for these latter instruments. Its tonal-compass ranges between that of the Flügel and Tenor Horns, serving as a natural connection of these two instruments.

Tonal-Compass.

Chromatic.

Sounds.

Two parts are usually written for this instrument; but where circumstances allow even three or four parts may be employed. The principal task of the Althorns consists in completing the accompanying harmony together with the second Tenor Horn, which may be possibly augmented by the third and fourth E flat Trumpets. But aside from this, and owing to its exceedingly beautiful and penetrating quality of tone, this instrument also adapts itself excellently for solo passages or for strengthening the melody in the lower registers; in addition to this the leading part may be entrusted to it at times.

The Alto-Cornet in F is pitched one tone higher, *the Alto-Cornet in D* one-half tone lower, than the *Alto-Cornet* in E flat. Both are rarely employed.

13. THE TENOR HORN IN B FLAT.

An indispensable instrument for both Military and Brass Bands. Its tones sound an octave lower than those of the Flügelhorns. Usually two parts are written, but sometimes even three (in the Bands of Saxony). The first is treated as a solo part, especially, in Brass Bands, and as such is entrusted with strengthening the principal melody of the Flügelhorns or Basses, or it progresses independently with a counter-melody, but can also be employed for perfecting the accompanying harmony. Accompaniments are principally allotted to the second and third parts in bass melodies; or for the continuation of certain bass passages, too high for the Basses, they can proceed in unison with the first part.

The round flexible tone of the Tenor Horns adapts itself excellently for the expression of serious, religious and melancholy solo melodies. Notation in the Violin clef.

Tenor Horns pitched in C and A have also been made but they are rarely used.

14. THE BARITONE.
(EUPHONION.)

This instrument is similar to the Tenor Horn but of somewhat larger build; its compass is the same as that of the latter, but its tone is stronger and more voluminous, especially in the lower registers.

Music for the Baritone is written in the bass clef.

The employment of this beautiful instrument, which may be fittingly compared with the voice of a baritone singer, is similar to the use of the Violoncello in the orchestra. Its tone can always be plainly distinguished from among the greatest mass of instruments; attention should therefore be constantly directed towards writing only independent and effective passages, counter or bass melodies for this instrument.

The Baroxyton, invented by Çervený, serves as a bass instrument in Russian Infantry bands.

The Kaiserbariton (Emperor Baritone), also invented by Çervený, pitched in C or B flat, possesses a Cello-like quality of tone.

15. THE TROMBONE.

The Slide Trombone is employed here in the identical manner as in the orchestra. In the majority of French Military and Brass Bands Valve-Trombones have been introduced, owing to greater ease in the execution of difficult passages, brought about by the valves, but with a partial loss of the peculiar tonal-quality of the Slide Trombone. Usually three Trombone parts are written, which are called upon to execute sustained notes, accompanying figures, expressive, grand, and religious melodies, etc. For triumphal marches, in fact, for every composition of a martial character, the Trombones are tremendously effective; they can also be employed to excellent advantage *p* and *pp*.

16. THE SAXOPHONE.

Six varieties of this instrument are in use, alike in form but very different as regards size, following in steps like organ-pipes and all possessing the same tonal-character.

1. Saxophone High Soprano in E flat.
2.   "   "   "   " B flat.
3.   "   Alto   " F or E flat.
4.   "   Tenor   " C or B flat.
5.   "   Baritone   " E flat.
6.   "   Bass   " B flat.

I have already discussed these peculiar instruments sufficiently, and they can be employed for military music in the identical manner as indicated in the foregoing respective chapter. Usually only a quartette of these instruments, consisting of a Soprano B flat, Alto E flat, Tenor B flat, and Baritone E flat, is employed.

17. THE SARUSOPHONE.*

New Brass instruments intended to replace the Oboes and Bassoons of the Military Band. The Sarusophones consist of a whole family of the following eight instruments:—

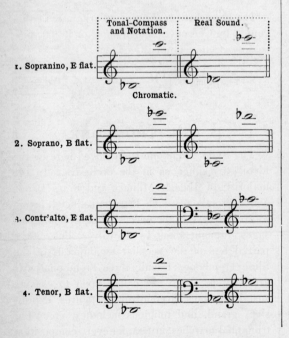

5. Baritone, E flat.

6. Bass, B flat.

7. Contra-Bass, E flat.

in C.

8. Contra-Basson C, or in B flat.

in B flat.

The tonal quality and character of these instruments is very similar to that of the Oboes and Bassoons, but possesses a much stronger and more penetrating tone; through the use of these instruments, either singly or in numbers, a large variety of new effects might be produced by composers. The fingering upon the Sarusophone is almost identical with that of the B flat Clarinet. The music for all these differently pitched Sarusophones is written in the G clef. The best-sounding Keys, for this instrument, are C, G, D, A, F, B flat, E flat Major and Minor. Music which does not abound in too many technical difficulties, expressive broad melodies, sustained harmonies, arpeggios, etc., will be found to be best adapted for these instruments.

The following example will illustrate the correct and practical treatment of the entire family of Sarusophones.

* The first idea for constructing these instruments is credited to Monsieur Sarus, Bandmaster of the 13th Infantry Regiment, France; credit is due to the Parisian manufacturers of Band instruments, Messrs. Gautrot & Co., for having carried out this idea in the shape of the above instruments.

FRAGMENT FROM THE FANTASIA IN C-MINOR FOR PIANOFORTE.

(Especially arranged for Six Sarusophones.)

MOZART.

18. THE OPHICLEIDE.

Is treated exactly as in the orchestra, but has luckily been abandoned in nearly all Military Bands, for reasons already explained (See Page 158.)

Pitched in C and B flat. The latter preferable.

19. THE BASS TUBA.

(BOMBARDON.)

A variety of Bass Tubas are in use pitched in F, E flat, C and B flat.

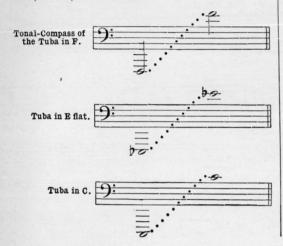

In Germany the Bass parts are written as they sound ; but in France their notation is an octave higher than their real sound, and within the following compass : —

Quick runs should be avoided for this instrument, as a clear and distinct execution thereof demands an accomplished artist. The following examples will illustrate the practical manner of writing for this instrument as well as for the Helicon or Contrabasstuba.

Examples showing notation and practical manner of writing for the Bass Tuba and Helicon or Contrabasstuba.

20. THE HELICON OR CONTRABASSTUBA.

A bass instrument like the above-mentioned one, with a powerful, sonorous, soft tone, owing to which it is nearly always used in preference to the Bass Tuba. Helicons pitched in F, E flat, C, and B flat are in use; tonal-compass, notation and treatment the same as for the Bass Tuba. See examples on this and preceding page.

In the following a complete table of the notation and compass of all the Brass Instruments is given.

NOTATION AND TONAL-COMPASS OF ALL THE BRASS INSTRUMENTS.

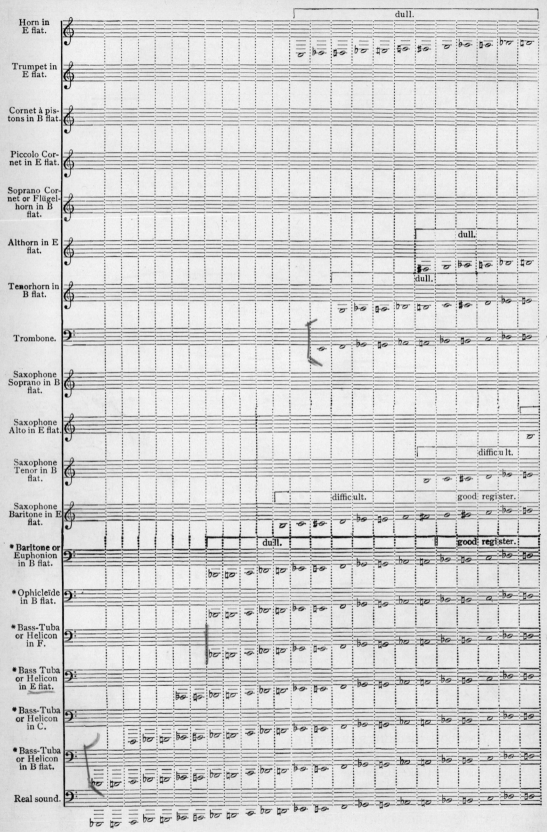

* (See Addenda (Page 318) for special remarks.

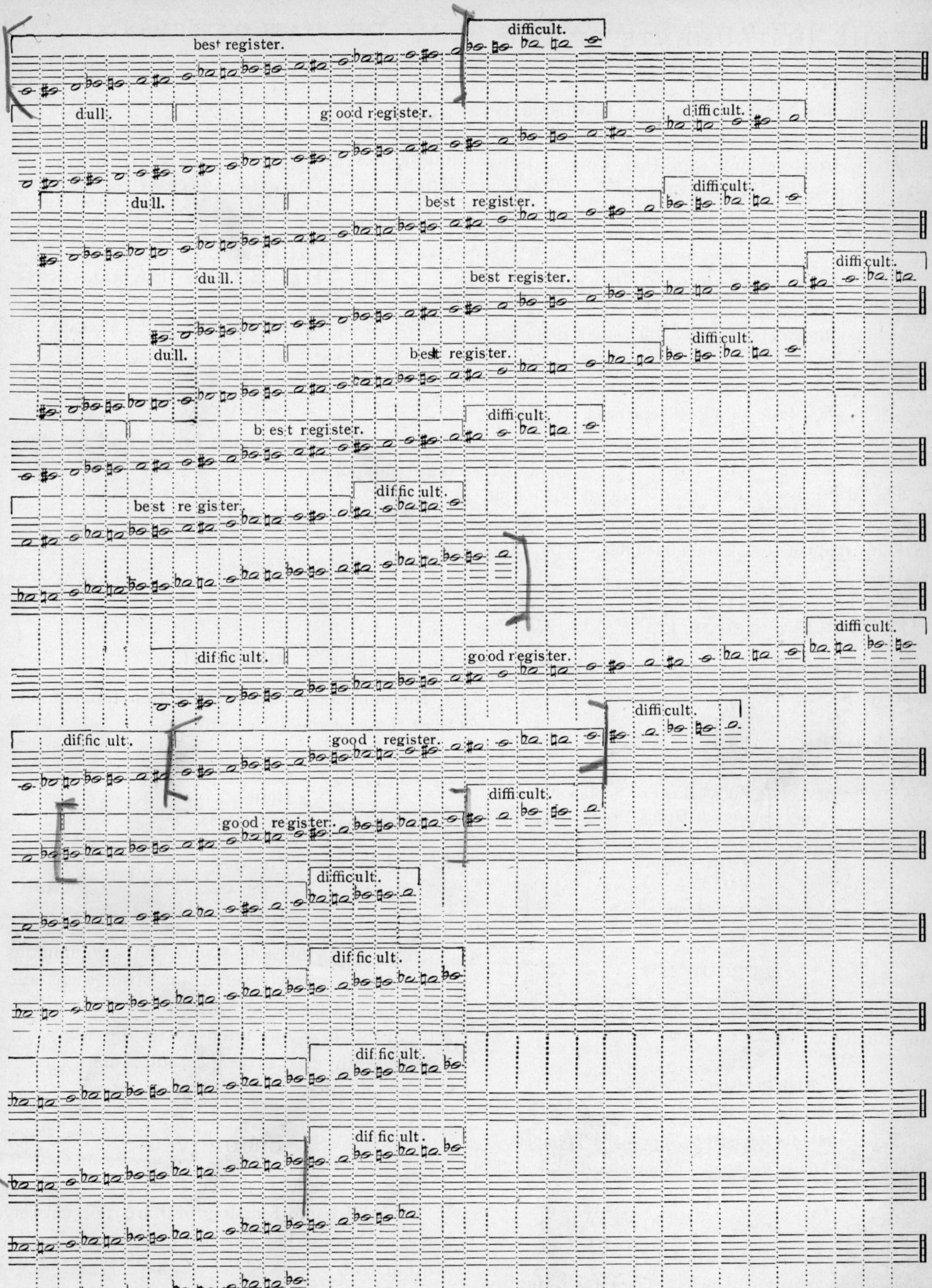
best register.
difficult.
dull.
good register.
difficult.
dull.
best register.
difficult.
dull.
best register.
difficult.
dull.
best register.
difficult.
best register.
difficult.
best register.
difficult.
difficult.
good register.
difficult.
difficult.
good register.
difficult.
good register.
difficult.
difficult.
difficult.
difficult.
difficult.

21. THE INSTRUMENTS OF PER- CUSSION.

All the instruments belonging to this class, and which I have already discussed so extensively in Groups 3 and 4 of this work, can be used in the same manner and to equal advantage in connection with the Military Band.

22. THE MILITARY BAND.

Military music is divided into two principal groups : —

1. Music for the Military Band.
2. Music for the Brass Band.

The Military Band is again divided into four different instrumental groups, which are classified in respect to tonal-character, type, and volume.

GROUP I.

Instruments of soft, round, and subdued tonal-quality.

High Register :   Flutes.

Middle Register :
{
Flügelhörner or Soprano-Cornets.
French Horns.
Alto Horns.
Tenor Horns.
Baritones.
Saxophones.
}

GROUP II.

Instruments of brilliant, bright, and penetrating tonal-quality.

High Register : Piccolos.
High and Middle Register : Clarinets.
Middle Register : Cornets and Trumpets.
Middle and Lower Register : Trombones.
Lower Register : Basses.

GROUP III.

Instruments of somewhat nasal tonal-quality, but which impart color and smoothness to the general combination of instruments.

High Register : Oboes.
Lower Register : Bassoons.
High, Middle, and Lower Register : Saxophones and Sarusophones.

GROUP IV.

All instruments of percussion.

The number of instruments necessary for a Military Band is entirely dependent upon the number of performers at the disposal of the Bandmaster. No fixed rules can be laid down in this respect.

23. THE BRASS BAND.

The Brass Band is divided into four different Instrumental groups.

GROUP I.

Instruments of brilliant, bright, and penetrating tonal-quality :

Piccolo-Cornets.
Soprano-Cornets.
Trumpets.
Trombones.
Basses.

GROUP II.

Instruments of somewhat softer tonal-quality than those of the above group :

Flügelhorns.
Horns.
Alto Horns.
Tenor Horns.
Baritones.

GROUP III.

Instruments of soft, round, and voluminous tonal-quality, which serve to strengthen and bring the harmony into prominence and impart more brilliancy and intensity to the whole ensemble (only used in France and America).

The Quartette of Saxophones.

GROUP IV.

All Instruments of Percussion.

The third and fourth group are not entirely necessary, and they may be used or dispensed with at will.

Exactly as with the Military Band, the number of instruments to be employed in a Brass Band depends entirely upon the number of performers at the disposal of the Bandmaster or Leader, as well as upon the individual accomplishment of each player.

24. ARRANGEMENT OF MILITARY MUSIC.

As a general rule Military music should possess characteristics of a manly, serious, martial, severe, resounding and brilliant nature; but then again it can be expressive in a joyous, light, graceful, etc., manner; its general style must be as simple and natural as possible, if a variety of effects are to be obtained. In composing and arranging for these combinations, one of the most important points to be observed by bandmasters and conductors is that the compositions are always specially written or arranged according to the number of instruments at the disposal of the writer and according to the individual abilities of the players, in order to show off the excellent qualities of such a band to the best advantage.

For the arrangement of an orchestral symphonic composition the following directions may be followed as a general guide : —

a) **For Military Band.** The part of the first Violins is taken by the first Clarinets; the second Violins by the second Clarinets; the Violas by the Alto and Tenor Horns; the Violoncellos by the Baritones or Tenor Tubas; the Double-Basses by the Helicons or Bass Tubas.

b) **For Brass Band.** The part of the first Violins is taken by the Piccolo-Cornets, the first cornets and Flügelhorns; the second Violins, by the second Cornets and second Flügelhorns; the Violas by the Alto or Tenor Horns; the Violoncellos by the Baritones or Tenor Tubas; the Double-Basses by the Helicons or Bass Tubas.

The Flutes, Horns, Trumpets, Cornets, Trombones, and Instruments of Percussion are employed in almost the identical manner as in an orchestral arrangement.

The following examples will serve to illustrate and present a complete idea of how to score correctly and effectively for the Military and Brass Band as employed in Germany, France, England, and America.

THE GERMAN MILITARY BAND.

a.) EXTRACT FROM THE OPERA "EURYANTHE."

C. M. von Weber.

b.) EXTRACT FROM THE OPERA "CARMEN."

Act IV.   Arranged by Louis Oertel.

G. BIZET.

EXTRACT FROM THE SIXTH SYMPHONY.

Marcia funèbre.   Arranged by H. Saro.   J. RAFF.

THE FRENCH MILITARY BAND.

EXTRACT FROM "ARIANE," OVERTURE MILITAIRE.

(Prize Composition.)

H. KLING.

Grandioso e con tutta la forza.

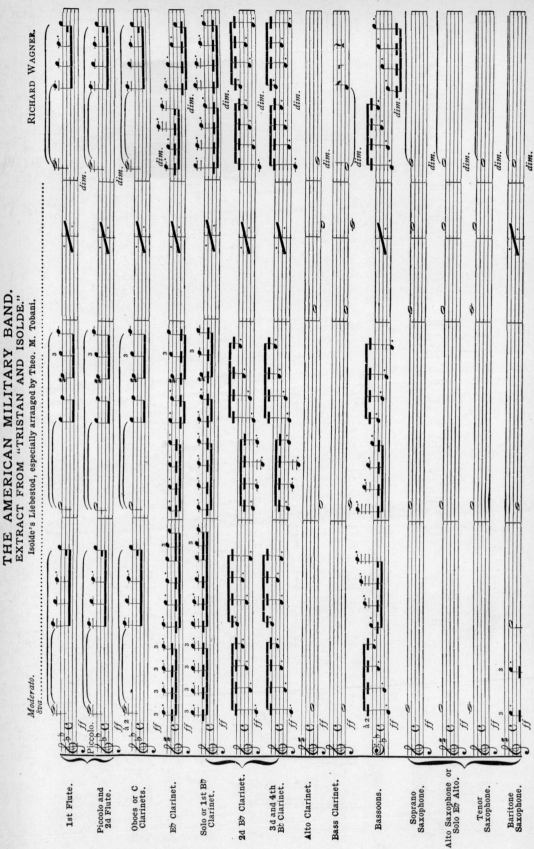

THE AMERICAN MILITARY BAND.
EXTRACT FROM "TRISTAN AND ISOLDE."
Isolde's Liebestod, especially arranged by Theo. M. Tobani.

RICHARD WAGNER.

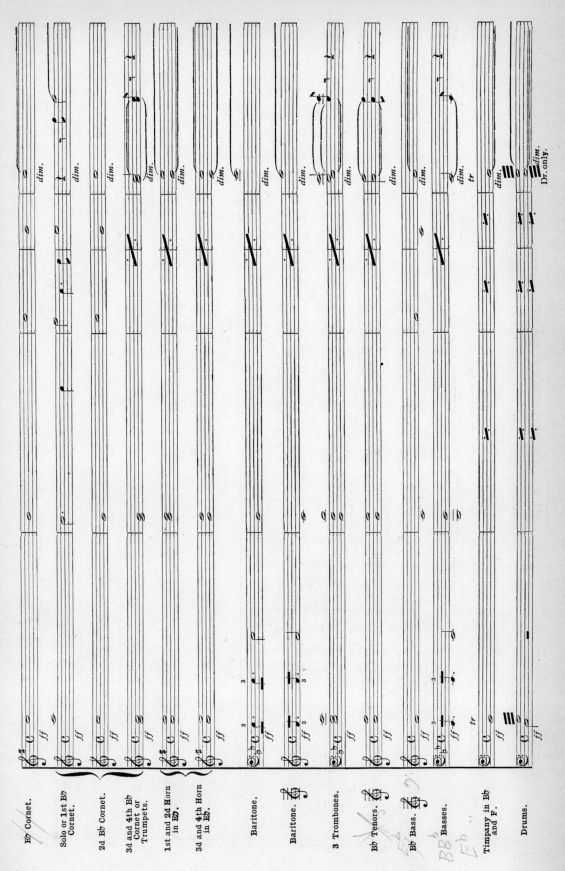

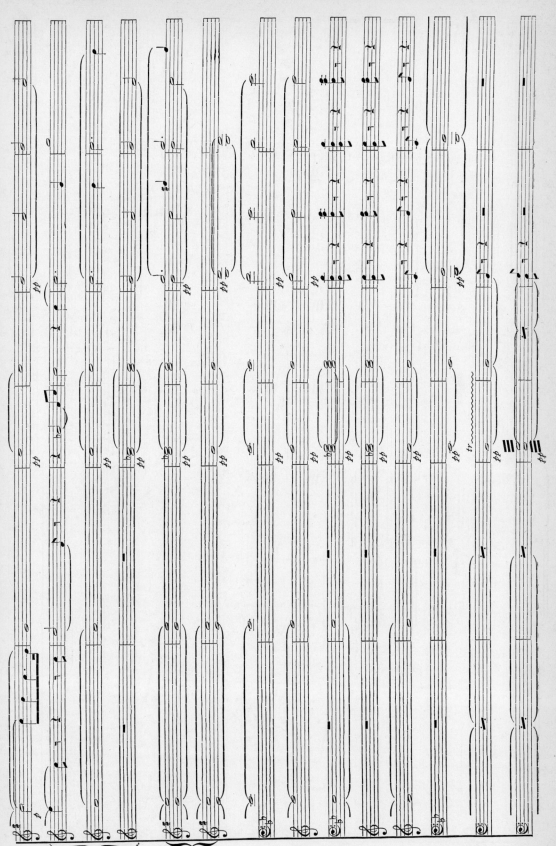

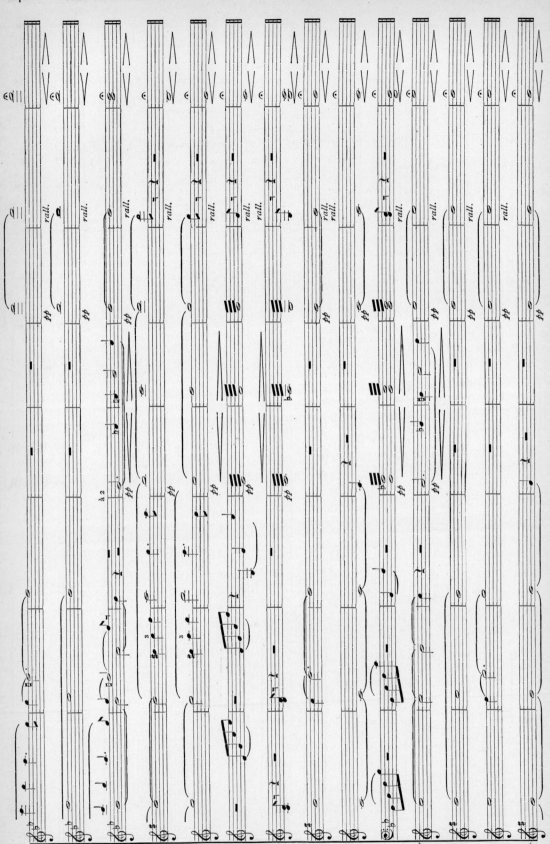

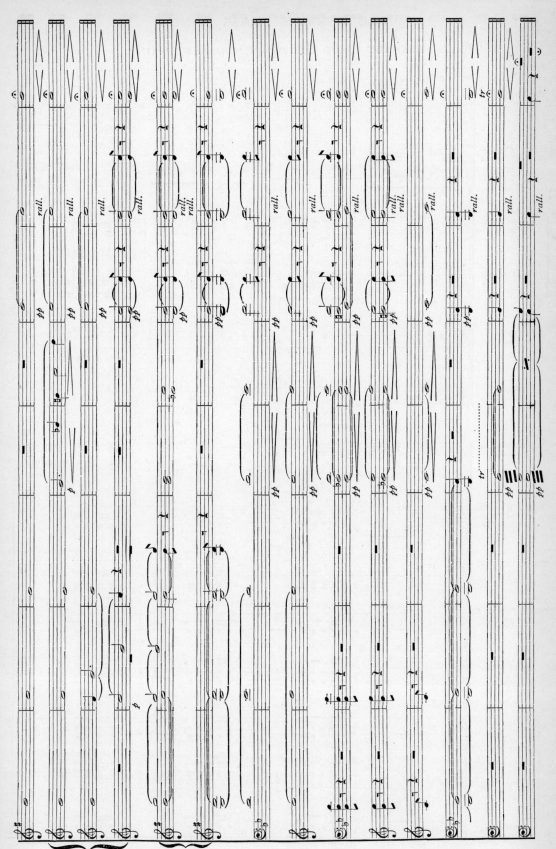

THE GERMAN BRASS BAND.

EXTRACT FROM THE OPERA "CARMEN," Act II.

G. BIZET.

THE FRENCH BRASS BAND.

EXTRACT FROM "LE ROI CHILDEBERT" OVERTURE MILITAIRE.

(Prize Composition.)

H. KLING.

Every conceivable style or kind of Musical composition known up to the present day can be arranged for these various combinations. They can also serve for accompanying a chorus, and as an additional aid for the general effectiveness of a dramatic scene, can be used in connection with an orchestra, as Meyerbeer has done in several of his operas with such telling effect. For instance, in the Prophet, North Star, L'Africaine, etc., when this master introduces the principal motive in the most brilliant manner, following it up by both orchestras executing his idea alternately, with the most artistic blending of the instruments; the Brass instruments alternating with the Wood Wind and Strings to such a point where both bodies combine into one grand and tremendous coda, the effect of which is overpowering.

Halévy, Verdi, Donizetti, as well as Berlioz in his Funereal and Triumphal Symphony, have employed combinations of this kind in a like manner.

"Above all, Wagner's instrumentation, the tremendous orchestral apparatus and its polyphonic treatment is both wonderful and astonishing. Not alone has Wagner used the greatest number of instruments, the like of which no operatic composer before him has ever attempted, probably with the exception of Berlioz, but he has introduced entirely new ones like the Bass Trumpet, etc. In the same manner he has made use of numerous wind instruments, especially the Tubas, which up to his time had only been employed in Military music. And what grand and tremendous effects has he produced with these Tubas which formerly were not thought fit to be used in the higher forms of music.

"In idyllic, tender scenes of course they are superfluous and their use would be entirely out of the question. Heroic, majestic, in fact all grand and overpowering situations require and demand new and original treatment from our composers in addition to enlarging their resources through the use of new musical instruments. But this in turn demands, and is only possible with the aid of new orchestral instruments and new instrumental combinations.

"The scene in 'Rheingold' where Wotan and Fricka appear for the first time, is illustrated by Wagner with the aid of three E flat Trumpets, one E flat Bass Trumpet, three Tenor Bass Trombones, two Tenor Tubas in B flat, two Bass Tubas in F, one Contrabass Trombone, one Contrabass Tuba, Harp, Tympani, twelve Cellos, eight first and second Double Basses, joined by three Flutes, two Oboes, three Clarinets, four French Horns, three Bassoons, etc., later on. It stands to reason that Wagner does not allow these numerous instruments to constantly play at full strength, and especially not while the singing is in progress. As soon as Fricka and Wotan begin to sing, the Brass instruments pause, and only the Cellos and Violas are retained and two Double Basses sustain E flat in the doubled octave.

"N. B. In this case the E string of the second Double Bass must be tuned to E flat.

"Wagner the almighty, perfectly routined master of the orchestra has disclosed such astonishing perfection in the art of orchestration, which in itself is worthy of the greatest respect and admiration. In all his thoughts and writings he certainly must have carefully figured and reckoned upon the effectiveness of every individual tone. This conclusion is best arrived at through the careful and conscientious study of his scores. To begin with, they disclose two fundamental principles, which our modern composers might adopt as rules in the creation of dramatic works. In Parlando scenes, whether in Monologues or Dialogues, where the singer must sing more in a speaking voice, and only fortissimo in exceptional exclamatory passages, while during Parlando scenes, probably mezzo-forte or as the occasion might require only Piano, in such cases Wagner has called upon the assistance of only a few instruments. It stands to reason that the spoken song or singing speech (as we might translate the Parlando) according to its nature cannot and must not be performed in a forced or screaming manner by the singer. The correct gauge, we might say the rule, would be the strength of the general speaking tone of the individual.

"But there, where pain and desperation are to be expressed, or where, like in the second act of Tristan and Isolde, the wild and impulsive fire of love breaks forth and expresses itself in words like: O rapture of spirit! O sweetest, highest, fairest, strongest, holiest bliss! Endless pleasure! Boundless treasure!

"Every known orchestral resource is brought into play. The lovers express their passion in fortissimo exclamations, assisted by the entire orchestral body to such an extent as to overpower the voices at times, echoing their expressions of love and passion in a very torrent of fortissimo passages, according to the intentions of the master who conceived this wonderful work. Of course Tristan and Isolde must be possessed of strong, in fact, very strong voices, otherwise they will be completely engulfed and lost in the overpowering fire and passion of the orchestra.

DR. J. SCHUCHT.
The Instrumentation of the Modern Opera, with special reference to the "Ring of the Nibelung."
(*Neue Zeitschrift für Musik, 1886.*)

Among the composers and accomplished arrangers for this special branch of music the names of: Wieprecht, Rosenkranz, Saro, Goldschmidt, Streck, Bender, Beer, Frank, Böttge, Oertel, Parlo, Sellenwick, Léon Chic, Magnier, Mohr, and a great many more, too numerous to mention, are regarded as among the most prominent and especially worthy of mention.

In conclusion, I will not omit to add that the personnel of the Military Bands of all countries is neither the same nor the outcome of a well-regulated system, every organization possessing its own particular combination of instruments, and these latter as a rule being determined according to the personal ideas of the bandmaster. In Prussia the organization and personnel of the different varieties of Military Bands (Infantry, Cavalry, and Jäger music) is under strict control and never varies. Consequently a composer writing for such an organization must take the exact number and variety of instruments into careful consideration.

25. INSTRUMENTS EMPLOYED IN GERMAN MILITARY ORGANIZATIONS.

The German Infantry (Military) Band is made up of the following instruments : —

Wood Wind Instruments

Piccolo.
Flute.
Clarinet in A♭ (not always in use).
2 Clarinets in E♭.
3–4 Clarinets in B♭.
Alto and Bass Clarinets (rarely used).
2 Oboes.
2 Bassoons.
1 Double Bassoon (not always used).

Brass Instruments.

2 Flügelhorns in B♭.
2 Alto Horns in E♭ (not always in use).
2 Tenorhorns in B♭ (in Saxony 3 Tenorhorns are employed).
1 Euphonium (Tenor Tuba).
2 Basses (Tuba, Helicon, Bombardon).
4 Trumpets in E♭ (or the first two in B♭, 3–4 in E♭).
2 Bass Trumpets in B♭ (only employed in Southern Germany).
4 French Horns in E♭.
3–4 Trombones.

Instruments of Percussion.

Drums and Cymbals (Tympani rarely employed).
Lyra.

HORN BAND.

(HUNTER, PIONEER, AND ARTILLERY MUSIC.)

Piccolo Cornet in E♭ (Piston in E♭).
2–3 Flügelhorns or Cornets in B♭.
2 Alto horns in E♭.
2 Tenor horns in B♭.
1 Euphonium (Tenor Tuba).
2 Basses (Tuba-Helicon).
4 Trumpets in E♭ (or 2 B♭ and 2 E♭ Trumpets).
4 French Horns in E♭ (sometimes only 2 are used).
3 Trombones (sometimes 4 are used).
Drums.

Of late years the bands of some of the Artillery Regiments have partly adopted the combination of the Infantry (Military) Bands.

TRUMPET (CAVALRY) BAND.

Piccolo in E♭ (Piston in E♭).
2 Flügelhorns or Cornets in B♭.
2 Alto Horns in E♭ (sometimes only one).
2 Tenor Horns in B♭.
1 Euphonium (Tenor Tuba).
2 Basses (Tuba-Helicon).
4 Trumpets in E♭.
Tympani (ad lib).

26. INSTRUMENTS EMPLOYED IN THE MILITARY ORGANIZATIONS OF FRANCE, BELGIUM, AND HOLLAND.

Wood Wind Instruments.

Piccolo D♭. | Saxophone Soprano B♭.
Flute. | " Alto E♭.
2 Oboes (†). | " Tenor B♭.
Clarinet E♭. | " Baritone E♭.
1. 2. 3. 4. Clarinets B♭. | 2 Bassoons (†).

Brass Instruments.

1 Small Bugle E♭ (†). | 3 Trombones.
2 Cornets, B♭. | Bass, E♭.
2 Bugles, B♭. | Bass Tuba B♭.
2 French Horns, E♭ (†). | Drums.
2 Trumpets, E♭ (†). | Sarrusophone (†) (very
3 Altos E♭. | rarely employed).
2 Barytones B♭. |

27. INSTRUMENTS EMPLOYED IN ITALIAN MILITARY ORGANIZATIONS.

Flute. | 3 Genes (Altos in E♭).
Piccolo E♭. | 2 Bassoons.
Oboes. | Double Bassoon.
Clarinet E♭. | 3 Trombones.
1. 2. 3. Clarinets B♭. | 1 Bass Trombone.
Saxophone Soprano B♭. | 2 Bombardini (Baritones).
" Alto E♭. | Bombardoni (Tuba in E♭).
" Tenor B♭. | Pelittoni (BB♭ Tuba or
Clarone (Bass Clarinet) B♭. | Helicon).
Pistone (Piccolo Cornet) E♭. | Tympani.
2 Cornets B♭. | Drums.
2 Flügelhorns B♭. | Bass Drum, Cymbals,
4 Trumpets E♭. | Triangle, Tam-Tam, etc.
4 French Horns E♭. |

28. INSTRUMENTS EMPLOYED IN AMERICAN MILITARY ORGANIZATIONS.

As the American Military Band Organizations are not governed by any uniform law, relative to a certain number of players or special instruments to be employed, we will cite the instru-

---

The instruments marked with (†) are not employed in all French Military Bands.

mentation of two representative American Bands, the 22d Regiment of New York, and John Philip Sousa's, the latter's having been the official American Band at the Paris Exposition, 1900, and of a special combination of brass-band instruments designated as a "Fanfare," grouped and conducted by John George Frank, Conductor of the 12th Regiment Band of New York.

22D REGIMENT BAND, N. Y.

Wood Wind Instruments.

2 Piccolos.	1 Alto Clarinet.
2 Flutes.	1 Bass "
2 Oboes.	1 Soprano Saxophone.
1 A♭ Piccolo Clarinet.	1 Alto "
3 E♭ Clarinets.	1 Tenor "
8 First B♭ Clarinets.	1 Bass "
4 Second B♭ Clarinets.	2 Bassoons.
4 Third B♭ Clarinets.	1 Double Bassoon.

Brass Instruments.

1 E♭ Cornet.	2 B♭ Tenor horns.
2 First B♭ Cornets.	2 Euphonions.
2 Second B♭ Cornets.	2 Trombones.
2 Trumpets.	5 Tubas.
2 Flügelhorns.	3 Drums.
4 French Horns.	1 Pair Cymbals.
2 E♭ Alto Horns.	

JOHN PHILIP SOUSA'S BAND.

(INSTRUMENTATION AS OFFICIAL AMERICAN BAND, PARIS EXPOSITION, 1900.)

Wood Wind Instruments.

1 Piccolo.	2 Alto Clarinets.
3 Flutes.	2 Bass Clarinets.
2 Oboes.	2 Alto Saxophones.
2 E♭ Clarinets.	2 Tenor Saxophones.
9 First B♭ Clarinets.	1 Baritone Saxophone.
4 Second B♭ Clarinets.	3 Bassoons.
3 Third B♭ Clarinets.	

Brass Instruments.

2 First B♭ Cornets (1 Solo).	1 Solo Euphonion.
2 Second B♭ Cornets.	1 Baritone Euphonion.
2 Trumpets.	4 Tubas.
2 Flügelhorns.	Tympani.
4 French Horns.	Drums.
4 Trombones (1 Solo).	Cymbals and Bells, etc.

JOHN GEORGE FRANK'S "FANFARE."

2 Solo B♭ Cornets.	2 Euphonions.
2 E♭ Flügelhorns.	1 F Tuba.
2 B♭ Flügelhorns.	2 Contra C Tubas.
2 B♭ Trumpets.	Tympani and Drums.
2 E♭ Altos.	1 Quartette of Saxophones
2 B♭ Baritones (in Treble clef).	(for increased Band).

HOW A SCORE FOR MILITARY BAND IS TO BE ARRANGED.

It is equally difficult to lay down any decided rules as to the exact manner in which a score for Military Band music is to be arranged and written; the score, as a rule, must be arranged in such a way as to present the instruments in groups similar to the score of the string orchestra, in order to enable the conductor to overlook it quickly; to accomplish this the instruments should follow somewhat in the following order:

Piccolo.
Flutes.
Oboes.
Clarinets in A♭.
Clarinets in E♭.
Clarinets in B♭ (Firsts).
Clarinets in B♭ (Seconds).
Bassoons.
Double Bassoon.
Soprano Cornets in B♭ (Flügelhorns).
Alto Cornets in E♭.
Tenor Horns in B♭.
Baritone (Euphonion).
French Horns.
Trumpets.
Trombones.
Tubas.
Instruments of Percussion.

The Flute and Oboe Registers are the most delicate of all, especially in the higher positions, and are always exceedingly effective. The registers of the Clarinets, Bassoons, and Double Bassoon in military music must be treated in a similar way, as the string-quintette of the string orchestra; manner of writing for these instruments is exactly the same as for their employment in the orchestra. The small Clarinets and the B♭ Clarinets lead the melody in the upper positions; the second Clarinets join the melody in thirds, sixths, in unison or in the lower octave, or they are employed for the execution of effective accompanying passages; sustained notes for these instruments, especially in the lower position, are very effective.

The following movement from Verdi's "Traviata" (Introduction) arranged for E♭ and B♭ Clarinets, creates a beautiful and most delicate effect.

The following movement is also exceedingly effective for Clarinets.

EXTRACT FROM "FESTIVAL OVERTURE."

L. FRANK.

Arpeggios can also be transferred in a very effective manner, and I will choose the following example as an illustration:

EXTRACT FROM "THE PROPHET."

MEYERBEER.

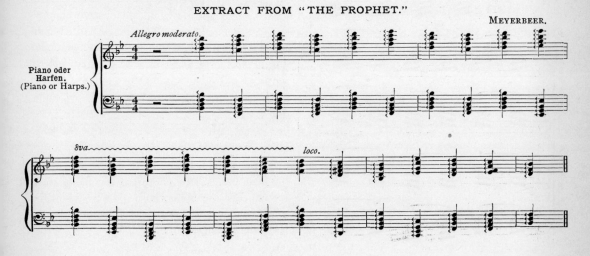

In his Prophet Phantasie, the renowned Royal Prussian Musical Director Wieprecht transferred the above part to the Clarinets, as follows:

Broken Chords, as shown in the following example, can also be executed very effectively by the Clarinets:

B-Klar.
(B♭ Clar.)

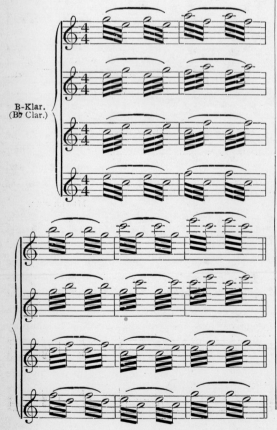

The Cornet Register embraces the different Cornets as well as the Tenor Horn and Baritone (Euphonion). The first Cornets are usually employed as leaders of the melody, and the other either as strengtheners of the principal melody in the lower octave, for the execution of accessory melodies, or for rhythmical accompanying figures. The French Horn Register should be employed in military music in the same way as in the String Orchestra. If used as accompanying instruments in military music the Horns receive appropriate accompanying figures according to the nature of the composition, as illustrated in the following examples:

MARCH.

POLKA.

WALTZ.

Sustained notes are exceedingly effective, both in Forte and Piano passages:

Corno I u. II.
(Horns I and II.)

Corno III u. IV.
(Horns III and IV.)

As the French Horns move in the register of the male voices, male choruses executed by these instruments are always very effective, both in tonal volume and beauty, as illustrated by the following arrangement:

THE HUNTER'S FAREWELL.

MENDELSSOHN.

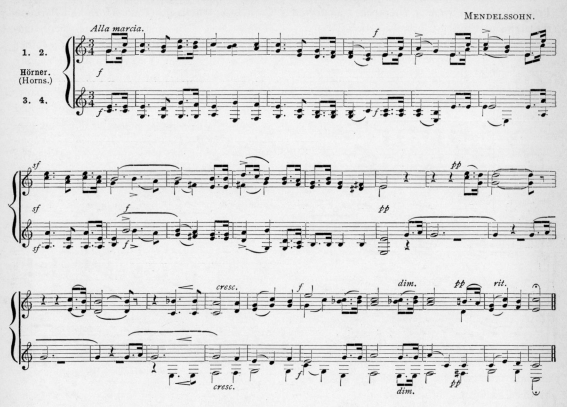

In arrangements and original compositions for Military Music, the composer should endeavor to write the Horn parts in as interesting and appropriate (as far as the tonal character of the instrument is concerned) a manner as possible. At intervals a melodious and effective solo-passage may be entrusted to the first Horn.

The tonal-quality of the Trumpet-Register is cutting, blaring, and penetrating; the first Trumpet is sometimes used to lead the melody, the others being employed for sustained notes, or rhythmical accompaniments, similar to the Horns, but in a somewhat more animated manner.

The Trombones are to be employed as in the String Orchestra. Expressive sustained harmonies are of touching effectiveness. The Trombones sound tremendously effective in forte or fortissimo, especially when all the instruments are employed unisono or in octaves.

Employed in *open harmony*, the Trombones are exceedingly effective:—

They also produce good effects in *close harmony*.

The Instruments of Percussion are to be treated as in the String Orchestra, but their parts should be written in an interesting and original manner, in order to render them as effective as possible.

The Bass-Tubas are treated in the exact manner as the Bass-instruments of the String-Orchestra.

The Euphonion or Baritone takes the place of the Violoncellos or Bassoons, and the Double-Bass parts are transferred to the Tubas, for which it is sometimes necessary to change original figures and passages in order to simplify their execution for the player. Leading melodies (especially such in slow tempo) executed by all Bass-Tubas (and strengthened by the Trombones) create a grand and impressive effect.

An example of this kind is illustrated in the following extract from a Fantaisie romantique, "Le Chemin des Étoiles," for Military Band, by H. Kling. (This composition was awarded a prize at Paris, 1885).

As the author has been repeatedly requested to illustrate how a Score for Military Music is to be written and practically arranged, he has added the following examples for the express purpose of showing and instructing a beginner, how to go to work in scoring either for Brass or Military Band. For this purpose he has chosen the following simple song for mixed chorus:—

(a.) SONG FOR FOUR MIXED VOICES.

As this song is written in C Major, I will also retain this Key in transferring it, although in doing so the chorus will in reality be heard a tone lower, owing to the B♭ instruments reading from parts written in C Major. If the chorus were to be transferred so as to really sound in C Major, the parts for the B flat instruments would have to be written a full tone higher, i.e., in D Major; and consequently leading the E flat instruments to A Major, causing the technical execution upon these instruments to become quite difficult.

It can be easily inferred from the above, that the greatest care must be exercised in selecting appropriate Keys for Military Band arrangements, on account of the Brass Instruments sounding to best advantage in the Keys of *C Major*, *A Minor*, *F Major*, *D Minor*, *B♭ Major*, *G Minor*, *E♭ Major* and *C Minor*.

We will now proceed to the first transcription of the above song, arranged for a quartet of Brass Instruments.

(b) ARRANGEMENT FOR A QUARTET OF BRASS INSTRUMENTS.

In this example the Cornets could either be replaced by Bugles, or strengthened through the latter's addition.

The following example shows the song in a ten-part arrangement for Brass Band.

(c) ARRANGEMENT FOR A COMBINATION OF TEN BRASS INSTRUMENTS.

And the next one in an arrangement for full Brass Band :—

d. ARRANGEMENT FOR FULL BRASS BAND.

In adding appropriate parts for the Wood-wind instruments and Saxophones, we now obtain an arrangement for full Military Band as exemplified in the following arrangement. It must furthermore be borne in mind, that in this last-shown arrangement the song will be equally effective either for small or large Brass Band or for small or large Military Band:

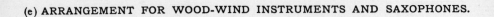

(e) ARRANGEMENT FOR WOOD-WIND INSTRUMENTS AND SAXOPHONES.

(f) PRACTICAL DIRECTIONS RELATIVE TO ARRANGEMENTS FOR AMERICAN BANDS.

In consequence of the uncertain and optional instrumentation of American Military Bands and particularly smaller band organizations, the knowledge of how to arrange correctly and effectively for small and oft-times unusual combinations is one of the most necessary accomplishments of every practical leader or band teacher. Circumstances will often force the substitution of instruments which were never intended to fill such vacancies, and in order to use them to best advantage the leader must know exactly how to write for them. Especially is this accomplishment necessary in smaller cities where players are limited both as to choice of instruments and accomplishments.

We will now illustrate a number of band arrangements for what might be termed as *typical American combinations* of from *eight to twenty-four* instruments, and have chosen the following sixteen bars of Theo. M. Tobani's famous composition "Hearts and Flowers," specially arranged by the composer for this purpose.

HEARTS AND FLOWERS.

The first illustration arranged for a combination of eight instruments (E flat Clarinet, B flat Clarinet, 1st B flat Cornet, 2nd B flat Cornet, 1st and 2nd E flat Alto, Baritone and Tuba) would be practically carried out in the following fashion:

A twelve-part arrangement of this melody consisting of the above-named instruments, together with a Piccolo, 2nd B flat Clarinet, 3d B flat Cornet, and 3d E flat Alto, would present itself as follows:—

The original eight instruments, augmented by a Piccolo, 2nd and 3d B flat Clarinets, 3d B flat Cornet, 3d E flat Alto, 1st Trombone (or 1st B flat Tenor), 2d Trombone (or 2nd B flat Tenor) and 3d Trombone (or B flat Bass) now lead us to the following Sixteen-part arrangement:—

Taking up the eight original instruments once more, and adding a Piccolo, Oboe, 2nd and 3d B flat Clarinet, Bassoon, E flat Cornet, 3d B flat Cornet, 3d E flat Alto, 1st Trombone (or 1st B flat Tenor), 2nd Trombone (or 2nd B flat Tenor,) 3d Trombone (or B flat Bass), and an extra Bass, we arrive at the following Twenty-part arrangement: —

For our final illustration the original eight instruments are again employed, this time with the addition of Piccolo, Oboe, 2nd and 3d B flat Clarinet, Bassoon, Soprano, Alto, Tenor, and Baritone Saxophone, E flat Cornet, 3d B flat Cornet, 3d E flat Alto, 1st Trombone (or 1st B flat Tenor), 2nd Trombone (or 2nd B flat Tenor), 3d Trombone (or B flat Bass), and extra Bass, which enables us to present the following arrangement for twenty-four instruments:—

THE HUMAN VOICE.

We distinguish 1) Purely Instrumental Music and 2) Instrumental and Vocal Music.

The former embraces the Concertos and the entire category of chamber-music, symphonies, etc.; the latter embraces the Cantatas, Masses, Oratorios, Operas, etc.

CHILDREN'S VOICES.

1.) **Girls' Voices.** They are divided into Soprano, Mezzo-Soprano, and Alto voices.

2) **Boys' Voices.** Exact division as the above.

The compass of these voices is as follows:—

Girls' voices possess a much softer quality than those of Boys, but are somewhat timid as compared with the latter, the tonal-character of which is a very strong and sometimes a very peculiar one, especially with boys possessing a cultivated voice. In former times Boys' voices were in great favor and demand, especially in church choirs and private musical organizations. Boys' voices are sometimes employed to excellent advantage in operatic writing, as for instance in Meyerbeer's "Prophet" and G. Bizet's "Carmen." In his last opera, "Parsifal," R. Wagner has assigned a most beautiful and effective part to Boys' voices.

Three and four-part choruses are usually written for these voices, particularly intended for use in schools. Under no condition must the ordinary tonal-compass of these voices be exceeded, as the higher notes are generally produced more through screaming than real singing, and the lower notes as a rule are nearly inaudible. It is therefore very necessary that the voices be distributed carefully and evenly, and to arrange the harmonic chord-intervals in such a well-balanced manner as to obtain a most harmonious and well-rounded ensemble. In order to bring this about, it is advisable to place all intervals as close to each other as possible, as shown in the following example:—

J. HAYDN.

Die Himmel er - z h - len die Eh - re Got - tes

The following examples:—

are not very appropriate for children's voices, as the intervals are placed at too great a distance from each other.

On the other hand, the following song presents a fine example of how to write most effectively for these voices:—

THE NEIGHBOR'S REQUEST.
(C. Anshütz.)

CARL ATTENHOFER, Op. 17.

Such writers as Reinecke, Attenhofer, Reissland, etc., have written large quantities of simple, easy, and melodious songs for solo children's voices with piano accompaniment, which every student should take up for careful study.

WOMEN'S VOICES.

These voices offer much greater tonal wealth than the above-mentioned, possess greater tonal volume and range, besides greater elasticity.

Both the very low and extremely high notes are not frequently employed for chorus-work, as the former sound too weak and the latter tire the voices too much, besides possessing a very shrill quality of tone.

They are divided into three principal groups:—

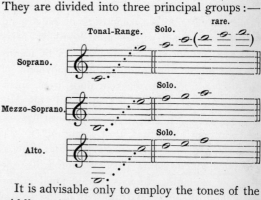

It is advisable only to employ the tones of the middle register of each voice, as much better results are obtainable therewith. Choral works for woman's voice are written for two, three, or four voices, sometimes also for five, as shown in the following example:—

"LICHT SEI DER ORT DEINER SEELE."
5 Part Female Chorus.

H. VON SENGER, Op. 3.

lib - li - cher We - sen als Du schwang, frei von ir - di - scher feh - le, dem Kreis sich der Sel' - gen zu. .

sich der Sel'-gen zu. .

For solo-singing the female voice takes first rank. The greatest composers of olden and modern times have written most wonderful arias and have produced astounding effects by means of their clever and appropriate employment of the different female voices in duos, trios, quartets, quintets, sextets, septets, and operatic finales. The Soprano voice is the most flexible and brilliant, adapting itself admirably to the performance of every conceivable kind of most complicated coloratura passages and trills; capable of executing the most varied tonal gradations and shadings, extending from the softest pianissimo to the strongest fortissimo, as well as possessing the requisite resources for the rendition of sweet and languishing Cantabile compositions.

For operatic purposes, the female voices are especially classed according to particular parts and treated and employed in accordance with their own individual tonal-compass and character.

SOPRANO VOICE.

1. **Coloratura-Singer.** Part of Rosina in Rossini's "Barber of Sevilla;" Violetta in Verdi's Traviata;" Queen of the Night in Mozart's "Magic Flute," etc.

2. **Grand Opera-Singer.** Part of Elizabeth in R. Wagner's "Tannhäuser;" Donna Anna in Mozart's "Don Juan;" Alice in Meyerbeer's "Robert le Diable;" Rachel in Halévy's "Jewess," etc.

3. **Second Coloratura-Singer** (Mezzo-Soprano). Part of Zerline in Mozart's "Don Juan;" Susanne in Mozart's "Marriage of Figaro," etc. In operettas the principal part is usually assigned to this singer.

4. **Third Soprano,** to which subordinate parts, such as Barbarine, in Mozart's "Marriage of Figaro," are assigned.

Among these different soprano voices some exceptional organs are sometimes found, which possess a tremendous range; but in order to present their particular capabilities, voices of such unusual range must be specially written for.

ALTO VOICE.

This voice possesses qualities and timbre similar in some respect to the male voice, and is exceptionally well adapted for the portrayal of such tragic parts, in which a mother's love dominates as the main subject; for instance, the part of Acuzena, the Gipsy-mother, in Verdi's "Il Trovatore"; Fides, in Meyerbeer's "Prophet," etc.

Our musical literature abounds in Romances, Arias, Songs, Duos, etc., of every conceivable variety for Female voices and piano accompaniment. Among these innumerable compositions, those by Mozart, Beethoven, Schubert, Mendelssohn, Schumann, Rob. Franz, Brahms, Abt, Bizet, Massenet, Gounod, Sullivan, Stainer, MacDowell, Foote, and many others, are especially worthy of particular mention.

MEN'S VOICES.

These are divided into three principal groups:—

The Tenor-part is usually written in the Violin-clef, but it must be remembered that the notes in reality sound an octave lower:—

Of late years choruses for men's voices have become very popular and greatly appreciated in all civilized countries, the best and cleverest composers having penned their choicest thoughts and conceptions for this form of music.

In writing for male voices, the greatest care as to the judicious and correct placing of the various triad-intervals must be observed above all. The principal melody must not extend over too great a tonal-range, and the placing of the already-mentioned triad-intervals between the different registers requires the most careful attention. Alternately the voices may cross each other, but if possible the middle voices should not extend beyond the first Tenor or second Bass.

The male chorus is subdivided into the following parts:—

1. Tenor; 2. Tenor; 1. Bass; 2. Bass.

Choruses for male voices demand an elegant, correct style, flawless harmonic progression, appropriate tonal-shading, and simplicity and good taste in particular; too many modulations, dissonances, and complicated chord-progressions must also be avoided.

I have already mentioned how much is dependent upon correct and flowing harmonic progression, and dwelt upon the importance of not exceeding the real compass of each voice. For instance, should we desire to arrange the Ave Verum, originally composed by Mozart for a chorus of mixed voices, for male chorus, and endeavor to retain Mozart's charming treatment of the voices, the third part (first Bass) would come to lie much higher than the first Tenor, and in consequence of the close position of the triad-intervals, the harmony produced would be a dull, indistinct, and disagreeable one, as shown in the following examples:—

AVE VERUM.

W. A. MOZART.

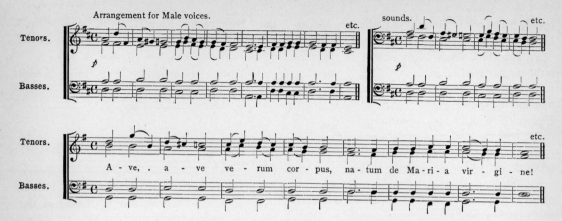

In order to produce a full and well-sounding tonal-coloring, similar to that of Mozart's own setting, a different key would have to be chosen, in which every voice could be employed in its best register, and consequently be heard to best advantage. For this purpose I should choose the key of G major, and write the voice parts in the same manner as in the last of the above examples.

Naturally this arrangement will not be nearly as effective as the original setting. My object in laying this example before the student has only been to convince him how highly important the correct placing of triad-intervals, as well as a thorough knowledge of the real compass of the male voices, is.

In order to learn how to write most effectively for male chorus, it will be of great benefit to study the choral-works of the following composers: Zöllner, Otto, Silcher, Adam, Tschirch, Liszt, Max Bruch, Faisst, Reinecke, Herbeck, Brambach, Abt, Palme, Brosig, Mendelssohn, Schumann, Nägeli, Saintis, Monnestier, L. v. Rillé, Gevaert, Limmander, Elwart, Massenet, Attenhofer, Billeter, Bessozi, O. H. Lange, C. Santner, Duke Ernst of Koburg, Stainer, Shelley, Buck, Chadwick, etc.

In addition to works for single chorus, choral-works for double or for three or four individual choruses may be written, which naturally necessitate a large body of singers. In his "Lovefeast of the Apostles," for male chorus, with orchestral accompaniment, R. Wagner has divided his voices into three choruses with great skill. One particular section of this work, where the entire body of voices is employed unisono, while the orchestra executes the principal part, is tremendously effective. In addition to the above, our musical literature is rich in quantities of lyric works for male chorus, with orchestra or Military Band accompaniment, by various composers. From among these I might advise the "Macedonian Triumphal Song," for male chorus and wind instruments, by Dr. Hermann Zopff, and "Festival Song to the Artists" by Mendelssohn, for particular study.

The chorus of male voices as employed in operatic works must be written for in a clear, easy, and comprehensive style, as the majority of chorus singers, especially in smaller cities, possess neither remarkable voices nor any particular musical education. The Soldier choruses from Meyerbeer's "Huguenots," Gounod's "Faust," as well as the Hunting choruses from A. Thomas's "Midsummer Night's Dream," and Weber's "Freischütz," may be considered as models in this particular field of writing.

For operatic purposes the solo voices are divided into various groups, according to their different tonal registers:—

1) **The Lyric Tenor,** who must be in possession of a light, clear, and flexible voice, which will enable him to execute coloratura passages if necessary (part of Wilhelm Meister in Thomas's "Mignon"; Duke Almaviva in Rossini's "Barber of Seville," etc.).

2) **The Heroic Tenor,** or **Tenor of Grand Opera,** possesses a much stronger and more voluminous voice than the first-mentioned tenor. (Part of Arnold in Rossini's "William Tell"; "Lohengrin"; "Tannhäuser"; Eleazer in Halévy's "The Jewess," etc.).

3) **The Second Tenor** of Comic Opera (Tenor Buffo) possesses a somewhat similar-sounding voice as the first-mentioned tenor. (In operettas the principal part as a rule is assigned to the second tenor.) Part of Daniel in Adam's

opera, "The Swiss House;" Raimbaut in Meyer-beer's "Robert le Diable," etc.)

4) **The Third Tenor** takes charge of the subordinate parts.

5) **The First Baritone,** flexible voice, pleasing tonal-color and quality. (Part of Don Juan, Figaro, Hamlet, King Alphonse in "La Favorita," William Tell, etc.)

6) **The Second Baritone** takes charge of the subordinate parts.

7) **The First Bass** of the Comic Opera, also named Buffo-Bass, flexible voice, of pleasing and well-sounding tonal-color and quality. (Part of Leporello in Mozart's "Don Juan," Bassilio in Rossini's "Barber of Seville," Casper in Weber's Freischütz," etc.)

8) **The Second Bass** takes charge of the smaller parts.

9) **The Bass of Grand Opera** possesses a voice of great range and tonal-beauty, and imbued with earnest granduer and dignity. (Part of Marcel in the "Huguenots," King Henry in "Lohengrin," the Cardinal in "The Jewess," Sarastro in the "Magic Flute," etc.)

The vocal literature for male voices is also very rich in romances, arias, songs, solo scenes, duos, trios, etc., by the best authors.

THE MIXED CHORUS

Consists of a combination of male and female voices. The art of writing for a mixed chorus requires a much wider or distant placing of the harmony, as in writing for an individual chorus of either male or female voices, and consequently places much greater tonal-wealth within reach of the writer. We have mixed choruses of four, six, eight and even more different parts. In order to show how a mixed chorus without accompaniment should be written, I add the following eight-part chorus by F. Mendelssohn-Bartholdy:—

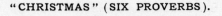

"CHRISTMAS" (SIX PROVERBS).

8 Part Chorus.

F. MENDELSSOHN.   Op. 79.

For operatic purposes the Mixed Chorus should be treated and written for in as easy and flowing a manner as possible. The vocal literature is rich in a tremendous amount of religious, worldly, lyric, and poetic music for mixed chorus with and without accompaniment by the best composers, of olden and modern times, which should be studied most carefully.

In the following a table of all the voices and their individual range is presented.

TABLE OF ALL THE VOICES AND THEIR INDIVIDUAL RANGE.

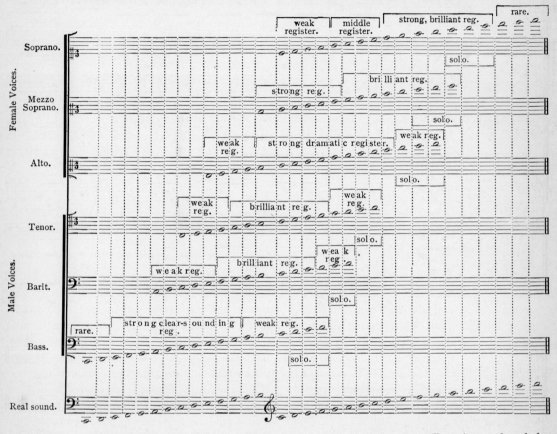

A FEW REMARKS AS TO VOCAL EFFECTS.

Various modern composers have introduced what might be termed as a species of vocal instrumentation of peculiar and odd effectiveness into their scores; the effect is produced by means of "Humming Voices," which, while a separate voice performs a solo, execute the parts of wind or string instruments by imitating sustained or pizzicato notes, as shown in the following example:

LES PECHEURS.

L. D. RILLIÉ.

man - te, le flot qui se la - men - te à nos pieds . . vient mourir   des va - peurs . . de ma

Entire parts of choral-works may be executed in this manner as shown below: —

LES VOIX DU LAC.

(Prize Composition.)

H. KLING.

But above all, these effects must not be employed too often, and especially not in too exaggerated a manner, f. i., in attempting to imitate (as is so often and so foolishly done by modern French writers) different tonal characteristics, absolutely foreign to the voices, — the manner of playing upon orchestral instruments or the organ, as well as the howling of the winds, storm, rain, ringing of bells, bellowing of cows, croaking of frogs, etc. Some French composers have even gone as far as to arrange the overtures of the "Freischütz," "Magic Flute," "Dame Blanche," the Andante from Beethoven's "A Major Symphony," etc., entirely for Humming Voices! But employed at the right time for dramatic or operatic scenes, or where the text allows of its appropriate use, very fine effects may be produced with the aid of these humming voices. Unisono employed with large choral-forces is always tremendously effective. A great deal of variety can be brought about in choral-works, through the introduction of solo voices in the shape of duets, trios or quartets, which are suddenly singled out from the mass of voices, forming a complete body in themselves, till all the voices again unite in a grand and overwhelming tutti. Effective contrasts are achieved through the sudden change from *piano* to *forte* and *vice versa*. Again, for the production of "echo-effects," a chorus may be employed in such a way that half of it will sing fortissimo, while the other half executes its part pianissimo, and in this way anticipating the echo, which will be much more effective if prepared in this manner. The usual transition from fortissimo to pianissimo will be obviated in such a way, that while half the chorus, which is suddenly stopped, the other half quietly keeps on singing pianissimo. (This effect can also be employed to excellent advantage in instrumental music. I have made use of same in my "Idylle" for orchestra, "An Evening in Spring.")

A peculiar style of singing designated as "*Jodeln*"[*] can also be employed to excellent advantage, especially in such productions in which a tender, simple, innocent, and sentimental character is to be expressed. It serves principally and is characteristic of Tyrolean songs. For this style of singing, syllables such as tra, la, la, ah! ha, ha, etc., on the different notes may be used, as shown in the following example:

[*] *Jodeln.*—A favorite style of singing among the inhabitants of the Alps, characterized by a frequent and unprepared alternation of falsetto tones with those of the chest-register.

HUNTER'S CHORUS FROM WEBER'S OPERA, "DER FREISCHÜTZ."

THE DRAMATIC ORCHESTRA.

The creator of the true dramatic orchestra was Mozart, who, in the conception of his Don Juan, introduced a style of instrumentation, which in its elegant masculine yet piquant effectiveness demonstrates and bears the stamp of a sentimental, expressive, melancholy, and profound genius. The masculinity of his style is brought into still greater prominence through the employment of particularly rich harmony, which is applied according to the individual strength or weakness of every orchestral instrument with such admirable mastery that it is more than evident and no over-drawn statement, to claim, that the highest pinnacle of perfection in instrumentation has been reached by Mozart in the scoring of his works. The successors of this great master have gradually and constantly enlarged and added to these effects; by degrees the tonal shadings were strengthened through the addition of new and through the improvement of old instruments to such an extent that now-a-days the entire instrumental apparatus of an orchestra is almost always called into action simultaneously; and for the accompaniment of the simplest Romance or Cavatina the score is arranged for two individual Violin parts, Viola, 'Cello, Bass, Flutes, Oboes, Clarinets, Bassoons, Horns, Trumpets, Tympani, etc. But in constantly employing all the resources of an orchestra, a most monotonous and tiresome effect is produced, resulting from the never-varying use of the same tonal-colors, the same accents, and the same tonal-characters, instead of lending an original physiognomy to every composition, through the aid of the varied and manifold types of sound peculiar to all the different orchestral instruments.

To exemplify the great diversity with which the instruments can be employed, we can have vocal arias, duets, romances, and even quartets, accompanied only by stringed instruments, for instance, by Violoncellos or Violins and Violas, or through a double-quartet, in which some instruments play sustained, others pizzicato notes. In the same way the Flutes and Clarinets may be employed separately, also Oboes with English Horns and Bassoons, the French Horns, with Trombones, or these various instruments again in mixed combinations, in just such proportions as might fit a dramatic situation to best advantage. In listening to vocal solos during operatic performances, it may often be noticed that particular parts sung without any accompaniment whatever, invariably prove exceedingly effective. This may be accounted for as a natural result of the variance of instrumental effects. If one or more solo voices are written for, care must be taken not to cover or crush them with too strong or weighty an instrumentation.

In operatic works many situations will demand the transferring of the principal part to the orchestra, while the singers execute a certain style of declamation in notes and words. A most beautiful example of this kind is the Register Aria of Leporello in Mozart's "Don Juan." Another kind of declamatory singing is when the voice constantly murmurs the same identical note upon one syllable, while the accompaniment surrounds and beautifies the monotonous chant. A fine example of this style of writing is shown in the following extract ·from Ambroise Thomas's opera "Mignon."

EXTRACT FROM "MIGNON."

Act I.

AMBROISE THOMAS.

The Melodrama, first introduced by J. J. Rousseau and Benda (the former in "Pygmalion," the latter in "Medea" and "Ariadne in Naxos)" consists of a declamation combined with dramatic action and accompanied throughout by an orchestra. The music, so to say, illustrates the principal situations of the drama and accompanies the declamation of the actor, endeavoring to express and bring into prominence his innermost feelings and passions. This style of music is also indicated by the term tone-painting. In theatrical productions, accompanying music never fails in heightening the effectiveness of dramatic situations, especially if the music is well-written and appropriately fitted to the action. In this particular field the well-known music to "Preciosa" by Weber may be taken as a model. Melodramatic effects have also been introduced and employed to excellent advantage in modern operatic works; and as examples it will be sufficient to mention the Devil's scene from the "Freischütz," a beautiful scene in the "Swiss Family," in "Robert le Diable" and "Fidelio."

The accompanying parts may be written in either simple or figurated, that is homophonic, or polyphonic style, in accordance with the individual character or expressiveness of the material to· be illustrated musically, and the selection of the accompanying instruments is also left to the discretion, taste, feeling, and imagination of the composer.

In conclusion, a word as to the invisible orchestra, which Wagner introduced for the performances of his operas at Bayreuth.

As I have never had the good fortune to witness any of these performances, I commissioned a good friend of mine (Mr. A. W.), a highly educated musician, who has attended the Bayreuth performances from the start, to give me his personal opinion as to the effectiveness of the invisible orchestra. His ideas relative to this subject were summed up somewhat in the following fashion, in a personal communication of his:—

"In answer to your question in reference to the invisible orchestra, I am prepared to say that the principal advantage derived from this new arrangement is, that the attention of the listeners can be concentrated entirely upon the dramatic developments of the stage. Through this innovation it is out of the question to have one's attention attracted by the antics of an eccentric conductor or the grimaces of a humorously inclined musician.

" The audience follows every occurrence upon the stage with intense interest, especially as in Bayreuth the house-lights are lowered considerably at the beginning of each act, in order to prevent the inattentive part of the audience from passing their time in idle conversation or with the reading of daily papers.

" In regard to tonal-volume I have noticed that all softer or mysterious parts are greatly enhanced by this innovation, but that the strong parts are robbed of a great deal of the warm and brilliant coloring to which we have become accustomed in those theatres where the orchestra is visible. I will not omit to add that as regards perfection of ensemble, the Wagnerian disposition brings about a most remarkable blending of all the instrumental forces, caused no doubt by the regular and systematic arrangement of the different instrumental groups.

" While the string instruments are placed upon a raised platform close against the wooden enclosure, which separates them from the first row of orchestra chairs, the brass instruments are placed entirely in the background, stretching far beneath the stage.

" As with all novelties in this direction, time will have to determine the practical value of the innovation, and it were reckless for the present, at least, to prophesy great or unusual success for the invisible orchestra.

" While the artistic effects obtained therewith must not be lost sight of, future improvements in this direction will probably determine its real worth, and place the orchestras somewhat lower than is the custom at present, without condemning the musicians to complete disappearance.

ON OPERATIC POETRY AND COMPOSITION IN PARTICULAR.

FROM RICHARD WAGNER'S PROSE WORKS.

[This article was originally published in the *Bayreuther Blätter*, for September, 1879.]

Apropos of sundry experiences, it has struck me how little the audience at opera-performances was acquainted with the matter of the plot. High-class operas, like " Don Juan " and " Figaro's Hochzeit," come out of it very well with uncorrupted youthful hearers, especially of the female sex, protecting them from any knowledge of the frivolities in the text, — a thing

which guardians and teachers may probably have counted on when they expressly commended those works to their pupils as a model of pure taste. That the happenings in " Robert the Devil " and the " Huguenots " were intelligible to none but the inmost circle of initiates, had much in its favor; but that the " Freischütz," too, should remain in shadow, as I lately discovered, amazed me till a little thought convinced me that, although I had conducted this opera any number of times in the orchestra, I myself was still quite hazy as to many a passage in the text. Some laid the blame on our singers' indistinctness of delivery. When I objected that in dialogic operas such as " Freischütz," " Zauberflöte " (Magic Flute), aye, and our German translations of " Don Juan " and " Figaro," everything that explains the action is simply spoken, I was reminded that the singers of our day speak indistinctly, too, and also that, for this very reason perhaps, the dialogue is abridged to unintelligibleness. Nay, that here one passed from bad to worse; for with operas " composed throughout " one at least could arrive at sufficient understanding of the scenic action by assistance of the text-book, whereas in " aria-books " of dialogic operas such an aid was not forthcoming. I have remarked that for most part the German audience learns nothing at all of what the poet really meant with his libretto; often enough, not even the composer appears to know. With the French it is otherwise; there the first question is as to the " *pièce* "; the play must be entertaining in and for itself save, perhaps, with the lofty *genre* of " Grand Opera," where Ballet has to provide the fun. The texts of Italian operas, on the other hand, are fairly trivial as a rule, the virtuoso-doings of the singer appearing to be the main concern; yet the Italian singer cannot rise to the level of his task without a remarkably drastic enunciation, quite indispensable to his vocal phrasing; and we do the Italian operatic *genre* a great injustice when we slur the text of arias in our German reproduction. Mechanical as is the Italian type of operatic composition, I still have found that it all will have a better effect when the text is understood than when it isn't, since a knowledge of the situation and exact emotion will advantageously ward off the effect of monotony in the musical expression. Only with Rossini's " Semiramide " was even this acquaintance of no help to me; Reissiger's "Dido abandonata," which earned its composer the favor of a Saxon monarch, I do not know — any more than F. Hiller's "Romilda."

According to the above observations, one might simply attribute the German public's love of opera-performances to its pleasure in hearing the separate "numbers" as purely melodic entities *per se*. Now, the Italians long ago attained great skill in manufacturing such pieces, so that it was very late before the German composer dared to vie with them. When Mozart had to compose the "Magic Flute," he was worried by a doubt if he would do it right, as he "had composed no magic operas before." With what aplomb, on the contrary, he treated "*le Nozze di Figaro*": on the set foundation of Italian *opera buffa* he reared a building of such perfect symmetry that he well might decline to sacrifice a single note to his cut-demanding Kaiser. What the Italian threw in as banal links and interludes between the "numbers" proper, Mozart here drastically employed to animate the situation, in striking harmony with just this exceptionally finished comedy-text that lay before him. As in the Symphony of Beethoven the very pause grows eloquent, so here the noisy half-closes and cadences which might well have held aloof from the Mozartian Symphony give quite an irreplaceable life to the scenic action, where craft and presence of mind fight — lovelessly ! — with passion and brutality. Here the dialogue becomes all music, whilst the music converses; a thing that certainly was only possible through the master's developing the orchestra to such a pitch as never before, and perhaps to this day, had been dreamt of. On the other hand, the earlier isolated pieces became thereby fused into what appeared so complete a work of music that the admirable comedy in which it stood might finally be altogether overlooked, and nothing heard but music. So it seemed to our musicians; and Mozart's "Figaro" was given more carelessly and indistinctly day by day, till at last we have dropped to a mode of performing this work itself that leaves our teacher no scruple about sending their pupils to the theatre on "Figaro" nights.

We will not discuss again to-day the effect of these instances of public vandalism on the German's sensibility to the genuine and correct; but it cannot be unimportant to note their misleading influence in the drafts and finished products of our operatic poets and composers.

Forsaking all their native field, they first must seek an entrance to the ready-made Italian Opera; which could only lead to the nearest possible imitation of the Italian "cabaletta," with the abandonment of every broader mode of musical conception. Upon due "rhyme and reason" of the whole no weight was to be laid. Had it done any harm to the "Magic Flute," composed for a German text and spoken with German dialogue, that the villain was suddenly changed to a hero, the originally good woman to a bad one, making utter nonsense of what had happened in the first act? Only it fell hard to the German genius to master the Italian "cabaletta." Even Weber in his earliest youth still tried in vain to make something of the "coloratura" aria, and it needed the heart-stirring years of the War of Liberation to set the singer of Körner's lays on his own feet. What we Germans received with the "Freischütz" has fallen to few nations' lot.

Yet we are not about to trace the historic evolution of German Opera, — which I have already discussed at length elsewhere, — but rather to explain the peculiar difficulty of that evolution by this opera's fundamental faults. The chief of these I find in the criminal *vagueness* that has disfigured all our opera-performances from the beginning to this day, as I stated from personal experience in my prefatory words, and whose cause — the librettist's and composer's involuntarily accustomed standard for the degree of plainness needful to an operatic story — has been touched on in the previous paragraphs. The so-called "*Tragédie lyrique*," which reached the German from abroad, remained indifferent and unintelligible to him so long as the "Aria" did not take his fancy by its marked melodic structure. This Aria form of melody passed over into German Opera as the sole aim and end of the composer, and necessarily also of the poet. The latter felt that he might take his ease in the text for an aria, as the composer had his own musical scheme of extension, interchange, and repetition of themes, and needed an entirely free hand with the words, which he would repeat at pleasure, either as a whole or in part. Long lines could only hamper the composer, whilst a strophe of about four lines was ample measure for one section of an aria. The verbal repetitions necessary to fill out the melody, conceived quite apart from the verse, even gave the composer opportunity for pleasant variations of the so-called "declamation," through a shifting of accents. In Winter's "Opferfest" we find this rule observed throughout; there the "Inka," for instance, sings one after the other:—

> "Mein *Leben* hab' ich ihm zu danken —
> Mein Leben *hab* 'ich ihm zu danken";

and repeats a question in the form of answer:—

> "Muss nicht der Mensch auch menschlich sein? —
> Der Mensch muss menschlich sein."

Marschner once had the grave misfortune, in his "Adolf von Nassau," to triplicate the part of speech, "hat sie" (has she), in a particularly incisive rhythmic aspect:—

"hat sie,   hat sie   hat sie"

Even Weber could not avoid the temptation to vary the accent; his "Euryanthe" sings: "Was is mein Leben gegen *diesen* Augenblick," and repeats it as, "Was ist mein Leben gegen diesen *Augenblick*"! This sort of thing leads the hearer away from any serious following of the words, without affording adequate compensation in the purely musical phrase itself; for in most cases it is a mere question of musico-rhetorical flourishes, such as show out the naïvest in Rossini's eternal "Felicità."

It seems, however, that it was not solely a delight in free command of flourishes that prompted the composer to his arbitrary dealings with morsels of the text; no, the whole relation of our imaginary Verse to the truthfulness of musical Accent placed the composer from the first in the alternative of either declaiming the text in strict accordance with the accent of daily speech and common sense, which would have resolved the verse with all its rhymes into naked prose, or, regardless of that accent, completely subjecting the words to certain dance-schemes, and giving free rein to melodic invention. The results of this latter method were far less disturbing, or even destructive, with the Italians and French, than with ourselves, because their speaking-accent is incomparably more accommodating, and, in particular, not bound to the root-syllable; wherefore, also, they do not weigh the feet in their metres, but simply count them. Through our bad translations of their texts, however, we had acquired from them that peculiar operatic jargon in which we now thought fit, and

even requisite, to declaim our German lines themselves. Conscientious composers were certainly disgusted at last with this frivolous maltreatment of our tongue; but it never yet struck them that even the verse of our first-class poets was no true, no melody-begetting verse, but a mere elaborate sham. Weber declared it his duty to faithfully reproduce the text, yet admitted that, were he always to do so, he must say good-bye to his melody. In fact, it was just this upright endeavor of Weber's to preserve the set divisions of the verse-text, and thereby make the thought intelligible, which, coupled with his adherence to a melodic pattern for the resulting incongruences, led to that indistinctness whereof I promised an example from my experience. This occurs in Max's *Arioso* in the "Freischütz"; "Durch die Wälder, durch die Auen." Here the poet had committed the egregious blunder of furnishing the composer with the following verse:—

> "Abends bracht' ich reiche Beute,
> Und wie über eig'nes Glück —
> Drohend wohl dem Mörder — freute
> Sich Agathe's Liebesblick."

Now, Weber really takes the trouble to phrase these lines in strict accordance with their sense and sequence; he therefore makes a break after the parenthesis, "drohend wohl dem Mörder," and begins with the closing line with "freute"; but as that makes the line much longer, he feels obliged to employ the verb — so important for a connection with the second line — as a preliminary "Arsis" (*Auftakt*); whereas the pronoun "*sich*," merely introduced to supplement the verb, receives the stronger accent of the following beat. This certainly has resulted in an entrancing strain of melody:—

"Abends bracht ich rei-che Beu-te   und wie
ü-ber eig-nes Glück, drohend wohl dem
Mör-der,   freu-te   sich   A-
ga-   the's   Lie-   bes-blick."

Not only is the poet's verse as such, however, revealed as an absurdity, but, for all the distinctness of its musical phrasing, the *sense* has become so hard of understanding that, accustomed to merely hear it sung, it was only after this unintelligibleness had one day struck me that I discovered the true connection of ideas. A similar difficulty arises in further course of the same aria through the favorite poetic trick of disassociating words for sake of rhyme ; and here the composer unfortunately makes things worse by repeating the parenthesis : —

" Wenn sich rauschend Blätter regen,
  Wähnt sie wohl, es sei mein Fuss,
  Hüpft vor Freuden, winkt entgegen —
  Nur dem Laub — nur dem Laub — den Liebesgruss."

Moreover *"Fuss"* and *"Liebesgruss"* are here intended to rhyme. The first time Weber accentuates thus :

the second time thus :

where the wrongful accent gives the rhyme, but the right discloses that these words do *not* rhyme. And so we have a flagrant instance of the utter folly of our whole literary scheme of Verse, which well-nigh always rests on end-rhymed lines, though it is only in the finest verses of our greatest and best-reputed poets that the rhyme, through being genuine, has a determinant effect. Nor has this genuineness or spuriousness much troubled our German composers heretofore ; rhyme to them was rhyme, and they paired off their last syllables in true street-minstrel fashion. A striking example is offered by Naumann's melody, so popular at one time, to Schiller's " Ode to Joy " : —

Now take Beethoven, the Truthful : —

For sake of the imaginary rhyme, Naumann put the verse's accents all away ; Beethoven gave the proper accent, and, doing so, revealed the fact that in German compound words it falls on the first component, so that the last section, being the weaker accent, cannot be used for rhyme ; if the poet does not hold to this, the rhyme is only present to the eye, a literature-rhyme ; to the ear, and thus to both the feeling and a vital understanding, it vanishes away. And what a bother this wretched rhyme creates in all musical composition to verbal texts ; twisting and disfiguring the phrases into utter gibberish, to be not so much as noticed in the end ! In Kaspar's great aria I lately searched for a prior rhyme to correspond with the last line, " *Triumph, die Rache gelingt,*" as I had never heard it in the singing, and therefore thought that Weber must have added this clause on his own authority ; however I succeeded in finding " *im Dunkel beschwingt,*" which, hastily strewn between " *umgeht ihn, ihr Geister,*" and, " *schon trägt er knirschend eure Ketten,*" without any musical caesura, had never struck me as a rhyme before. In truth, what use had the composer for this rhyme, when he merely wanted words, eh ! Syllables to give the singer his share in a tempestuous musical phrase that properly belongs to the characteristic orchestral accompaniment alone ?

I believe this example, which I only hit upon at random, will afford the easiest introduction to a further inquiry into the mysteries of operatic melody. The meagre doggerel verse, often built of simply empty phrases ; the verse whose sole affinity to music, its rhyme destroyed the words' last shred of meaning, and thereby made its best conceits quite valueless to the musician —this verse compelled him to take the pattern and working out of characteristic melodic motives from a province of music which had hitherto developed in the orchestral accompaniment to a *lingua franca* of the instruments. Mozart had raised this symphonic accompaniment to such high expressiveness that, wherever consistent with dramatic naturalism, he could let the singers merely speak to it in musical accents, without disturbance of the rich melodic woof of themes or break in the musical flow. And herewith disappeared that violence towards the word-text; whatever in it did not call for vocal melody was understandably intoned.

Yet the incomparable dramatic talent of the glorious musician alone, accomplished this perfectly in so-called *opera buffa*, not to the same degree in *opera seria*. Here his followers were left with a great difficulty. They could see nothing for it but to keep the utterance of passion invariably melodious; since the threadbare text gave them little help, and willful repetition of its words had already made them deaf to any claims of the librettist; they finally set the prose part of the text itself, with just as many repetitions as the purpose needed, to melodic-looking phrases such as Mozart had originally assigned to his characterizing orchestral accompaniment. In this wise they thought to give their singers always "melody" to sing; and to keep it in perpetual motion they often buried all the text, if there was rather too much of it, beneath such a mass of scales and runs that neither song nor text could be discerned. Whoever wants a fairly striking instance, let him study the Templar's great air in "Marschner's "Templer und Jüdin," say the *allegro furioso* from "*mich fasst die Wuth*," onwards, where the composition of the finale verses is specially instructive, for in one breath, without the smallest pause, stream forth the words:—

> " Rache nur woll't ich geniessen;
> Ihr allein mein Ohr nur leihend
> Trennt' ich mich von allen süssen,
> Zarten Banden der Natur,
> Mich dem Templerorden weihend."

Here the composer halts, for the poet's having tacked on a

> " Bitt're Reue fand ich nur "

after a full-stop, just to make a rhyme for "*Natur*," seemed really too bad; only after two bars of interlude does Marschner allow this strange addendum to appear, of course in breathless roulades as before.

Thus the composer believed he had "melodised" everything, even the wickedest. Nor was it better with the elegiac-tender, whereof the same air of the "Templer" affords us evi-

dence in its Andante ($\frac{3}{4}$); "*in meines Lebens Blüthezeit*"—the second verse, "*einsam in das dunkle Grab*," being sung in ballad fashion to the exact tune of the first, saving for that elegance of melodic embellishment which has brought this *genre* of German vocal music to the verge of the ridiculous. The composer opined that the singer would always like "something to sing;" the great bravura fireworks of the Italians did not go off quite briskly with the German; on "*Rache*" (revenge) at most did one feel incumbent to risk a run up and a run down. In the "Cantabile," on the contrary, one found those minor prettinesses, particularly the "Mordente" and its derivative grace-notes, which would show one had one's taste as well. Spohr brought the *agréments* of his violin-solos into his singers' airs, and if the melody, apparently composed of these extras, turned out a nothing-saying weariness, at the same time it strangled the verse that had been making signs of having something to say. With Marschner—beside the manifest traits of genius that occur so frequently (in that great Templar-air for instance), and now and then ascend to positive sublimity (for instance in the chorusses introducing the second finale of the same opera)—we meet an almost preponderant mawkishness and an often astounding incorrectness, mostly due to the unfortunate delusion that things must always go melodiously," i. e., must everywhere be "tuney." My departed colleague Reissiger complained to me of the failure of his "Schiffbruch der Medusa," in which, as I myself must admit, there was "so much melody,"—which, at the same time, I had to take as a bitter allusion to the success of my own operas, in which you know there was "so little melody."

This wondrous wealth-of-melody which emptied its horn of plenty on the just and unjust, made good its squandered riches by an—alas! not always skillful—annexation of all the musical gew-gaws current in the world, mostly filched from French or Italian operas and huddled up pell-mell. Against Rossini there was many an outcry. Yet it was merely his originality that vexed us; for as soon as Spohr's violin-solo was exhausted for the trimming of the "Cantabile," Rossini's march-and-ballet rhythms and melismi flocked into the freshening *allegro* almost of themselves; nothing again but yards of "melody." The overture to the "Felsen-mühle" still lives at our garden-concerts and change-of-guards, though we hear no more the march from " Mosé; " in this case German patriotism, to the shade of Reissiger's great satisfaction, would seem to have gained the victory.

Yet it was not solely those ineffective importations of Italian and French melismic and rhythmic nicknacks that feathered German operatic melody, but the sublime and hearty further taxed the four-part male chorus so passionately practiced since the last half-century. Spontini attended a performance of Mendelssohn's " Antigone " in Dresden, against his will; he soon left it in contemptuous dudgeon. *"C'est de la Berliner Liedertafel!"* 'Tis a sad tale the incursion of that miserably thin and monotonous beer-chant, even when raised to the rank of a Rhine-wine song, with which the Berlin composer of the opera, " die Nibelungen," himself could not dispense. It was the genius of Weber that led the opera into noble pathways of the National by introducing the German men's-chorus, to which he had given so splendid an impetus by his songs of the War of Freedom. Its uncommon success moved the master to lend its character to the chorus that takes a dramatic part in the action; in his " Euryanthe " the dialogue of the principal characters is repeatedly arrested by the chorus, which unfortunately sings entirely in the strain of the four-part glee by itself, unrelieved by any characteristic movement in the orchestra, almost as if these passages were intended to be cut out as they stand for the Liedertafel books. What here was most surely meant nobly, perhaps in opposition to the stereotyped employment of the Italian chorus to merely accompany the aria or ballet, led Weber's successors into that eternal nothing-saying " melodic " chorusing which, together with the aforesaid aria-tuning, makes out the entire substance of a German opera. Whole breadths are covered by this " melodic " general-muster, without a single striking moment to tell us the cause of the unbroken drench of melody. For an example I return to the operas of that else so highly talented Marschner, and point to his so-called Ensembles, such as the *Andante con moto* ($\frac{9}{8}$) in the second finale of his *Templer*, " lässt den Schleier mir, ich bitte "; as also (for a model) the introduction to the first act of the same work, with special reference to the first strophe of the male chorus, " Wir lagern dort im stillen Wald, der Zug muss hier vorbei, er ist nicht fern, er nahet bald und glaubt die Strasse frei," sung

to a hunting-tune; and in further progress of the piece, the extraordinary melodizing of the strictest dialogue by aid of unimaginable repetitions. Here dramatic melodists may learn how long a fair number of men can indulge in an " aside " on the stage; naturally it can only be done through their standing in rows with their backs to the forest, and facing the audience — which in its turn pays no heed to a man of them, but patiently waits for the end of the general " melody."

To the intelligent spectator the spoken dialogue in such an opera often comes as a positive relief. On the other hand, this very dialogue betrayed composers into the belief that the musical numbers imbedded in the prose must always be of a lyric kind; an assumption quite justified in the " Singspiel " proper, for there one only wanted vocal " Intermezzi," while the piece itself was recited in intelligible prose, just as in Comedy. Here, however, it was " Opera "; the vocal pieces lengthened out, arias changed places with concerted " Ensemble " numbers, and at last the " Finale," with all the text, was put at the musician's disposal. And the separate " numbers " must all be telling in themselves; their " melody " must never flag, and the closing phrase must be rousing, clamorous for applause. Already the music-dealer had been taken in eye; the more effective or merely pleasing single pieces that one could extract, the more valuable the work to the trade. Even the pianoforte-score must begin with a table of contents cataloguing the numbers under the rubric of "Aria," " Duet," " Trio," " Drinking-song," and so on throughout the whole length of the opera. This continued when " Recitative " already had ousted the dialogue, and the whole had been given a certain show of musical cohesion. To be sure, these recitatives weren't much to speak of, and contributed no little to the *ennui* of the *opera-genre;* while Nadori in Spohr's " Jessonda," for instance, delivered himself of the recitative, " Still lag ich an des Seees Fluthen," —

und las   im Ve-da"

one simply was all impatience for re-entry of the full orchestra with definite tempo and a set "melody," let it be put together ("composed") as it might. At the end of these redeeming numbers one must be able to applaud, or things looked black and the number would have to be omitted in time. In the "Finale," however, quite a little tempest of delirium must be caused; a kind of musical orgy was needed, to bring the act to a satisfying close; so "Ensemble" was sung; every man for himself, all for the audience; and a jubilant burst of melody with a soaring final cadence, appropriate or not, must waft the whole into due ecstasy. If this also fell flat, the thing had failed, and the opera was withdrawn.

Coupling the above considerations with the utterly chaotic vocalizing of most of our singers, —their want of finish aggravated by the want of style in such tasks,—we must candidly admit that German Opera indeed is bungler's work. We must confess it even in comparison with French and Italian Opera; but how much more when we apply the requirements that should necessarily be met by a drama on the one hand, an independent piece of music on the other, to this pseudo-art work kept in hopeless incorrectness! In this Opera, taken strictly, everything is absurd, up to what a god-given musician offers up therein as original melodist. For definitely so-called "German Opera" such a one was Weber, who sent to us his most enkindling rays of genius through this opera-mist, which Beethoven shook off in anger when he scored his diary with, "No more operas and such like, but *my* way!" And who shall dispute our verdict on the *genre* itself, when he recalls the fact that Weber's finest, richest, and most masterly music is as good as lost to us because belonging to the opera "Euryanthe"? Where shall we find this work performed to-day, when even sovereign heads are more easily inclined to the "Clemenza di Tito" or "Olympia"—if something heavy must really be dug up for their wedding or jubilee festivities — than to this "Euryanthe," in which, spite all its name for tedium, each single number is worth more than all the *Opera seria* of Italy, France, and Judea? Such preferences, beyond a doubt, are not to be simply set down to the somnolent discrimination of the Prussian Operatic College of Directors; but, as everything there is governed by a certain dull but stiffnecked academic instinct, from such a choice we may gather that beside those works of undeniably firm-set style, though very cramped and hollow genus, the best of "German operas" must needs look incomplete, and therefore unpresentable at court. Certainly all the sins of the *opera-genre* come out most strongly in this

work, yet solely because its composer was in mortal earnest this time, but still could do no more than try to cover up the failings, nay, absurdities, of the *genre* by a supreme exertion of his purely musical productiveness. To revive my old figure of speech, that in the marriage to beget the grand United Art-work the poet's work is the masculine principle, and music the feminine, I might compare the outcome of the penetration of the "Euryanthe" text by Weber's genius with the fruit of the union of a "Tschandala" with a "Brahminess"; for according to Hindu belief and experience a Brahmin might beget from a Tschandala woman a quite goodly child, though not one fitted for the rank of Brahmin, whereas the offspring of a Tschandala male from the superbly truth-bearing womb of a Brahmin female revealed the outcast type in plainest, and consequently in most revolting, imprint. Moreover, in the conception of this unlucky "Euryanthe" you must remember the poet-father was a lady, the music in the fullest sense a man! When Goethe thought that Rossini could have written quite passable music for his "Helena," it was the Brahmin casting his eye on a buxom Tschandala maiden; only in this case it is scarcely to be supposed that the Tschandala girl would have stood the test.

In the first part of my larger treatise on "Opera and Drama," I long ago tried to expound the mournful, nay, heart-rending, lessons to be drawn from Weber's work last named; in particular I endeavored to show that even the most richly-gifted melodist was in no position to turn a collection of verseless German verses for a poetic-posing operatic text into a sterling art-work. And Weber, beyond being one of the most pre-eminent of melodists, was a bright-witted man with a keen eye for all trash and humbug. With the young musicians who came after, he soon fell into a certain disesteem. God knows what mysteries of Bach, Händel, and so forth, they concocted as the very newest recipes, but none of them ventured to face the problem which Weber seemed to have left unsolved; or if any did, he gave it up after a brief but labored attempt. Only Kapellmeisters went gayly on composing "operas." In their installation-contracts it was written that they must enrich the Court opera conducted by them with a new product of their fancy every year. My operas "Rienzi," "Der Fliegende Holländer," "Tannhäuser," and "Lohengrin" are given gratis at the Dresden Court theater to this day, because they are reckoned to me as Kapellmeister operas from the period of my life-appointment there; I therefore have to pay a curious penalty for these operas having fared better than those of my colleagues. Happily, this calamity affects myself alone; I know of no other Dresden opera-composer whose works have survived his Kapellmeistership, except my great predecessor, Weber; but from him they asked no opera expressly written for the Court theater, as in his time Italian Opera alone was deemed compatible with human dignity. His three famous operas Weber wrote for theaters elsewhere.

Apart from this nice enrichment of the Royal Saxon Court theater's repertoire by my modest, but now over thirty-years' enduring work, not one of the afterbirths of Weberian Opera has had any real subsistence at the other Court theaters either. Incomparably the most significant of them, were the first operas of Marschner; for some time their author was kept erect by the great unconcern with which, untroubled by the problem of Opera itself, he let his melodic talent and a certain idiomatic trick of maintaining his music, not always very new, in constant, active flow, work out their own salvation. But the contagion of the new French Opera caught him as well, and soon he lost himself past rescue in the shallows of the poorly-schooled and not-highly-gifted. In face of Meyerbeer's successes one and all stood· still and timid, were it only for good manners; not until recent times did one dare to follow up the creations of his style with Old Testament abortions.* German Opera, however, was on its deathbed till it happened at last that the still opposed, but less and less disputed, successors of my own works seemed to have set pretty well the whole German composer-world in alarm and eager competition.

Long years ago I noticed symptoms of this movement. My successes at the Dresden Court-theater even then drew F. Hiller, and later R. Schumann also, into my vicinity; at first no doubt just to see how it arrived that on an important German stage the operas of a thitherto entirely unknown German composer should lastingly attract the public. That I was no remarkable musician, both friends believed they had soon detected, so that my success appeared to be founded in the texts I had penned

for myself. Indeed I also was of opinion that, as they now were brooding operatic plans they should first of all procure good poems. For this they begged my help, but declined it again when things came to the point — I presume for fear of shabby tricks that I might play them. Of my text for "Lohengrin" Schumann remarked that it could never be composed as an opera; wherein he differed from Upper-Kapellmeister Taubert of Berlin, who later on, after my music also had been finished and performed, declared that he should like to set its text all over again for himself. When Schumann was compiling the book of his "Genovefa" no argument of mine could dissuade him from retaining the lamentably foolish third act as he had framed it; he took offense and certainly imagined that I wished to spoil his very best effects. For *effect* he aimed at; everything "German, chaste, and pure," but with a piquant dash of mock unchastity to be harrowingly supplied by the most un-human coarsenesses and lownesses of the second finale. A few years ago I heard a most carefully prepared performance of this "Genovefa," in Leipzig, and could but find that the revolting and offensive scene which ends the third act of Auber's "Bal masque," founded on similar motives, was quite a dainty *bon mot* compared with this sickening brutality of the chaste German effect-composer and librettist. And — marvelous ! Never have I heard a solitary complaint about it.† With such energy does the German control his inborn purer feelings when he means to pit one man — Schumann for instance — against another; e.g., myself. For my part, I perceived that I could have been of no earthly use to Schumann.

But this was in the good old times. Since then the Thirty-years' Zukunftsmusic War broke out, as to which I cannot quite ascertain whether it is yet deemed ripe for a Westphalian treaty. At any rate, there was a fair amount of opera-composing again in the years of war themselves, prompted perhaps by the very circumstance that our theaters were doing less and less business with the French and Italian wares they used to live on, whereas a number of German texts from my dilettantish pen, and actually composed by my own unaided self, for long had furnished them with good receipts.

---

* Goldmark's "Queen of Sheba," for instance.

† It is frequently used for performances, by the young ladies and gentlemen of prominent English Academies.

Unfortunately I have been unable to gain any closer acquaintance with the creations of the neo-German Muse. They tell me that the influence of my " innovations " in the dramatic style of music may there be remarked. Notoriously I am credited with a " manner " (or " line "— "*Richtung* ") against which the deceased Kapellmeister Rietz of Dresden was predisposed, and the departed Musikdirektor Hauptmann of Leipzig directed his choicest sallies. I fancy they were not the only ones, but quite a number of masters of all sorts were, and probably still are, unfriendly toward this " line." In the Music-schools and Conservatories it is said to be sternly tabooed. What " line " may be taught there is not clear to myself ; all I know is, that mighty little is learnt ; someone who had studied composition for six whole years at one of these establishments gave it up at the end. It almost seems that the learning of Opera-composition must proceed in secret outside the High Schools, so that he who falls into my " line " had best keep a lookout ! But it is less a study of my works than their success that appears to have sent many an academically untaught to my " manner." In what the latter consists, to myself is most unclear of all. Perhaps in the recent predilection for medieval subjects ; the Edda and the rugged North in general have also been taken in eye as quarries for good texts. Yet it is not only the choice and character of its opera-texts that seem to have been of weight to the by all means " new " line, but several things besides ; in particular that " composing throughout," and above all a never-ceasing interference of the orchestra in the singers' affairs — a mode with which one was the more liberal, as a good deal of " manner " had lately arisen in the instrumentation, harmony, and modulation of orchestral compositions.

I scarcely think that in all these things I could give much useful instruction ; as I luckily am neither asked for it by anyone, at most I might give — unbidden — the following little counsel out of pure good nature.

A German prince with a turn for composing operas * once asked friend Liszt to procure my aid in the instrumentation of a new opera by his Highness ; in particular he wanted the good effect of the Trombones in " Tannhäuser " applied to his work, in which regard my friend felt bound to divulge the secret that something al-

ways occurred to me before I set it for the trombones. On the whole it would be advisable that sundry composers adopted this " manner ; " to myself, indeed, it is of scanty profit, for I never can compose at all when nothing "occurs " to me ; and perhaps the generality are wiser not to wait for such " ideas." With regard to the dramatic branch, however, I would indicate the best device for positively forcing such " occurrences."

A young musician whom I also once advised to wait for ideas asked skeptically how he was ever to know that the idea he might get, under circumstances, was really his own. This doubt may arrive to the absolute Instrumental composer ; in fact, our great Symphonists of the " now-time " might be counseled to turn any doubt as to the ownership of their stray ideas into downright certainty, ere others do it for them. *Dramatic* composers of my " manner," on the other hand, I would recommend to never think of adopting a text before they see in it a plot, and characters to carry out their plot that inspire the musician with a lively interest on some account or other. Then let him take a good look at the one character, for instance, which appeals to him the most the very day : bears it a mask — away with it ; wears it the garment of a stage-tailor's dummy — off with it ! Let him set it in a twilight spot where he can merely see the gleaming of its eye ; if that speaks to him the shape itself will now most likely fall a-moving, which perhaps will even terrify him — but he must put up with that ; at last its lips will part, it opens its mouth, and a ghostly voice breathes something quite distinct, intensely seizable, but so unheard-of (such as the " Guest of stone," and surely the page Cherubino, once said to Mozart) that he wakes from out his dream. All has vanished ; but in the spiritual ear it still rings on : he has had an "idea " ("*Einfall*"), a so-called musical " Motiv ; " God knows if other men have heard the same, or something similar before ? Does it please Christianity, or displease Christ ? What's that to him ? It is *his* motiv, legally delivered to and settled on him by that marvelous shape in that wonderful fit of absorption.

But one only gets these inspirations when one doesn't ply for opera-texts with theater-dummies ; to invent " new " tunes for such, is uncommonly hard. We may take it that Mozart has ex-

* The Late Duke of Coburg.

hausted all the music for those same dramatic masquerades. Clever men have praised his texts, that of "Don Juan," for instance, as the half-sketched programmes for a stage masque, with which they say his music corresponds so admirably because it reproduces even the most passionate of human situations as an always pleasantly diverting game. Though this view is easy of misconstruction, and above all may wound as derogatory, it was seriously meant, and involved that widely-accepted verdict of our æsthetes on Music's true office which it is so hard to combat till this day. Only I think that Mozart, while elevating his art — exposed in a certain and very deep sense to the charge of frivolity — to an æsthetic principle of Beauty, at like time completely exhausted it; it was his own; whoever thought to follow him merely bungled and bored.

The stock of "pretty melodies" is out, and without "new ideas" there cannot be much originality remaining. Wherefore I advise the "new-mannered" to keep a keen eye on his text, his plot, and characters, for inspirations. But whoso has no time to wait for the results of such a scrutiny (to many it has so happened with their "Armin"s and "Konradin"s!), and finally contents himself with stage-dummies, processions, shrieks of vengeance, storms in a teacup, and all the dance of death and devils, at least I warn him not to employ for the musical outfit of such mummery those attributes of the "manner" which have issued from communion with the true-dream shapes I spoke of above, as he would only make a muddle of it. For he who has looked those figures in the face has had a difficulty in drawing on the store-room of our masking music to plainly re-compose the motive they had given him; frequently there was nothing to be done with the squaring of rhythm and modulation, since it is somewhat different to say "It is," from "Let us say," or "He believes so." Here the straits (*Noth*) of the Unheard-of often bring new necessities to light, and the music may haply weave itself into a style that might much annoy our Quadrature musicians. Not that that matters much; for if he who makes strange and startling modulations without that Want is certainly a bungler, so he who does not recognize the compulsion to modulate forcibly in the proper place is a —— "Senator." The worst of it is that the "new-mannerist" assumes that those occasional unheard-of-nesses have now become the common property of all who have footed the "line," and that if he only lays them on thick enough his dummies will at once look like something. But they look very bad, and I can't blame many an honest soul of the German Reich for still preferring to hear masque-music correctly built according to the lines of Quadrature. If only there were *Rossinis* to be had! I am afraid, however, they have come to an end.

After all, there won't be much to learn from my jottings of to-day; my counsels, in particular, will prove quite useless. Indeed, under no conditions would I pretend to teach how men should make, but merely to guide them to a knowledge of how the made and the created should be rightly understood. Even for this a really lasting intercourse were requisite; for only by examples, examples, and again examples, is anything to be made clear, and eventually something learnt; but effectually to set examples in our domain we need musicians, singers, finally an orchestra. All these the minions of our Culture-ministries have at their hand in schools of the great cities; how they have contrived that nothing right will yet come of our music, and that even at the change-of-guard the pieces played grow daily worse, must remain a modern mystery of state. My friends are aware that two years back I thought it would be useful if I mixed a little in the thing myself; what I wished, however, seemed to be viewed as undesirable. I have been left in peace, for which I may be thankful in some respects. Only I regret to have to remain so incomplete and hard of understanding when I feel moved at times, as with the above, to throw a ray of light on much that touches our world of music. May it be adjudged to this evil if the present article is found more agitating than instructive; luckily it is written for neither the *Kölnische*, the *National*, — nor any other world — *Zeitung*, and whatever is amiss in it thus stays among ourselves.

ON THE APPLICATION OF MUSIC TO THE DRAMA.

(FROM RICHARD WAGNER'S PROSE WORKS.)

[This article was originally published in the *Bayreuther Blätter*, for November, 1879.]

My last article on Opera-writing contained an allusion to the necessary difference in musical style between a dramatic and a purely musical composition. I now should like to put this plainer, as it seems to me that one thus might rectify great misconceptions, both in the judgment of music and, more particularly, in our composer's ideas of production. I spoke of "bunglers" who needlessly indulge in strange and startling modulation, and of "senators" who are unable to perceive the necessity of apparent extravagances in that department. The euphemism "Senator" was furnished me at a critical moment by Shakespeare's "Iago," who wished to avoid the application of an epithet from the animal world to a person of official status; * in a similar predicament of respect towards art-scientific worthies, I will in future employ the more becoming term " Professor." The weighty question here involved, however, had better be discussed without any reference to " Professors," purely among artists and true, i.e., unsalaried, friends of art. To such alone I therefore propose to address the following upshot of my experiences and meditations in the exercise of my artistic calling.

As Example always teaches best, I at once adduce a speaking instance from art-history, namely, that Beethoven shows such daring in his Symphonies, such caution in his (only) opera, "Fidelio." The cramping structure then accepted as the mould of Opera I assigned in my preceding essay as the reason of the master's turning a sullen back on further attempts with the dramatic genre. Why he did not seek to broaden the whole style of Opera itself into correspondence with his mighty genius, was manifestly that he found no instigation in the only case that lay before him; that he did not strive to gain him such a stimulus by hook or crook, we must explain by the all-unknown New having already opened up to him as Symphonist. If we watch him in the fullness of his innovating force, we can but recognize that he fixed for once and all the character of independent Instrumental music by the plastic barriers his impetuous genius never overstepped. Let us now endeavor to perceive and understand these barriers, not as limitations, but conditions of the Beethovenian Art-work.

I have called these barriers plastic; I will further denote them the pillars through whose ordering, as symmetrical as to the purpose, the Symphonic edifice is bounded, borne, and made distinct. In the construction of the Symphonic movement, already planned by Haydn, Beethoven altered nothing; and for the same reason that forbids an architect to displace the columns of a building at discretion, or to use forsooth the horizontal parts as vertical. If it was a conventional order, the very nature of the art-work had dictated that convention; for the basis of the Symphonic art-work is the Dance-tune. It is impossible for me to here repeat what I have said upon this theme in earlier essays, and, as I believed, established. Merely I would point once more to the character stamped for good and all on the Haydn and Beethoven Symphony by that foundation. Dramatic pathos is completely excluded, so that the most intricate involvements of the thematic motives in a symphonic movement could never be explained in the analogy of a dramatic action, but solely by the mazes of an ideal dance, without a suspicion of rhetorical dialectics. Here there is no "conclusion," no problem, no solution. Wherefore all these Symphonies bear one and all the character of lofty glee (*Heiterkeit*). Never are two themes of diametrically opposite character confronted here; diverse as they may seem, they always supplement each other as the manly and the womanly element of one whole character. Yet the undreamt variety in which these elements may break, re-form, and re-unite with one another is proved to demonstration by such a Beethovenian movement; the first in the "Eroica" reveals this to the absolute bewildering of the uninitiate, although to the initiate this movement bears the unity of its root-character the most convincingly of all.

It has been very rightly remarked that Beethoven's innovations are far rather to be sought in the field of rhythmic distribution than on that of harmonic modulation. Remote changes of Key are scarcely used except in wanton fun, whereas we find an invincible power of constantly reshaping rhythmic-plastic motives, of ordering and ranging them in ever richer piles. Here we light, so it seems, on the line of cleavage of the Symphonist from the Dramatist. Mozart was new and startling to his contemporaries through his love of daring flights in modulation, inspired by deepest need; we know their horror at the harmonic acridities in the introduction to that Quartet which he dedicated to Haydn. Here, as in so many characteristic passages where

* "Othello," Act I, Scene 1: *Brabantio*, " Thou art a villain." *Iago*, " You are—a senator."

the contrapuntal theme is raised to the expression of anguished yearning through an ascending series of accented suspending-notes, the craving to exhaust all Harmonic possibilities appears to border on dramatic pathos. In effect it was from the realm of dramatic music, already widened by himself to undreamt capability of expression, that Mozart first entered on the Symphony; for those few symphonic works of his, whose peculiar worth has kept them living to this day, we owe to that creative period when he had fully unfolded his genius as opera-composer. To the composer of "Figaro" and "Don Giovanni" the framework of the Symphonic movement only offered a curb on that mobile love of figure-painting (*gestaltungsfrohe Beweglichkeit*) which had found such congenial scope in the passionately changeful situations of those dramatic drafts. Viewing his art as Symphonist a little closer, we observe that here he shines by wellnigh nothing save the beauty of his themes, whilst in their application and refashioning he distinguishes himself merely as a practised contrapuntist; to breathe life into connecting links he missed the accustomed dramatic stimulus. Now, his dramatic art of music had really fed on nothing but the so-called *Opera buffa*, the melodic comedy; true "Tragedy" was still a stranger to him, and only in single lofty features, as *Donna Anna* and the *Marble Guest*, had she turned on him her quickening countenance. Was he seeking for it in the Symphony? Who shall answer for the latent parts and possible developments of a genius who passed his earthly life, itself so brief, beneath the scalpel of the vivisector?

But now the Tragic Muse has actually laid hands on Opera. Mozart knew her only in the mask of Metastasio's "*Opera seria*," stiff and arid — "Clemenza di Tito." Her true visage she appears to have but gradually unveiled to us; Beethoven saw it not yet, and abode "by *his way*." I believe I may aver that, with the advent of full earnestness in the conception of Tragedy and the realizing of the Drama, quite new necessities arose for music; requirements which we must accurately measure against those demanded of the Symphonist in preservation of the pureness of his art-style.

Though the absolute instrumental-composer found no musical forms to hand save those in which he originally had had to "strike up," more or less for the enlivenment, or even the encour-

agement, of others at festal dances and marches, if this formed the basal character of the symphonic art-work, at first compounded of such Dance and March tunes which dramatic pathos could only confuse by the posing of questions without a possibility of answers, yet certain vividly gifted instrumentalists nursed the irrepressible desire to enlarge the bounds of musical form and expression by superscribing their pieces with a dramatic incident, and endeavoring to present it to the imagination through purely musical means. The reasons why a pure artistic style could never be attained in this path have doubtless been discerned in course of the manifold attempts thereon; but to us it seems that the admirable service thus rendered by exceptionally gifted musicians has not yet been sufficiently regarded. The excesses to which his guardian dæmon drove a Berlioz were nobly tempered by the incomparably more artistic genius of Liszt to the expression of soul and world events too great for words; and to the disciples of their art it might appear that a new order of composition was placed at their immediate disposal. In any case, it was astonishing to see what boundless faculties sheer Instrumental music had acquired under guidance of a dramatic synopsis. Theretofore the Overture to an opera or play alone had offered occasion for the employment of purely musical means of expression in a form departing from the symphonic movement. Beethoven himself had here proceeded very circumspectly; feeling impelled to introduce an actual stage-effect in the middle of his "Leonora" overture, he still repeated the first section of the tonal-piece, with the customary change of key, exactly as in a symphonic movement, heedless that the dramatic excitement of the middle section, reserved for thematic working-out, had already led us to expect the *dénoument* — a manifest drawback to the receptive hearer. Far more concisely, and in a dramatic sense correctly, did Weber plan his "Freischütz" overture, where the so-called middle section rushes on at once to the conclusion through a drastic climax in the thematic conflict. Now, though in the larger Programme works of the more recent tone-poets named above we find clear traces of the Symphony construction proper — indelible for natural reasons — in the fashioning of the themes, their contrast and remodeling, there already appears a passionate and "eccentric" character such as pure Symphonic instrumental music seemed called to hold entirely aloof; indeed, the Programmist felt bound to give this eccentric characterization particularly high relief, as a poetic shape or episode was always present to his mind, and he believed he could not set it plain enough before the eye, as it were. At last this obligation led to downright melodrama music, with pantomime to be supposed, and quite consistently to instrumental recitatives, whilst horror at the pulverizing formlessness filled all the critical world, so that nothing really remained but to help the new form of Musical Drama itself to light of day from such birth-agonies.

This latter is as little to be compared with the older operatic form as the newer instrumental music conducting to it is to be likened with the Classic Symphony, because impossible to our composers. But we will defer for a while our inquiry into that so-called " Musikdrama," and first cast a glance on the " classical " instrumental composition of our latest times, all unaffected by that process of gestation; we shall find that this " classic survival " is an empty pretense, and has planted beside our great Classic masters a highly unattractive hybrid from " I would " and "yet I cannot."

That Programme music on which "we" looked with timid glances from the corner of our eye had imported so much novelty in harmonization, theatrical and landscape effects, nay, historical painting, and had worked it all out with such striking brilliance, in power of an uncommonly virtuosic art of instrumenting, that to continue in the earlier style of Classic Symphony one lacked alas! the Beethoven who would have known how to make the best of it. " We " held our tongues. When at last we took heart to open our Symphonic mouth again, just to show what still was in us, we found we had grown so turgid and wearisome that there was nothing for it but to deck ourselves with fallen feathers from the Programme petrel. In our symphonies, and that sort of thing, all now goes world-distraught and catastrophic; we are gloomy and grim, then mettlesome and daring; we yearn for the fulfillment of youthful dreams; daemonic obstacles encompass us; we brood, we even rave; and then the world-ache's tooth is drawn; we laugh, and humorously show the world its gaping gum; brisk, sturdy, blunt, Hungarian, or Scotch,— alas! to others dreary. To be serious: we cannot believe that a happy future has been secured

to instrumental music by the creations of its latest masters; above all, it must be bad for us to recklessly tack on these works to the legacy of Beethoven, in view of the utter un-Beethovenism which we ought, on the contrary, to be taught to discern in them — a lesson that should not come so very hard in the matter of kinship to the Beethovenian spirit, in spite of all the Beethovenian themes we here meet once again; though in the matter of form it could scarcely be easy to the pupils of our Conservatories, as under the rubric of " Æsthetic Forms," they are giving nothing but a list of different composers' names, and left to form a judgment for themselves without further comparison.

The said symphonic compositions of our newest school — let us call it the Romantic-classical — are distinguished from the wild stock of our so-called Programme-music, not only by the regretted absence of a programme, but in especial by a certain clammy cast of melody which its creators have transplanted from their heretofore retiring " Chamber-music." To the " Chamber," in fact, one had withdrawn. Alas! not to the homely room where Beethoven once poured into the ears of few and breathless friends all that Unutterable he kept for understanding here alone, instead of in the ample hall-space where he spoke in none but plastic masses to the Folk, to all mankind in this hallowed " chamber " silence long had reigned; for one now must hear the master's so-called " last " Quartets and Sonatas either badly, as men played them, or not at all — till the way at last was shown by certain outlawed renegades, and one learnt what that chamber-music really said. No, those had already moved *their* chamber to the concert-hall; what had previously been dressed as Quintets and the like, was now served up as Symphony: little chips of melody like an infusion of hay and old tea-leaves, with nothing to tell you what you are swallowing but the label " Best; " and all for the required taste of World-ache. On the whole, however, the new tendency to the eccentric, the requiring-a-programme, retained the upper hand. With fine discernment Mendelssohn had gone to Nature for his subjects, and executed them as a kind of landscape epic; he had traveled much, and brought home many a thing that others could not lightly come by. But the latest phase is to take the cabinet-pictures of our local Exhibitions and set them to music straightway; enabling one to seize those quaint instrumental effects which are now at every one's command, disguise embezzled melodies in harmonizations that are a constant surprise and play the outcome to the world as Plastic music.

The results of our survey may be summed up as follows : —

Pure Instrumental, no longer content with the legalized form of the Classical Symphonic Movement, sought to extend her powers in every respect and found them easily increased by poet's fancies ; the reactionary party was unable to fill that Classic form with life, and saw itself compelled to borrow for it from the wholly alien, thereby distorting it. Whilst the first direction led to the winning of new aptitudes and the second merely exposed inaptitudes, it became evident that the further evaluation of those aptitudes was only to be saved from boundless follies, threatening serious damage to the spirit of Music, by openly and undisguisedly turning that line towards the *drama*. What there remained unutterable could here be spoken definitely and plainly, and thereby " Opera " redeemed withal from the curse of her unnatural descent. And it is here, in what we may call for short the " Musical Drama," that we reach sure ground for calmly reckoning the application of Music's new-won faculties to the evolution of noble, inexhaustible artistic forms.

The science of Æsthetics has at all times laid down Unity as a chief requirement from the artwork. In the abstract this Unity is difficult to define dialectically, and its misapprehension has led to many and grave mistakes. It comes out the plainest in the perfect art work itself, for it is it that moves us to unbroken interest and keeps the broad impression ever present. Indisputably this result is the most completely attained by the living represented drama; wherefore we have no hesitation in declaring the Drama the most perfect of art-works. The farthest from this art-work stood the "Opera," and perhaps for the very reason that she made a pretence of drama, but split it into countless disconnected fragments for sake of the Aria form : in Opera there are pieces embracing all the structure of a symphonic Movement in briefest lapse of time with first and second themes, return repetition and so-called "Coda;" but self-included they remain without one whit of reference to all the other pieces like them. In the

Symphony, on the contrary, we have found this structure so developed and enlarged that its master turned in anger from the cramping form of Operatic numbers. In this Symphonic movement we recognized the unity that has so determinant an influence on us in the perfect drama, and the downfall of that art-form so soon as foreign elements, all unassimilable with that unity were introduced therein. But the element most foreign to it was the Dramatic, which needed infinitely richer forms for its unfolding than could naturally present themselves on the basis of the Symphonic Movement, i.e., Dance music. Nevertheless, to be an art-work again *quâ* music the new form of dramatic music must have the unity of the Symphonic Movement; and this it attains by spreading itself over the whole drama in the most intimate cohesion therewith, not merely over single, smaller, arbitrarily selected parts. So that this Unity consists in a tissue of root-themes pervading all the drama, themes which contrast, complete, re-shape, divorce, and intertwine with one another as in the Symphonic Movement, only that here the needs of the dramatic action dictate the laws of parting and combining which were there originally borrowed from the motions of the dance.

Upon the new form of musical construction as applied to the Drama I have expressed myself sufficiently in earlier articles and essays, yet sufficiently merely in the sense that I imagined I had plainly pointed out the road in which a true, and alike a useful judgment of the musical forms now won from Drama by my own artistic labors might be attained by others. To the best of my knowledge that road has not been trodden yet, and I can remember nothing but the studies of one of my younger friends* who has viewed the characteristics of what he calls my " *Leitmotive* " rather in the light of their dramatic significance, than in that of their bearing on musical construction (since the specific art of music was not the author's province). On the contrary, I have lived to see our Music-schools all inculcating horror at the wild confusion of my periods, while young composers, fired by the success of public representations of my works, and guided by a superficial private reading of my scores, have unintelligently tried to copy me. As the State and Parish only pay for un-teachers of my art, such as Professor Rheinberger of Munich (to remain within the

* Freiherr Hans von Wozgogen.

circle of my supposititious influence), instead of founding something like a chair for it, as may some day happen in England or America, — the present little article will not have been labor thrown away if it only gives those said composers an inkling of what they might learn and copy from my works.

So, whoever till now has trained himself by listening to our newest Romantic-classical instrumental-music, and wants to try his skill with the dramatic genre, I would above all advise him not to aim at harmonic and instrumental Effects, but to await sufficient cause for any effect of the kind, as otherwise they will not come off. You could not insult Berlioz more profoundly than by bringing him abortions of this sort on paper and expecting them to please the composer of " Witches-Sabbaths," and the like. Liszt used to polish off these stupid suggestions with the remark that cigar-ash and sawdust steeped in *aqua fortis* did not make pleasant soup. I have never yet made the acquaintance of a young composer who did not think to gain my sanction for "audacities" before all things. On the other hand, it has been a real surprise to me that the restraint I have striven for with increasing vigilance in the modulation and instrumentation of my works has not met the smallest notice. In the instrumental introduction to " Rheingold," for instance, it was impossible for me to quit the fundamental note simply because I had no reason for changing it ; a great part of the not un-animated scene that follows for the *Rhine-daughters* and *Alberich* would only permit of modulation to Keys the very nearest of kin, as Passion here is still in the most primitive *naïvete* of its expression. I do not deny that I certainly should have given to the first entry of *Donna Anna* — denouncing the shameless seducer *Don Juan* in the height of passion — a stronger coloring than Mozart held appropriate to the conventions of the operatic style and those means of expression he himself was the first to enrich. But there sufficed that simple austerity which I had as little to abandon when the " Walküre " was to be introduced with a storm, the " Siegfried " with a tone-piece conducting us into the silent depths of Nibelheim's Hoard-smithy by a reminiscence of certain plastic motives from the previous dramas : all three were *elements* from which the drama had to quicken into life. Something different was demanded for an introduction to the Norn's scene

of " Die Götterdämmerung ; " here the destinies of the ure-world are weaving themselves into that rope one must see the hooded sisters swing when the curtain rises, to understand its meaning : wherefore this prelude could only be brief and preparatory, though the expectant use of motives made intelligible in the earlier sections of the work allowed a richer harmonic and thematic treatment. And it is important how one commences. Had I used in an Overture a motive cast like that which is heard in the second act of " Die Walküre " at *Wotan's* surrender of world-sovereignty to the possessor of the Nibelungen-hoard : —

according to my notions of distinctness of style I should have perpetrated a piece of downright nonsense. But after in course of the drama the simple nature-motive : —

had been heard at the earliest gleam of the shining Rheingold ; at the first appearance of the Gods'-burg " Walhall," shimmering in the morning's red, the no less simple motive

and each of these motives had undergone mutations in closest sympathy with the rising passions of the plot, — with the help of a digression in the harmony. I could present them knit in such a way that, more than Wotan's words, this tone-figure should give to us a picture of the fearful gloom in the soul of the suffering god. Again, I am conscious of having always endeavored to prevent the acerbity of such musical combinations from making a striking effect as such, as a special " audacity " we will say ; both by my marks of expression and by word of mouth I sought to so tone down the change, whether by a timely slackening of tempo or a preliminary dynamic compensation, that it should invade our willing feeling as an artistic moment in strict accordance with the laws of nature. So that it may be imagined how nothing enrages me more, and keeps me away from strange performances of my music, than the insensibility of most of our conductors to the requirements of Renderings in such combinations in particular ; needing the most delicate treatment they are given to the ear in false and hurried tempo, without the indispensable dynamic shading, and mostly unintelligible. No wonder they are a bugbear to our " Professors."

I have dealt at some length with this example because it has an application to all my dramas, only far more extended, and shows the characteristic distinction between the Dramatic and the Symphonic use and working out of motives. But I will take a second of like nature, and draw attention to the metamorphoses in that motive with which the *Rhine-daughters* greet the glancing Gold in childish glee :—

„Rhein - gold!   Rhein - gold!

One would have to follow this uncommonly simple theme — recurring in manifold alliance with almost every other motive of the drama's widespread movement — through all the changes it receives from the diverse character of its resummoning to see what type of variations the Drama can engender ; and how completely the character of these variations departs from that of those figured, rhythmic or harmonic alterations, of a theme which our masters ranged in immediate sequence to build up pictures of an often intoxicatingly kaleidoscopic effect. This effect was destroyed at once, and with it the classic form of Variation so soon as motives for-

eign to the theme were woven in, giving something of a dramatic development to the Movement's progress and fouling the purity, or let us say self-evidence, of the tone-piece. But neither a mere play of counterpoint, nor the most fantastic art of figuration and most inventive harmonizing, either could or should transform a theme so characteristically, and present it with such manifold and entirely changed expression — yet leaving it always recognizable — as true dramatic art can do quite naturally. Hardly anything could afford a plainer proof of this than a pursuit of that simple motive of the " Rhine-daughters," through all the changing passions of the four-part drama down to *Hagen's* Watch-song in the first act of the " Götterdämmerung," where it certainly takes on a form which, to me at least, makes it inconceivable as theme of a Symphonic Movement, albeit it still is governed by the laws of harmony and thematism, though purely in their application to the Drama. To attempt to apply the results of such a method to the Symphony, however, must lead to the latter's utter ruin ; for here would appear as a far-fetched effect what follows there from well-found motives.

It cannot be my present purpose to repeat what I have said at length in earlier writings about the application of Music to the Drama, even though regarded from a fresh point of view ; rather, my main object has been to mark the difference between two modes of music from whose commingling have sprung disfigurement of the one variety of art, false judgment of the other. And to me this seemed of weight, if we are ever to arrive at a proper æsthetic estimate of the great events in the evolutionary career of Music — the one still truly living and productive art of our era — whereanent the greatest confusion prevails to this day. Starting from the structural laws of the Symphony, Sonata, or the Aria, when we hitherto have made for Drama we never got beyond that Operatic style which trammeled the great symphonist in the unfolding of his faculties ; on the other hand, in our amazement at the boundlessness of these faculties when unfolded in right relation to the Drama we confound those laws if we transfer the fruits of musical innovations on the dramatic field to the Symphony and so forth. However, as I have said that it would lead us too far to display these innovations in all their mutual bearings ; and as that task would also fall more fitly to another, I will conclude with one more illustration — namely of the characteristics demanded by the Drama, forbidden by the Symphony not only in the use and transformation, but also in the first modeling of the Motive itself.

Properly speaking, we cannot conceive of a chief motive of a Symphonic Movement as a piece of eccentric modulation, especially if it is to present itself in such a bewildering dress at its first appearance. The motive which the composer of "Lohengrin" allots as closing phrase of a first arioso to his *Elsa* plunged in memory of a blissful dream, consists almost solely of a tissue of remote harmonic progressions; in the Andante of a Symphony we will say it would strike us as far-fetched and highly unintelligible; here it does not seem strained, but quite arising of itself, and therefore so intelligible that to my knowledge it has never been decried as the contrary. *Elsa* has slowly approached in gentle grief, with timid, down-bent head; one glance at her transfigured eye informs us what is in her soul.

Questioned she replies by nothing save the vision of a dream that fills her with a sweet belief: "With signs so soft and courteous he comfort gave to me;" that glance had already told us something of the kind. Now, boldly passing from her dream to assurance of fulfillment in reality she adds: "That Knight I will await then; he shall my champion be." And after all

* Theodor Uhlig.

its wanderings the musical phrase now passes back to its mother-Key.

At the time a young friend of mine,* to whom I had sent the score for arrangement of a pianoforte edition, was much astonished by the look of this phrase which had so many modulations in so few bars, but still more when he attended the first performance of "Lohengrin" at Weimar, and found that this self same phrase appeared quite natural — which at any rate was due in part to the musical conducting of Liszt, who by a proper rendering had turned the transient eye-sore into a well-favored shape of Tone.

It seems that already a very large portion of the public finds much, nay, almost everything in my dramatic music quite natural, and therefore pleasing, at which our "Professors" still cry Fie! Were the latter to seat me in one of their sacred chairs, however, they perhaps might be seized with even greater wonder at the prudence and moderation, especially in the use of harmonic effects, which I should enjoin upon their pupils; as I should have to make it their foremost rule never to quit a Key so long as what they have to say can still be said therein. If this rule were complied with we possibly might again hear Symphonies that gave us something to talk about; whereas there is simply nothing at all to be said of our latest Symphonies.

Wherefore I too will be silent till some day I am called to a Conservatorium — only, not as "Professor."

PRACTICAL DIRECTIONS FOR CONDUCTING.

A good conductor should be possessed of the following capabilities : —

A correct ear; the capability of distinguishing tonal-colors; knowledge of harmony and composition ; facility in transposing; extensive knowledge of scores of every description. Furthermore, a conductor must be capable of indicating the most complicated kinds of time distinctly and clearly, enter into and grasp the spirit of a composition to be performed quickly and correctly, and be able to dominate and keep together a large number of executants, sometimes composed of the most varied elements, with such energy and cleverness as to bring about an ensemble perfect in every detail.

On page 319, Hector Berlioz' treatise on conducting has been added. The arguments, principles, and the practical advice laid down in this discussion, stamp it as invaluable to every musician, desirous of wielding the baton, at the same time calling attention to the artistic importance of what a conductor should strive after and aim at, in his professional career.

THE DIFFERENT KINDS OF TIME.

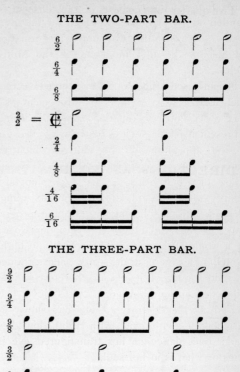

THE FOUR-PART BAR.

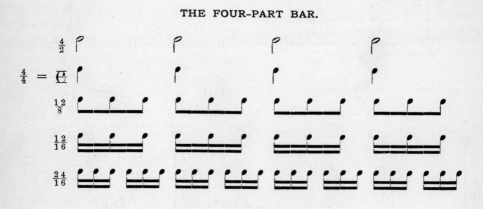

MISCELLANEOUS KINDS OF TIME.

FIVE AND SEVEN-PART TIME.

Five-quarter time consists of the consecutive change of a three-quarter with a two-quarter bar:—

Seven-quarter time consists of the consecutive change of a four-quarter with a three-quarter bar:—

DIRECTIONS AS TO BEATING TIME.

For beating time the conductor makes use of a baton and sometimes also of a violin bow. Owing to its length the latter is not as practical as the baton, as every beat should cut the air quickly and precisely. Irregular, indistinct, and particularly all ludicrous or unnecessary movements with the baton should be avoided, as they only interfere with the precision and clearness necessary for the correct beat. The various kinds of time should be beaten as follows:—

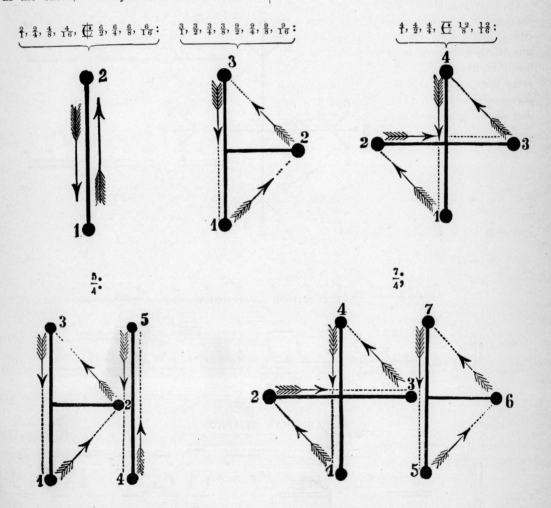

For rapid tempis like Scherzo, Waltz, Vivace, Presto or Prestissimo only the first beat of the bar is given. For slow tempis, like Adagio, Largo, etc., in two- three- or four-part time, all the subdivisions are indicated as follows:—

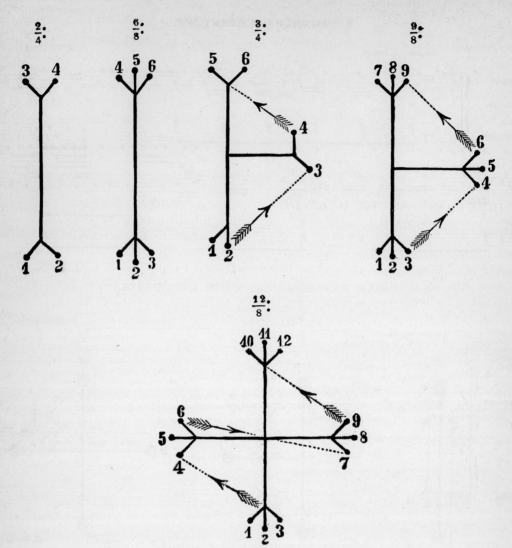

At times we meet certain compositions containing two different kinds of time, as illustrated in the following examples:—

1. G MINOR SYMPHONY.

MOZART.

Violins.

Violas.

Basses.

2. PASTORAL SYMPHONY.

BEETHOVEN.

Violins.

Violas.

Basses.

3. TANNHÄUSER OVERTURE.

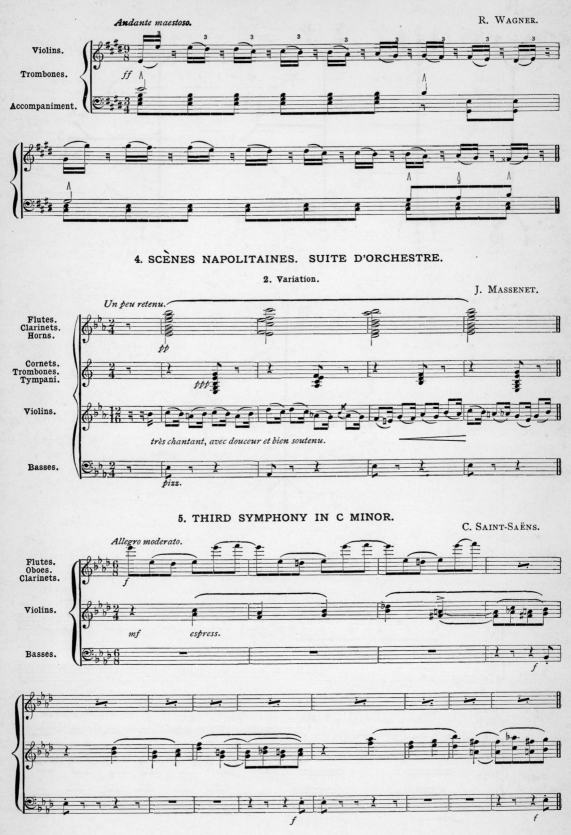

4. SCÈNES NAPOLITAINES. SUITE D'ORCHESTRE.

2. Variation.

5. THIRD SYMPHONY IN C MINOR.

6. DON JUAN FINALE.

The above cited ball-room scene in the Finale of "Don Juan" is not difficult to conduct as everyone of the three beats of the Menuet must be marked by a down-beat of the baton. When once started the three-eight bars (of which a whole bar is equal to a third or one beat of the Menuet), and the three-quarter bars (of which every half bar is also equal to one beat of the Menuet), fits exactly to each other, and to the Menuet, and proceeds without any difficulties. A principal point is that the beginning be marked very decidedly.

If a two-part bar contains Triplets:—

TANNHÄUSER OVERTURE.

this does not indicate that the rhythm should be taken any slower. In slow tempo a separate beat can be given to every note of the triplet, but the duration of the bar must therefore not be lengthened. In quicker tempo the particular marking of the first note will suffice.

THE ORCHESTRAL CONDUCTOR.

The conducting of a stringed orchestra is very difficult, and demands a high degree of routine and experience, together with extensive musical knowledge. In particular the orchestral conductor should cultivate the study of the classic master works. In this respect our modern musical conditions leave much to be wished for, the majority of conductors being absolutely ignorant of how the works of Haydn, Mozart, and Beethoven should be performed. As a rule, the tempis are hurried, the dynamic marks of expression as well as accents, *f*, *p*, *mf*, *cresc.*, and *dim.*, etc., ignored, not to mention the entire lack of taste displayed in conception and style.

In order to obtain a clear, æsthetic oversight as to the exact manner in which the classic tonal giants and their immortal works are to be interpreted and performed, it will be advisable and of great benefit to study R. Wagner's "*Treatise on Conducting*" and H. Berlioz "*The Orchestral Conductor.*"

GENERAL REMARKS.

In the majority of orchestral organizations the following observances are not enforced with sufficient severity; it is the duty of every conductor to pay special attention that: —

1.) The String and Wind Instruments are tuned, both individually and together, with the greatest care and exactness.

2.) Wherever the use of A or C Clarinets is indicated, these instruments should be really employed by Clarinetists.

3.) In the same way the Horn and Trumpet players should use the identical instruments indicated in the score, and not be allowed to execute everything upon the F Horn or Trumpet by simply transposing the music.

4.) The Flutists must not be allowed to play the notes of the lower registers an octave higher for the sake of convenience.

5.) The Bass Drum and Cymbals should be played each separately, as the tonal-color of the Cymbals becomes most ordinary and poor when attached to the Drum.

6.) Double-Bass players must make a rule of practicing difficult passages and not endeavor to simplify the same.

7.) The tremolo of the String Instruments must not be executed too slowly, and not that instead of thirty-seconds or sixty-fourths only eighths or sixteenths become audible.

8.) A great fault, which cannot be condemned too strongly, is the continuous preluding, tuning or practicing of difficult passages before the beginning of or during the intervals of a performance. In case any of the parts contain unusually difficult passages, runs, etc., it is the duty of the conductor to remind the individual musicians to practice their parts at home.

In conclusion, I will remark that the orchestral conductor should endeavor above all to beware of growing one-sided in his artistic views and tendencies, that he should encourage young and striving composers, in fact, assist every rising or struggling talent to the best of his ability.

THE CHORAL CONDUCTOR.

Above all the duties of such a conductor demand a thorough and dignified interpretation of classic and modern choral works, either for mixed, male, female or children's chorus.

As conductors in this particular field are usually dependent upon amateurs, among which many are possessed of a fine voice, but deficient in reading the notes, it becomes a necessity to impress the various parts upon the singers' memory through playing them either upon a violin or piano.

In consequence, it would be advisable if every conductor were to impress his chorus with the following important points: —

1.) To open the mouth to such an extent as to enable a free and clear tonal emission;

2.) To learn the text by heart and principally to enter into the spirit of the same;

3.) To articulate very clearly;

4.) To observe free and unrestrained breathing, and not get accustomed to careless gasping for breath, and especially to take the latter in such places where the words and their special sense will allow of it;

5.) To strictly observe all dynamic signs of expression, etc., which are of such great consequence in adding to the beauty of song;

6.) To constantly keep a watchful eye upon the conductor.

The following hints are added for the careful consideration of singing-society conductors; they will find them of practical value: —

1.) While beating time the conductor must not execute his movements in accordance with the time-value of the notes; as a rule, those notes receiving a down-beat should be specially accented.

2.) In conducting, smaller movements indicate " piano," more extended ones "forte," for the singers. The conductor should accustom his chorus to always take note of this, as it will do away with loud exclamations of "forte," " piano," on his part while the singing is going on.

3.) The proper observance of the above necessitates that the singers keep a watchful eye upon their conductor as soon as a song is taken up for practice and particularly during a concert performance of same. The conductor's aim should be to get his singers so proficient and independent in their text and notes, as to enable them to render a concert by heart. To begin with, it looks anything but well if the eyes of the singers are constantly fastened upon their books, and secondly a member may spoil everything through carelessness or improper attack.

And now if a conductor should query: How can I manage to train my singers that they will always strictly observe such rules? I would offer the following hint. Take a simple song for practice. Make a point of it that while a part is taken through with one section the others are already acquainting themselves with the text. When every section has been carefully rehearsed, and the song is about to be taken up by all, then insist upon having all eyes directed towards the conductor, and allow no one to cast his eyes persistently upon his book. If this is not followed out in every instance, stop and start again from the beginning.

At the start such severity might seem unwarranted and exaggerated. But finally the singers will get accustomed to it, and watch their conductor closely over their books.

The above will prove how mistaken it is to have the singers grouped around the conductor in a circle, the latter standing in the centre; everyone will admit that those who are placed behind the conductor's back cannot watch him as attentively as those placed in front of him.

4.) Some conductors will lead with one hand while holding the score in the other. This is not advisable. At times the conductor is obliged to lead with both hands, and if he executes his movements book in one hand and batôn in the other it is apt to create an unfavorable impression upon the audience. The conductor should always provide himself with a music-stand upon which to place his score, or otherwise memorize the composition so perfectly as to be able to do without music or text.

5.) Too rapid or nervous movements with the arm should be avoided, as the conductor must be careful not to be taken for a fencing-master. Stamping with the feet is to be entirely condemned. The conductor need have no reason for nervousness during a concert as long as the rehearsals thereto have been entirely satisfactory. To quote the words of a dear friend of mine : — "It must be possible to conduct a chorus with your thumb."

6.) It also creates a bad impression if the conductor sings along during a performance. If possible, he should refrain from doing so.

7.) All affected, offensive, or unnatural actions through which a conductor, either consciously or unconsciously might attract the attention of an audience, while conducting, must be avoided.

It is well known that the number of tenors is always smaller than that of bass singers, every singing society being able to boast of a larger number of basses than tenors. In order to preserve the voices of his tenors in good condition, the conductor should persuade them to refrain from smoking and drinking to excess ; at any rate, smoking should be entirely done away with during rehearsals, as the effect of tobacco smoke upon the voices is a decidedly bad one, the tenors in particular partaking somewhat of the bass character, through continuous inhalation of the smoke.

After every one of the voice-parts has been carefully rehearsed with the aid of a piano or violin, the entire chorus should proceed to sing without accompaniment.

No persons with poor or unmusical voices should be accepted as active members of a singing society.

The chorus should be placed in such positions that every individual singer can plainly see the conductor, and with special attention towards compact grouping of the different voices.

THE MILITARY BAND CONDUCTOR.

The conductor of a Military Band must be thoroughly acquainted with the elementary principles of his art, as well as harmony, transposition, etc., together with the individual usage of the various instruments which constitute the ensemble of his organization.

Above all, he must endeavor to obtain true and correct pitch, which is always such a difficult matter in a military band organization. He must also insist that all dynamic marks of expression, etc., which may be indicated in the score, be carefully observed and executed.

He must, furthermore, be very careful in the selection of compositions which he wishes to have performed ; in this respect everything depends upon the musical taste of the conductor. In the majority of cases it were best if every conductor could arrange his scores, for his particular combination, himself ; but wherever this cannot be accomplished, only works and arrangements of recognized authorities should be chosen.

Many of the hints as well as much of the advice contained in the article " *The Orchestral Conductor* " are of equally practical value in this particular field. In amateur bands it is of frequent occurrence that the brass instrument-players produce their notes more through forcing, than through a free and unrestrained action of the tongue; this disgusting tone-production must never be tolerated; the execution upon an instrument becomes heavy and clumsy, and every performance is marred thereby.

The conductor must also remind his men to keep their instruments in a neat and clean condition. Even the water which accumulates in the tubing, if not regularly withdrawn, will affect the tone in a disagreeable way.

It is also most necessary that all members pay close attention to the conductor's batôn.

No definite rules can be given as to the grouping of the men; it must be left to the judgment of the conductor to place his men in such positions as will enable their performance to sound to best advantage, and as in every other particular branch, practical experience will ultimately aid in indicating the best grouping of his forces.

ADDENDA.

COMPLETE ARRANGEMENT OF THE ANDANTE AND FIRST VARIATION FOR STRING QUINTETTE.

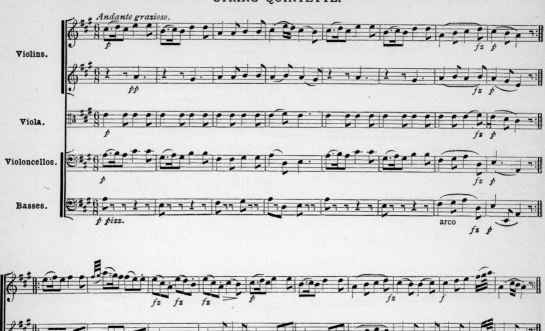

3. THE FLUTE D'AMOUR.

This member of the Flute family is met with now-a-days only on very rare occasions. It is a transposing instrument, its notes sounding a minor third lower than written. It was frequently employed by the writers of Bach's time, and the tonal quality of the instrument is said to have been very tender and full.

4. THE FLAGEOLET.

This instrument is a remnant of the old Flute-á-bec. In shape it resembles a present-day Flute, but in playing it is held away from the body like the Oboe. The tone is easily produced, for the instrument is fitted with a mouth piece resembling that on a child's whistle.

Its notation is in the violin clef, and it is a transposing instrument, sounding a fifth higher. Its compass is as follows:

A complete method has been published for this instrument by Bousquet, and a duet for two Flageolets, "La Favettes," by the same author is very popular and frequently played on two Piccolos.

Little use has been made of it as an orchestral instrument. Mozart used it to good advantage in his opera "Entführung aus dem Serail" (Seraglio) but at present it is only played by amateurs.

6. THE OBOE D'AMORE.

This style of Oboe has become almost obsolete. It might be described as a Mezzo-Soprano Oboe, although in shape it was larger, its pitch deeper, and its tone of different quality and fuller than the original Oboe. It was provided with a hollow globular bell, through which a veiled and pathetic quality was imparted to the tone. Its range exceeded two octaves. It was pitched a minor third lower than the Oboe as follows:

It is frequently met with in the works of J. S. Bach, who employed it mostly in sharp Keys. Prominent examples of its use may be found in his Cantata No. 8, St. Matthew Passion, Magnificat in D, and Christmas Oratorio. As an instance of the modern use of this instrument it may be cited that Rich. Strauss has written a part for it in his "Symphonia Domestica." Notwithstanding the fact that so prominent a composer should interest himself in this instrument it is difficult to say whether or not it will come into general use again.

7. THE OBOE DI CACCIA.

This instrument, almost obsolete at the present time, resembled the English Horn, but was less perfect in construction. It was pitched in F and its compass was as follows:

In the opening of Bach's Christmas Oratorio Part I. this instrument is used to excellent advantage in a combination of two Oboes d'Amore and two Oboes di Caccia with the strings.

SPECIAL REMARKS REFERRING TO CHART OF NOTATION AND TONAL COMPASS OF ALL THE BRASS INSTRUMENTS, Page 224.

In American Military Band arrangements, the Baritone or Euphonion is always provided with a part written in the Treble Clef, in which case it reads like a B flat Cornet part, but actually sounds a Major Ninth lower.

In English Military Band arrangements the Euphonion is scored in the Bass Clef as a non-transposing instrument, and the B flat Baritone in the Treble Clef, sounding a Major Ninth lower.

In Military Band arrangements the Ophicleide is frequently scored as a transposing instrument, but for Orchestral scoring this has not been followed, the performer being required to transpose in order to produce the *real tones*.

The very lowest or pedal notes of the various Tubas as marked on page 222 are difficult to produce and weak in sound. In some European countries (Belgium and France) all Tubas but the one in C, are written for as transposing instruments, the music, however, being scored for in the Bass Clef.

THE

Orchestral Conductor

THEORY OF HIS ART

BY

HECTOR BERLIOZ.

EIGHTH EDITION

CARL FISCHER, Inc.

COOPER SQUARE, NEW YORK

1929

THE ORCHESTRAL CONDUCTOR.

THEORY OF HIS ART.

By HECTOR BERLIOZ.

MUSIC appears to be the most exacting of all the Arts, the cultivation of which presents the greatest difficulties, for a consummate interpretation of a musical work so as to permit an appreciation of its real value, a clear view of its physiognomy, or discernment of its real meaning and true character, is only achieved in relatively few cases. Of creative artists, the composer is almost the only one who is dependent upon a multitude of intermediate agents between the public and himself; intermediate agents, either intelligent or stupid, devoted or hostile, active or inert, capable — from first to last — of contributing to the brilliancy of his work, or of disfiguring it, misrepresenting it, and even destroying it completely.

Singers have often been accused of forming the most dangerous of these intermediate agents; but in my opinion, without justice. The most formidable, to my thinking, is the conductor of the orchestra. A bad singer can spoil only his own part; while an incapable or malevolent conductor ruins all. Happy indeed may the composer esteem himself when the conductor into whose hands he has fallen is not at once incapable and inimical; for nothing can resist the pernicious influence of this person. The most admirable orchestra is then paralyzed, the most excellent singers are perplexed and rendered dull; there is no longer any vigor or unity; under such direction the noblest daring of the author appears extravagant, enthusiasm beholds its soaring flight checked, inspiration is violently brought down to earth, the angel's wings are broken, the man of genius passes for a madman or an idiot, the divine statue is precipitated from its pedestal, and dragged in the mud. And what is worse, the public, and even auditors endowed with the highest musical intelligence, are reduced to the impossibility (if a new work is rendered, and they are hearing it for the first time) of recognizing the ravages perpetrated by the orchestral conductor — of discovering the follies, faults, and crimes he commits. If they clearly perceive certain defects of execution, not he, but his victims, are in such cases made responsible. If he has caused the chorus-singers to fail in taking up a point in a finale, if he has allowed a discordant wavering to take place between the choir and the orchestra, or between the extreme sides of the instrumental body, if he has absurdly hurried a movement, or allowed it to linger unduly, if he has interrupted a singer before the end of a phrase, they exclaim : " The singers are detestable ! The orchestra has no firmness; the violins have disfigured the principal design; everybody has been wanting in vigor and animation; the tenor was quite out, he did not know his part; the harmony is confused; the author is no accompanist; the voices are —— " etc.

Except in listening to great works already known and esteemed, intelligent hearers can hardly distinguish the true culprit, and allot to him his due share of blame; but the number of these is still so limited that their judgment has little weight; and the hostile conductor — in presence of the public who would pitilessly hiss a *vocal accident* of a good singer — reigns, with all the calm of a bad conscience,

1

in his baseness and inefficiency. Fortunately, I here attack an exception ; for the malevolent orchestral conductor — whether capable or not — is very rare.

The orchestral conductor full of goodwill, but incapable, is on the contrary very common. Without speaking of innumerable mediocrities, directing artists who frequently are much their superiors, an author for example, can scarcely be accused of conspiring against his own works. Yet how many are there who, fancying they are able to conduct, innocently injure their best scores !

Beethoven, it is said, more than once ruined the performance of his symphonies; which he would conduct, even at the time when his deafness had become almost complete. The musicians, in order to keep together, agreed at length to follow the slight indications of time which the concertmeister (first violin-player) gave them ; and not to attend to Beethoven's conducting-stick. Moreover, it should be observed, that conducting a symphony, an overture, or any other composition whose movements remain continual, vary little, and contain few nice gradations, is child's play in comparison with conducting an opera, or like work, where there are recitatives, airs, and numerous orchestral designs preceded by pauses of irregular length.

The example of Beethoven, which I have just cited, leads me at once to say that if the direction of an orchestra appears to be very difficult for a blind man, it is indisputably impossible for a deaf one, whatever may have been his technical talent before losing his sense of hearing.

The orchestral conductor should *see* and *hear ;* he should be *active* and *vigorous*, should know the *composition* and the *nature* and *compass* of the instruments, should be able to *read* the score, and possess — besides the especial talent of which we shall presently endeavor to explain the constituent qualities — other indefinable gifts, without which an invisible link cannot establish itself between him and those he directs ; otherwise the faculty of transmitting to them his feeling is denied him, and power, empire, and guiding influence completely fail him. He is then no longer a conductor, a director, but a simple beater of the time, — supposing he knows how to beat it, and divide it, regularly.

The performers should feel that he feels, comprehends, and is moved : then his emotion communicates itself to those whom he directs, his inward fire warms them, his electric glow animates them, his force of impulse excites them ; he throws around him the vital irradiations of musical art. If he is inert and frozen, on the contrary, he paralyzes all about him, like those floating masses of the polar seas, the approach of which is perceived through the sudden cooling of the atmosphere.

His task is a complicated one. He has not only to conduct, in the spirit of the author's intentions, a work with which the performers have already become acquainted, but he must also introduce new compositions and help the performers to master them. He has to criticise the errors and defects of each during the rehearsals, and to organize the resources at his disposal in such a way as to make the best use he can of them with the utmost promptitude ; for, in the majority of European cities nowadays, musical artisanship is so ill distributed, performers so ill paid and the necessity of study so little understood, that *economy of time* should be reckoned among the most imperative requisites of the orchestral conductor's art.

Let us now see what constitutes the mechanical part of this art.

The power of *beating the time*, without demanding very high musical attainments, is nevertheless sufficiently difficult to secure ; and very few persons really possess it. The signs that the conductor should make — although generally very simple — nevertheless become complicated under certain circumstances, by the division and even the subdivision of the time of the bar.

The conductor is, above all, bound to possess a clear idea of the principal points and character of the work of which he is about to superintend the performance or study ; in order that he may, without hesitation or mistake, at once determine the time of each movement desired by the composer. If he has not had the opportunity of receiving his instructions directly from the composer, or if the *times* have not been transmitted to him by tradition, he must have recourse to the indications of the metronome, and study them well ; the majority of composers, nowadays, taking the precaution to write them at the beginning, and in the course, of their pieces. I do not mean to say by this that it is necessary to imitate the mathematical regularity of the metronome , all music so performed would become of freezing stiffness, and I even doubt whether it would be possible to observe so flat a uniformity during a certain number of bars. But the metronome is none the less excellent to consult in order to know the original time, and its chief alterations.

If the conductor possess neither the author's instructions, tradition, nor metronome indications, — which frequently happens in the ancient masterpieces, written at a period when the metronome was not invented, — he has no other guide than the vague terms employed to designate the time to be taken, and his own instinct, his feeling — more or less distinguishing, more or less just — of the author's style. We are compelled to admit that these guides are too often insufficient and delusive. Of this we have proof in seeing how old operas are given in towns where the traditional mode of performance no longer exists. In ten different kinds of time, there will always be at least four taken wrongly. I once heard a chorus of *Iphigenia in Tauride* performed in a German theatre *allegro assai, two in the bar*, instead of *allegro non troppo, four in the bar ;* that is to say, exactly twice too fast. Examples might be multiplied of such disasters, occasioned either by the ignorance or the carelessness of conductors of orchestras ; or else by the real difficulty which exists for even the best-gifted and most careful men to discover the precise meaning of the Italian terms used as indications of the time to be taken. Of course, no one can be at a loss to distinguish a Largo from a Presto. If the Presto be two in a bar, a tolerably sagacious conductor, from inspection of the passages and melodic designs contained in the piece, will be able to discern the degree of quickness intended by the author. But if the Largo be four in a bar, of simple melodic structure, and containing but few notes in each bar, what means has the hapless conductor of discovering the true time ? And in how many ways might he not be deceived ? The different degrees of slowness that might be assigned to the performance of such a Largo are very numerous ; the individual feeling of the orchestral conductor must then become the sole authority ; and, after all, it is the author's feeling, not his, which is in question. Composers therefore ought not to neglect placing metronome indications in their works ; and orchestral conductors are bound to study them closely. The neglect of this study on the part of the latter, is an act of dishonesty.

I will now suppose the conductor to be perfectly well acquainted with the times of the different movements in the work of which he is about to conduct the performance or rehearsals ; he wishes to impart to the musicians acting under his orders the rhythmical feeling within him, to decide the duration of each bar, and to cause the uniform observance of this duration by all the performers. Now this precision and this uniformity can only be established in the more or less numerous assemblage of band and chorus by means of certain signs made by their conductor.

These signs indicate the principle divisions, the accents of the bar, and, in many cases, the subdivisions, and the half-accents. I need hardly here explain what is meant by the " accents " (accented and unaccented parts of a bar) ; I am presupposing that I address musicians.

The orchestral conductor generally uses a small light stick, of about a foot in length, and rather whitish than of a dark color (it is seen better), which he holds in his right hand, to make clearly distinct his mode of marking the commencement, the interior division, and the close of each bar. The bow, employed by some violinist-conductors (leaders), is less suitable than the stick. It is somewhat flexible, and this want of rigidity, together with the slight resistance it offers to the air, on account of its appendage of hair, renders its indications less precise.

The simplest of all times — two in a bar — is beaten simply.

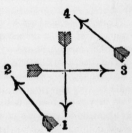

The arm and the stick of the conductor are raised, so that his hand is on a level with his head, he marks the first beat, by dropping the point of his stick perpendicularly (*bending his wrist* as much as possible; and not lowering the whole arm), and the second beat by raising the stick by a contrary gesture.

The time — one in a bar — being in reality, and particularly for the conductor, but the time of an extremely rapid two in a bar, should be beaten like the preceding. As the conductor is obliged to raise the point of his stick, after having lowered it, he necessarily divides this into two portions.

In the time — four in a bar — the first gesture, or down beat, is universally adopted for marking the first accented part, the commencement of the bar.

The second movement made by the conducting-stick, from right to left, rising, indicates the second beat (first unaccented part). A third, transversely, from left to right, (second accented part); and indicates the third a fourth, obliquely, from down to up, indicates the fourth beat (second unaccented part). The combination of these four gestures may be figured thus : —

It is of importance that the conductor, in thus delivering his different directions, should not move his arm much ; and consequently, not allow his stick to pass over much space ; for each of these gestures should operate nearly instantaneously ; or at least, take but so slight a movement as to be imperceptible. If the movement becomes perceptible, on the contrary, and multiplied by the number of times that the gesture is repeated, it ends by throwing the conductor behind in the time he is beating, and by giving to his conducting a tardiness that proves injurious. This defect, moreover, has the result of needlessly fatiguing the conductor, and of producing exaggerated evolutions, verging on the ridiculous, which attract the spectators' attention, and become very disagreeable to witness.

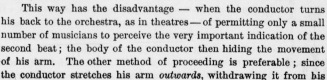

In the time, three in a bar, the first gesture made, from up to down, is likewise universally adopted for marking the first beat ; but there are two ways of marking the second. The majority of orchestral conductors indicate it by a gesture from left to right ; thus : —

Some German Kapel-meisters do the contrary ; and carry the stick from right to left ; thus : —

This way has the disadvantage — when the conductor turns his back to the orchestra, as in theatres — of permitting only a small number of musicians to perceive the very important indication of the second beat ; the body of the conductor then hiding the movement of his arm. The other method of proceeding is preferable ; since the conductor stretches his arm *outwards*, withdrawing it from his chest ; and his stick, which he takes care to raise slightly above the level of his shoulder, remains perfectly visible to all eyes. When the conductor faces the players, it is immaterial whether he marks the second beat to the right, or to the left.

However, the third beat of the time, three in a bar, is always marked like the last of the time, four in a bar ; by an oblique movement upwards.

The times, — five and seven in a bar, — would be more comprehensible for the performers, if instead of indicating them by a particular series of gestures, they were treated as though the one was composed of three and two in a bar, and the other composed of four and three.

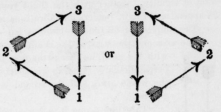

Then, these times would be beaten thus : —

Example of seven in a bar : —

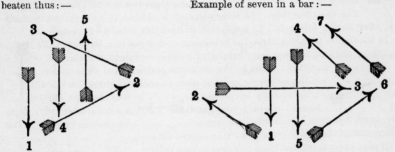

These different times, in order to be divided in this way, are assumed to belong to movements of moderate measure. The advice would not hold good if their measure were either very quick or very slow.

The time, two in a bar, I have already signified, cannot be beaten otherwise than as we have before seen—whatever its degree of rapidity. But if, as an exception, it should be very slow, the conductor ought to subdivide it.

A very rapid four in a bar, on the contrary, should be beaten two in a bar ; the four accustomed gestures of a moderate movement becoming then so hurried as to present nothing decided to the eye, and serving only to confuse the performer instead of giving him confidence. Moreover, — and this is of much more consequence, — the conductor, by uselessly making these four gestures in a quick movement, renders the pace of the rhythm awkward, and loses the freedom of gesture which a simple division of the time into its half would leave him.

Generally speaking, composers are wrong to write in such a case the indication of the time as four in a bar. When the movement is very brisk, they should never write any other than the sign 𝄵, and not that of 𝄴, which might lead the conductor into error.

It is exactly the same for the time, three in a bar, fast ¾ or ⅜. Then the conductor must omit the gesture of the second beat, and, by remaining the period of a beat longer on the first, only raise the stick at the third.

It would be absurd to attempt to beat the three in a bar of one of Beethoven's scherzos.

In slow movements the rule for these two times is like that for two in a bar. If the movement is very slow, each time must be divided ;

and consequently eight gestures must be made for the time, four in a bar, and six for the time, three in a bar, repeating (and shortening) each of the principal gestures we have before instanced.

Example of four in a bar, very slow :

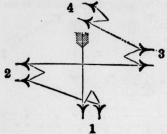

Example of three in a bar, very slow :

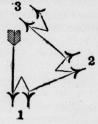

The arm should take no part in the little supplementary gesture indicating the subdivision of the bar ; merely the wrist causing the stick to move.

This division of the different times is intended to prevent the rhythmical divergences which might easily take place among the performers during the interval which separates one beat from the other. The conductor not indicating anything during this period (rendered somewhat considerable by the extreme slowness of the movement), the players are then entirely left to themselves, *without conductor;* and as the rhythmical feeling is not the same with all, it follows that some hurry, while others slacken, and unity is soon destroyed. The only exception possible to this rule is that of a first-rate orchestra, composed of performers who are well acquainted with each other, are accustomed to play together, and know almost by heart the work they are executing. Even then, the inattention of a single player may occasion an accident. Why incur its possibility ? I know that certain artists feel their self-love hurt when thus kept in leading-strings (like children, they say) ; but with a conductor who has no other view than the excellence of the ultimate result, this consideration can have no weight. Even in a quartet, it is seldom that the individual feeling of the players can be left entirely free to follow its own dictates. In a symphony, that of the conductor must rule. The art of comprehending it, and fulfilling it with unanimity, constitutes the perfection of execution ; and individual wills — which can never agree one with another — should never be permitted to manifest themselves.

This being fully understood, it will be seen that subdivision is still more essential for very slow times ; as those of $\frac{6}{4}$, $\frac{6}{8}$, $\frac{9}{8}$, $\frac{12}{8}$ etc.

But these times — where the triple rhythm plays so important a part — may be divided in various ways.

If the movement is brisk or moderate, it is rarely well to indicate other than the simple beats of these times, according to the procedure adopted for the analogous simple times.

The times of $\frac{6}{8}$ allegretto, and of $\frac{6}{4}$ allegro, therefore, are to be beaten like those of two in a bar : — ₵ = or 2 = or $\frac{2}{4}$; the time, $\frac{9}{8}$ allegro, should be beaten like that of three in a bar — $\frac{3}{4}$ moderato, or like that of $\frac{3}{8}$ andantino ; and the time, $\frac{12}{8}$ moderato or allegro, like the time, simple four in a bar. But if the movement be adagio, largo assai, or andante maestoso, either all the quavers, or a crotchet followed by a quaver, should be beaten, according to the form of the melody, or the predominant design.

Larghetto Grazioso.

It is unnecessary, in this three in a bar, to mark all the quavers ; the rhythm of a crotchet followed by a quaver in each beat suffices.

As to the subdivision, the little supplementary gesture for simple times should be made ; this subdivision will however separate each beat into two unequal portions, since it is requisite to indicate visibly the value of the crotchet, and that of the quaver.

If the movement is still slower, there can be no hesitation; the only way to ensure unity of execution is to beat all the quavers, whatever be the nature of the written bar.

Taking the three measures shown above in order, the conductor must beat three quavers down, and three up, for the time of $\frac{6}{8}$: —

Three down, three to the right, and three up, for the time of $\frac{9}{8}$: —

Three down, three to the left, three to the right, and three up, for the time of $\frac{12}{8}$: —

A dilemma sometimes presents itself when certain parts—for the sake of contrast—are given a triple rhythm, while others preserve the dual rhythm.

Wind
Instruments.

Violin.

If the wind-instrument parts in the above example are confided to players who are good musicians, there will be no need to change the manner of marking the bar, and the conductor may continue to subdivide it by six, or to divide it simply by two. The majority of players, however, seeming to hesitate at the moment when, by employing the syncopated form, the triple rhythm clashes with the dual rhythm, require assurance, which can be given by easy means. The uncertainty occasioned them by the sudden appearance of the unexpected rhythm, contradicted by the rest of the orchestra, always leads the performers to cast an instinctive glance towards the conductor, as if seeking his assistance. He should look at them, turning somewhat towards them, and marking the triple rhythm by very slight gestures, as if the time were really three in a bar, but in such a way that the violins and other instruments playing in dual rhythm may not observe the change, which would quite put them out. From this compromise it results that the new rhythm of three-time, being marked furtively by the conductor, is executed with steadiness ; while the two-time rhythm, already firmly established, continues without difficulty, although no longer indicated by the conductor. On the other hand, nothing, in my opinion can be more blamable, or more contrary to musical good sense, than the application of this procedure to passages where two rhythms of opposite nature do not co-exist, and where merely syncopations are introduced. The conductor, dividing the bar by *the number of accents he finds contained in it,* then destroys (for all the auditors who see him) the effect of syncopation ; and substitutes a mere change of time for a play of rhythm of the most bewitching interest. If the accents are marked, instead of the beats, in the following passage from Beethoven's Pastoral Symphony, we have the subjoined : —

whereas the four previously maintained display the syncopation and make it better felt : —

This voluntary submission to a rhythmical form *which the author intended to thwart* is one of the gravest faults in style that a beater of the time can commit.

There is another dilemma, extremely troublesome for a conductor, and demanding all his presence of mind. It is that presented by the super-addition of different bars. It is easy to conduct a bar in dual time placed above or beneath another bar in triple time, if both have the same kind of movement. Their chief divisions are then equal in duration, and one needs only to divide them in half, marking the two principal beats : —

But if, in the middle of a piece slow in movement, there is introduced a new form brisk in movement, and if the composer (either for the sake of facilitating the execution of the quick movement, or because it was impossible to write otherwise) has

adopted for this new movement the short bar which corresponds with it, there may then occur two, or even three short bars super-added to a slow bar : —

No. 1. No. 2.

Three bars to one. No. 3.

The conductor's task is to guide and keep together these different bars of unequal number and dissimilar movement. He attains this by dividing the beats in the an-

Bar No. 1.

dante bar, No. 1, which precedes the entrance of the allegro in ⁶⁄₈, and by continuing to divide them; but taking care to mark the division more decidedly. The players of the allegro in ⁶⁄₈ then comprehend that the two gestures of the conductor represent the two beats of

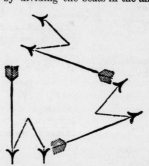

Bars Nos. 2, 3, and so on.

their short bar, while the players of the andante take these same gestures merely for a divided beat of their long bar.

It will be seen that this is really quite simple, because the division of the short bar, and the subdivisions of the long one, mutually correspond. The following example, where a slow bar is super-added to the short ones, without this correspondence existing, is more awkward : —

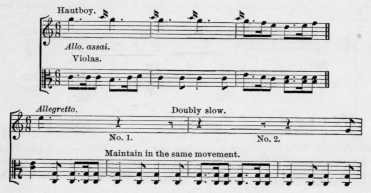

No. 1. No. 2.

Maintain in the same movement.

Here, the three bars allegro-assai preceding the allegretto are beaten in simple two time, as usual. At the moment when the allegretto begins, the bar of which is double that of the preceding, and of the one maintained by the violas, the conductor marks *two divided beats* for the long bar, by two equal gestures down, and two others up : —

The two large gestures divide the long bar in half, and explain its value to the hautboys, without perplexing the violas, who maintain the brisk movement, on account of the little gesture which also divides in half their short bar.

From bar No. 3, the conductor ceases to divide thus the long bar by 4, on account of the triple rhythm of the melody in ⅜, which this gesture interferes with. He then confines himself to marking the two beats of the long bar ; while the violas, already launched in their rapid rhythm, continue it without difficulty, comprehending exactly that each stroke of the conductor's stick marks merely *the commencement* of their short bar.

This last observation shows with what care dividing the beats of a bar should be avoided when a portion of the instruments or voices has to execute triplets upon these beats. The division, by cutting in half the second note of the triplet, renders its execution uncertain. It is even necessary to abstain from this division of the beats of a bar just before the moment when the rhythmical or melodic design is divided by three, in order not to give to the players the impression of a rhythm contrary to that which they are about to hear : —

In this example, the subdivision of the bar into six, or the division of beats into two, is useful; and offers no inconvenience *during bar No. 1,* when the following gesture is made : —

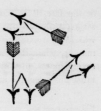

But from the beginning of bar No. 2 it is necessary to make only the simple gestures : —
on account of the triplet on the third beat, and on account of the one following it which the double gesture would much interfere with.

In the famous ball-scene of Mozart's *Don Giovanni,* the difficulty of keeping together the three orchestras, written in three different measures, is less than might be thought. It is sufficient to mark downwards each beat of the *tempo di minuetto* : —

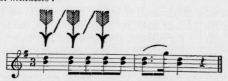

Once entered upon the combination, the little allegro in ⅜, of which a whole bar represents one-third, or one beat of that of the minuetto, and the other allegro in ¾, of which a whole bar represents two-thirds, or two beats, correspond with each other and with the principal theme; while the whole proceeds without the slightest confusion. All that is requisite is to make them come in properly.

A gross fault that I have seen committed, consists in enlarging the time of a piece in common-time, when the author has introduced into it triplets of minims : —

In such a case, the third minim adds nothing to the duration of the bar, as some conductors seem to imagine. They may, if they please, and if the movement be slow or moderate, make these passages by beating the bar with three beats, but the duration of the whole bar should remain precisely the same. In a case where these triplets occur in a very quick bar in common-time (allegro-assai), the three gestures then cause confusion, and it is absolutely necessary to make only two, — one beat upon the first minim, and one upon the third. These gestures, owing to the quickness of the movement, differ little to the eye, from the two of the bar with two equal beats, and do not affect the movement of those parts of the orchestra which contain no triplets.

We will now speak of the conductor's method of beating in recitatives. Here, as the singer or the instrumentalist is reciting, and no longer subject to the regular division of the bar, it is requisite, while following him attentively, to make the orchestra strike, simultaneously and with precision, the chords or instrumental passages with which the recitative is intermingled ; and to make the harmony change at the proper instant, when the recitative is accompanied either by holding-notes or by a tremolo in several parts, of which the least apparent, occasionally, is that which the conductor must most regard, since upon its motion depends the change of chord : —

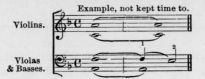

In this example, the conductor, while following the reciting part, not kept time to, has especially to attend to the viola part, and to make it move, at the proper moment, from the F to the E, at the commencement of the second bar ; because otherwise, as this part is executed by several instrumentalists playing in unison, some of them would hold the F longer than the rest, and a transient discord would be produced.

Many conductors have the habit, when directing the orchestra in recitatives, of paying no heed to the written division of the bar, and of marking an up beat before that whereon a brief orchestral chord occurs, even when this chord comes on an unaccented part of the bar : —

In a passage such as this, they raise the arm at the rest which commences the bar, and lower it at the time of the chord.

I cannot approve of such a method, which nothing justifies, and which may frequently occasion accidents in the execution. Neither do I see why, in recitatives, the bar should not be divided regularly, and the real beats marked in their place, as in music beaten in time. I therefore advise — for the preceding example — that the first beat should be made down, as usual, and the stick carried to the left for striking the chord upon the second beat ; and so on for analogous cases ; always dividing the bar regularly. It is very important, moreover, to divide it according to the time previously indicated by the author, and not to forget, — if this time is *allegro* or *maestoso*, and if the reciting part has been some time reciting unaccompanied, — to give to all the beats, when the orchestra comes in again, the value of those of an allegro or of a maestoso. For when the orchestra plays alone, it does so generally in time ; it plays without measured time only when it accompanies a voice or instrument in recitative.

In the exceptional case where the recitative is written for the orchestra itself, or for the chorus, or for a portion of either orchestra or chorus, it being then requisite to keep together, whether in unison or in harmony, but without regular time, a certain number of performers, *the conductor himself becomes the real reciter*, and gives to each beat of the bar the duration he judges fit. According to the form of the phrase, he divides and subdivides the beats, now marks the accents, now the semiquavers, if there are any, and, in short, indicates with his stick the melodic form of the recitative.

It must of course be understood that the performers, knowing their parts almost by heart, keep their eye constantly upon him, otherwise, neither security nor unity can be obtained.

In general, even for timed music, the conductor should require the players he directs to look towards him as often as possible.

An orchestra which does not watch the conducting-stick has no conductor. Often, after a pedal-point for instance, the conductor is obliged to refrain from marking the decisive gesture which is to determine the coming in of the orchestra until he sees the eyes of all the performers fixed upon him. It is the duty of the conductor, during rehearsal, to accustom them to look towards him simultaneously at the important moment.

If the rule just indicated were not observed in the above bar, of which the first beat, marking a pedal-point, may be prolonged indefinitely, the passage —

could not be uttered with firmness and unity ; the players, not watching the conductor's stick, could not know when he decides the second beat and resumes the movement suspended by the pedal-point.

The obligation upon the performers to look at their conductor necessarily implies an equal obligation on his part to let himself be well seen by them. He should, — whatever may be the disposal of the orchestra, whether on rows of steps, or on a horizontal plane, — place himself so as to form the centre of all surrounding eyes.

To place himself well in sight, a conductor requires an especial platform, elevated in proportion as the number of performers is large and occupies much space. His desk should not be so high that the portion sustaining the score shall hide his face for the expression of his countenance has much to do with the influence he exercises If there is no conductor for an orchestra that does not and will not watch him, neither is there any if he cannot be well seen.

As to the employment of noises of any kind whatever, produced by the stick of the conductor upon his desk, or by his foot upon the platform, they call for no other than unreserved reprehension. It is worse than a bad method ; it is a barbarism. In a theatre, however, when the stage evolutions prevent the chorus-singers from seeing the conducting-stick, the conductor is compelled — to ensure, after a pause, the taking up a point by the chorus — to indicate this point by marking the beat which precedes it by a slight tap of his stick upon the desk. This exceptional circumstance is the only one which can warrant the employment of an *indicating noise*, and even then it is to be regretted that recourse must be had to it.

While speaking of chorus-singers, and of their operations in theatres, it may here be observed that chorus-masters often allow themselves to beat time at the side-scenes, without seeing the conductor's stick, frequently even without hearing the orchestra. The result is that this time, beaten more or less ill, and not corresponding with that of the conductor, inevitably induces a rhythmical discordance between the choral and instrumental bodies, and subverts all unity instead of tending to maintain it.

There is another traditional barbarism which lies within the province of an intelligent and active conductor to abolish. If a choral or instrumental piece is performed behind the scenes, without accompaniment from the principal orchestra, another con-

ductor is absolutely essential. If the orchestra accompany this portion, the first conductor, who hears the distant music, is then strictly bound to *let himself be guided* by
the second, and to follow his time *by ear.* But if — as frequently happens in modern
music — the sound of the chief orchestra hinders the conductor from hearing that
which is being performed at a distance from him, the intervention of a special conducting mechanism becomes indispensable, in order to establish instantaneous communication between him and the distant performers. Many attempts, more or less ingenious,
have been made of this kind, the result of which has not everywhere answered expectations. That of Covent Garden Theatre, in London, moved by the conductor's
foot, acts tolerably well. But the *electric metronome*, set up by Mr. Van Bruge in the
Brussels Theatre, leaves nothing to be desired. It consists of an apparatus of copper
ribbons, leading from a Voltaic battery placed beneath the stage, attached to the conductor's desk, and terminating in a movable stick fastened at one end on a pivot before
a board at a certain distance from the orchestral conductor. To this latter's desk is
affixed a key of copper, something like the ivory key of a pianoforte ; it is elastic, and
provided on the interior side with a protuberance of about a quarter of an inch long.
Immediately beneath this protuberance is a little cup, also of copper, filled with quicksilver. At the instant when the orchestral conductor, desiring to mark any particular
beat of a bar, presses the copper key with the forefinger of his left hand (his right
being occupied in holding, as usual, the conducting-stick) this key is lowered, the protuberance passes into the cup filled with quicksilver, a slight electric spark is emitted,
and the stick placed at the other extremity of the copper ribbon makes an oscillation
before its board. The communication of the fluid and the movement are quite simultaneous, no matter how great a distance is traversed.

The performers being grouped behind the scenes, their eyes fixed upon the stick
of the electric metronome, are thus directly subject to the conductor, who could,
were it needful, conduct, from the middle of the Opera orchestra in Paris, a piece of
music performed at Versailles.

It is merely requisite to agree upon beforehand with the chorus-singers, or with
their conductor (if as an additional precaution, they have one), the way in which the
orchestral conductor beats the time — whether he marks all the principal beats, or
only the first of the bar — since the oscillations of the stick, moved by electricity,
being always from right to left, indicate nothing precise in this respect.

When I first used, at Brussels, the valuable instrument I have just endeavored to
describe, its action presented one objection. Each time that the copper key of my
desk underwent the pressure of my left forefinger, it struck, underneath, another
plate of copper, and, notwithstanding the delicacy of the contact, produced a little
sharp noise, which, during the pauses of the orchestra, attracted the attention of the
audience, to the detriment of the musical effect.

I pointed out the fault to Mr. Van Bruge, who substituted for the lower plate
of copper the little cup filled with quicksilver, previously mentioned. Into this the
protuberance so entered as to establish the electric current without causing the
slightest noise.

Nothing remains now, as regards the use of this mechanism, but the crackling
of the spark at the moment of its emission. This, however, is too slight to be heard
by the public.

The metronome is not expensive to put up ; it costs £16 at the most. Large lyric
theatres, churches, and concert-rooms should long ago have been provided with one.
Yet, save at the Brussels Theatre, it is nowhere to be found. This would appear
incredible, were it not that the carelessness of the majority of directors of institutions

where music forms a feature is well known; as are their instinctive aversion to whatever disturbs old-established customs, their indifference to the interests of art, their parsimony wherever an outlay for music is needed, and the utter ignorance of the principles of our art among those in whose hands rests the ordering of its destiny.

I have not yet said all on the subject of those dangerous auxiliaries named chorus-masters. Very few of them are sufficiently versed in the art, to conduct a musical performance, so that the orchestral conductor can depend upon them. He cannot therefore watch them too closely when compelled to submit to their coadjutorship.

The most to be dreaded are those whom age has deprived of activity and energy. The maintenance of vivacious times is an impossibility to them. Whatever may be the degree of quickness indicated at the head of a piece confided to their conducting, little by little they slacken its pace, until the rhythm is reduced to a certain medium slowness, that seems to harmonize with the speed at which their blood flows, and the general feebleness of their organization.

It must in truth be added, that old men are not the only ones with whom composers run this risk. There are men in the prime of life, of a lymphatic temperament, whose blood seems to circulate *moderato.* If they have to conduct an allegro assai, they gradually slacken it to *moderato;* if, on the contrary, it is a largo or an andante sostenuto, provided the piece is prolonged, they will, by dint of progressive animation, attain a *moderato* long before the end. The *moderato* is their natural pace, and they recur to it as infallibly as would a pendulum after having been a moment hurried or slackened in its oscillations.

These people are the born enemies of all characteristic music, and the greatest destroyers of style. May Fate preserve the orchestral conductor from their co-operation.

Once, in a large town (which I will not name), there was to be performed behind the scenes a very simple chorus, written in $\frac{6}{8}$, allegretto. The aid of the chorus-master became necessary. He was an old man.

The time in which this chorus was to be taken having been first agreed upon by the orchestra, our Nestor followed it pretty decently during the first few bars; but, soon after, the slackening became such that there was no continuing without rendering the piece perfectly ridiculous. It was recommenced twice, thrice, four times; a full half-hour was occupied in ever-increasingly vexatious efforts, but always with the same result. The preservation of allegretto time was absolutely impossible to the worthy man. At last the orchestral conductor, out of all patience, came and begged him not to conduct at all; he had hit upon an expedient : — He caused the chorus-singers to simulate a march-movement, raising each foot alternately, without moving on. This movement, being in exactly the same time as the dual rhythm of the $\frac{6}{8}$ in a bar, allegretto, the chorus-singers, who were no longer hindered by their director, at once performed the piece as though they had sung marching; with no less unity than regularity, and without slackening the time.

I acknowledge, however, that many chorus-masters, or sub-conductors of orchestras, are sometimes of real utility, and even indispensable for the maintenance of unity among very large masses of performers. When these masses are obliged to be so disposed as that one portion of the players or chorus-singers turn their back on the conductor, he needs a certain number of sub-beaters of the time, placed before those of the performers who cannot see him, and charged with repeating all his signals. In order that this repetition shall be precise, the sub-conductors must be careful never to take their eyes off the chief conductor's stick for a single instant.

If, in order to look at their score, they cease to watch him for only three bars, a discrepancy arises immediately between their time and his, and all is lost.

In a festival where 1200 performers were assembled under my direction, at Paris, I had to employ four chorus-masters, stationed at the four corners of the vocal mass, and two sub-conductors, one of whom directed the wind-instruments, and the other the instruments of percussion. I had earnestly besought them to look towards me incessantly; they did not omit to do so, and our eight sticks, rising and falling without the slightest discrepancy of rhythm, established amidst our 1200 performers the most perfect unity ever witnessed.

With one or more electric metronomes, it seems no longer necessary to have recourse to this means. One might, in fact, thus easily conduct chorus-singers who turn their back towards the chief conductor; but attentive and intelligent sub-conductors are always preferable to a machine. They have not only to beat the time, like the metronomic staff, but they have also to speak to the groups around them, to call their attention to nice shades of execution, and, after bar-rests, to remind them when the moment of their re-entry comes.

In a space arranged as a semicircular amphitheatre, the orchestral conduct may conduct a considerable number of performers alone, all eyes then being able to look towards him. Nevertheless, the employment of a certain number of sub-conductors appears to me preferable to individual direction, on account of the great distance between the chief conductor and the extreme points of the vocal and instrumental body.

The more distant the orchestral conductor is from the performers he directs, the more his influence over them is diminished.

The best way would be to have several sub-conductors, with several electric metronomes beating before their eyes the principal beats of the bar.

And now, — should the orchestral conductor give the time standing or sitting down?

If, in theatres where they perform scores of immense length, it is very difficult to endure the fatigue of remaining on foot the whole evening, it is none the less true that the orchestral conductor, when seated, loses a portion of his power, and cannot give free course to his animation, if he possess any.

Then, should he conduct reading from a full score, or from a first violin part (leader's copy), as is customary in some theatres? It is evident that he should have before him a full score. Conducting by means of a part containing only the principal instrumental cues, the bass and the melody, demands a needless effort of memory from a conductor; and moreover, if he happens to tell one of the performers, whose part he cannot examine, that he is wrong, exposes him to the chance of the reply: "How do you know?"

The disposal and grouping of the players and chorus-singers come also within the province of the orchestral conductor; particularly for concerts. It is impossible to indicate arbitrarily the best method of grouping the performers in a theatre or concert-room; the shape and arrangement of the interior of these places necessarily influence the course to be taken in such a case. Let us add, that it depends, moreover, upon the number of performers requiring to be grouped; and, on some occasions, upon the style of composition adopted by the author whose work is to be performed.

In general, for concerts, the following disposal of the orchestra seems best: — An amphitheatre of eight, or at least, five rows is indispensable. The semicircular form is the best for the amphitheatre. If it is large enough to contain the whole orchestra, the entire mass of instrumentalists can be disposed of along these rows, the first violins in front on the right, facing the public ; the second violins in front on the left ; the violas, in the middle, between the two groups of violins ; the flutes hautboys, clarinets, horns, and bassoons behind the first violins ; a double rank of violoncellos and double-basses behind the second violins ; the trumpets, cornets, trombones, and tubas behind the violas ; the rest of the violoncellos and double-basses behind the wooden wind instruments ; the harps in the foreground, close to the orchestral conductor ; the kettle-drums, and other instruments of percussion behind or in the centre of the brass instruments ; the orchestral conductor, turning his back to the public, at the base of the orchestra, and near to the foremost desks of the first and second violins.

There should be a horizontal flooring, or stage, more or less wide, extending in front of the first rows of the amphitheatre. On this flooring the chorus-singers should be placed, in form of a fan turned three-quarters towards the public, so that all shall be able easily to see the motions of the orchestral conductor. The grouping of the chorus-singers, in consonance with their respective order of voice, will differ according as the author has written in three, four, or six parts. At any rate, the women — sopranos and contraltos — should be in front, seated ; the tenors standing behind the contraltos ; and the basses standing behind the sopranos.

The solo-singers should occupy the centre, and foremost, part of the front stage, and should always place themselves in such a way as to be able, by slightly turning the head, to see the conducting-stick.

For the rest, I repeat, these indications can be but approximate ; they may be, for many reasons, modified in various ways.

At the Conservatoire, in Paris, where the amphitheatre is composed of only four or five rows, not circular, and cannot therefore contain the whole orchestra, the violins and violas are on the stage ; while the basses and wind instruments alone occupy the rows ; the chorus is seated on the front of the stage, facing the public, and the women, sopranos and contraltos, turning their backs directly upon the orchestral conductor, are utterly unable to see his motions. The arrangement is very inconvenient for this portion of the chorus.

It is of the greatest consequence that the chorus-singers placed on the front of the stage shall occupy a plane somewhat lower than that of the violins ; otherwise they would considerably deaden the sound of these instruments.

For the same reason, if there are no other rows for the choir in front of the orchestra, it is absolutely needful that the women should be seated, and the men remain standing up ; in order that the voices of the tenors and basses, proceeding from a more elevated point than those of the sopranos and contraltos, may come forth freely, and be neither stifled nor intercepted.

When the presence of the chorus-singers in front of the orchestra is not necessary, the conductor must take care to send them away ; since this large number of human bodies injures the sonority of the instruments. A symphony performed by an orchestra thus more or less stifled, loses much of its effect.

There are yet other precautions, relative especially to the orchestra, which the conductor may also take, to avoid certain defects in performance. The instruments of percussion, placed, as I have indicated, upon one of the last rows of the orchestra, have a tendency to modify the rhythm, and slacken the time. A series of strokes on the drum struck at regular intervals in a quick movement, like the following : —

will sometimes lead to the complete destruction of a fine rhythmical progression, by checking the onward bound of the rest of the orchestra, and destroying the unity. Almost always, the drum player, through not observing the original time given by the conductor, is somewhat behindhand in striking his first stroke. This retardment, multiplied by the number of strokes which follow the first one, soon produces — as may be imagined — a rhythmical discrepancy of the most fatal effect. The conductor, — all whose efforts to re-establish unanimity are then in vain — has only one thing left to do ; which is, to insist that the long drum player shall count beforehand the number of strokes to be given in the passage in question, and that, knowing his part, he shall no longer look at his copy, but keep his eyes constantly fixed upon the conducting-stick ; by which means he will follow the time without the slightest want of precision.

Another retardment, arising from a different cause, frequently takes place in the trumpet-parts ; it is when they contain a quick flow of passages such as this : —

The trumpet-player, instead of taking breath *before* the first of these three bars, takes breath at their commencement, during the quaver-rest, A ; and, not counting for anything the short time it has taken him to breathe, gives its whole value to the quaver-rest, which thus becomes superadded to the value of the first bar. The result of this is the following : —

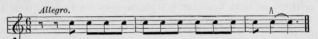

an effect all the worse because the final accent, struck at the commencement of the third bar by the rest of the orchestra, comes a third of the time too slow in the trumpets, and destroys unity in the striking of the last chord.

To obviate this, the conductor must first previously warn the players against such inexactness, into which they almost all are led to fall unawares ; and then, while conducting, must cast a glance towards them at the decisive moment, and *anticipate a little*, by beating the first beat of the bar where they come in. It is incredible how difficult it is to prevent trumpet-players from doubling the value of a quaver-rest thus placed.

When a long *accelerando, little by little*, is indicated by the composer, for passing from an allegro moderato to a presto, the majority of orchestral conductors hurry the time *by jerks*, instead of quickening it equally throughout, by an insensible onward rate. This should be carefully avoided.

The same remark applies to the converse proposition. It is even more difficult to slacken a quick time smoothly, and without checks, so as to transform it little by little into a slow time. Often, from a desire to testify zeal, or from defect of delivery in his musical feeling, a conductor demands from his players *an exaggeration of nice gradations*. He comprehends neither the character nor the style of the piece. The gradations then become so many blemishes ; the accents, yells ; the intentions of the poor composer are totally disfigured and perverted ; while those of the orchestral conductor — however politely meant they may be — are none the less injurious : like the caresses of the ass in the fable, who crushed his master while fondling him.

And now let us instance many deplorable abuses that are obtained in almost all

the orchestras of Europe — abuses which reduce composers to despair, and which it is
the duty of conductors to abolish as soon as possible.

Performers playing stringed instruments will rarely give themselves the trouble
to play a *tremolo;* they substitute for this very characteristic effect, a tame repetition
of the note, half, and sometimes three-quarters slower than the one whence results
the tremolo : instead of demisemiquavers, they make triple or double ones; and in
lieu of producing sixty-four notes in a bar in four-time (adagio), they produce only
thirty-two, or even sixteen.   The action of the arm necessary for producing a true
tremolo, demands from them too great an effort.   This idleness is intolerable.

Many double-bâss players permit themselves — from idleness, also, or from a
dread of being unable to achieve certain difficulties — to simplify their part.   This
race of simplifiers has existed for forty years; but it cannot endure any longer.   In
ancient works, the double-bass parts were extremely simple ; therefore there can be
no reason to impoverish them still more : those in modern scores are rather more
difficult, it is true ; but, with very few exceptions, there is nothing in them impossible
of execution ; composers, masters of their art, write them with care, and as they
ought to be executed.   If it is from idleness that the simplifiers pervert them, the
energetic orchestral conductor is armed with the necessary authority to compel the
fulfilment of their duty.   If it is from incapacity, let him dismiss them.   It is his
best interest to rid himself of instrumentalists who cannot play their instrument.

Flute-players, accustomed to having their parts written in the upper octave, and
not admitting that their part can be written below that of clarinets or hautboys, frequently transpose entire passages an octave higher.   The conductor, if he does not
carefully peruse his score, if he is not thoroughly acquainted with the work he is conducting, or if his ear lacks keenness, will not perceive the strange liberty thus taken.
Nevertheless, multitudes of such instances occur, and care should be taken to banish
them entirely.

It happens everywhere (I do not say in some orchestras only) — that when ten,
fifteen, or twenty violinists have to play the same part in unison, that they do not
count the bars' rest; each, from idleness, relying on the others doing it.   Whence it follows that scarcely half of them come in again at the right moment ; while the rest still
hold their instrument under their left arm, and look about them.   Thus the point
is greatly weakened, if not entirely missed.   I invoke the attention and vigor of
orchestral conductors to this insufferable habit.   It is, however, so rooted that they
will only ensure its extirpation by making a large number of violinists amenable for
the fault of a single player ; by inflicting a fine, for example, upon a whole row, if one
of them misses coming in.   Even were this fine no more than half-a-crown, I will
answer for it that each of the violinists would count his rests, and keep watch that his
neighbors did the same, since it might be inflicted five or six times upon the same
individuals in the course of one performance.

An orchestra, the instruments of which are not in tune individually, and with
each other, is a monstrosity ; the conductor, therfore, should take the greatest care
that the musicians tune accurately.   But this operation should not be performed in
presence of the public ; and, moreover, every instrumental noise — every kind of
preluding between the acts — constitutes a real offence to all civilized auditors.   The
bad training of an orchestra, and its musical mediocrity is to be inferred from the
impertinent noise it makes during the periods of quiet at an Opera or Concert.

It is also imperative for a conductor not to allow clarinet-players to use always
the same instrument (the clarinet in *B♭*), without regard to the author's indications ;
just as if the different clarinets — those in *D* and *A*, particularly — had not a special

character of their own, of which the intelligent composer knows the exact value ; and as if the clarinet in *A* had not moreover a low semitone more than the clarinet in *B♭* —, the C♯, of excellent effect,

produced by the E,   which E gives only the D,

on the clarinet in *B♭*.

A habit as vicious, and still more baneful, has crept into many orchestras since the introduction of horns with cylinders and pistons : it is that of playing *in open sounds;* by means of the new mechanism adapted to the instrument, those notes intended by the composer to be produced *in closed sounds*, by means of the right hand within the bell.   Moreover, the horn-players nowadays, on account of the facility afforded by the pistons or cylinders for putting their instrument into different keys, use only the *horn in F* whatever may be the key indicated by the author.   This custom gives rise to a host of inconveniences, from which the conductor should use all his efforts to preserve the works of composers *who know how to write*.

He should also set his face against the economical fashion adopted by certain theatres — called lyric — of causing the cymbals and the long drum to be played by the same performer.   The sound of the cymbals when attached to the drum — as they must be to render this economy feasible — is an ignoble noise, fit only for bands at tea-gardens.   This custom, moreover, leads mediocre composers into the habit of never employing one of these instruments without the other, and considering their use as solely confined to forcibly marking the accented parts of the bar.   This is an idea fruitful in noisy platitudes ; and one that has brought upon us the ridiculous excesses beneath which, if a stop be not put to them, dramatic music will sooner or later sink.

I conclude by expressing sincere regret at beholding choral and orchestral stud ies still so badly organized.   Everywhere, for grand choral and instrumental compositions, the system of rehearsals in the mass is maintained.   They make all the chorus-singers study at once, on the one hand ; and all the instrumentalists at once, on the other.   Deplorable errors, innumerable mistakes, are thus committed — particularly in the intermediate parts — errors which the chorus-master and the conductor do not perceive.   Once established, these errors degenerate into habits, and become part and parcel of the execution.

The hapless chorus-singers, moreover, are by far the worst treated of all the performers during their studies, such as they are.   Instead of giving them *a good conductor*, knowing the times of the different movements accurately, and proficient in the art of singing, to beat the time, and make critical observations : *a good pianist*, playing *from a well-arranged pianoforte score*, upon *a good piano ;* and *a violinist*, to play in unison or in octave with the voices as each part is learned alone — instead of these three *indispensable artists*, they commit them (in two-thirds of the lyric theatres of Europe) to the superintendence of a single man, who has no more idea of the art of conducting than of that of singing, who is generally a poor musician, selected from among the worst pianists to be found, or who cannot play the pianoforte at all — some old superannuated individual, who, seated before a battered out-of-tune instrument, tries to decipher a dislocated score which he does not know, strikes false chords major, when they are minor, or vice-versa, and under the protext of conducting and of accompanying by himself, employs his right hand in setting the chorus-singers wrong in their time, and his left hand in setting them wrong in their tune.

One might believe one's self in the Dark Ages, on witnessing such an exhibition of Gothish economy.

A faithful, well-colored, clever interpretation of a modern work, even when confided to artists of a higher order, can only be obtained, I firmly believe, by partial rehearsals. Each part of a chorus should be studied singly until it is thoroughly known, before combining it with the others. The same step should be taken with regard to the orchestra, for a symphony at all complicated. The violins should first be practised alone ; the violas and basses by themselves ; the wooden wind instruments (with a small band of stringed instruments, to fill in the rests, and accustom the wind instruments to the points of re-entrance) and the brass instruments the same ; and very often it is necessary to practise the instruments of percussion alone ; and lastly, the harps, if they be numerous. The studies in combination are then far more profitable, and more rapid ; and there is then good hope of attaining fidelity of interpretation, now, alas, but too rare.

The performances obtained by the old method of study are merely *approaches* to achievement ; beneath which so very many masterpieces have succumbed. The superintending conductor, after the butchering of a master, none the less serenely lays down his stick with a satisfied smile ; and if some few misgivings remain with him as to the mode in which he has fulfilled his task, should no one venture at the close to dispute its accomplishment, he murmurs aside : "Bah ! væ victis !"

HECTOR BERLIOZ.

INDEX.

INDEX

Of Score Examples, Solo Passages, Special Arrangements, and Comparative Tables of Notation and Tonal Compass of all the Stringed, Wood-wind, and Brass Instruments.

A LIST OF THE BEST BOOKS FOR BAND AND ORCHESTRA LEADERS

The Orchestral Conductor . . *Hector Berlioz* Net $0.25
The most famous of all treatises on the art
of conducting.|

**An Abridged Treatise on Modern Instru-
mentation and Orchestration**
Hector Berlioz Net 1.00
The best-known work on instrumentation
in concise and abridged form.

**The Amateur Band Guide and Aid to Leaders by
Edwin Franko Goldman**

The object of this little volume is to provide for
Bandmasters, Band Teachers, and Bandsmen in
general a handbook which will prove of value in the
organizing and proper maintaining of Bands. Designed primarily for the purpose of giving advice,
information and suggestions for young bands, the
book contains many points which may well prove of
advantage and interest to older and more experienced players.
The Bandmaster will find use for this book, for
in it his position and work are explained fully and
in detail. Wind Instrument players will find use
for it because, aside from describing the entire
workings of a band, it offers suggestions for the care
of instruments, how and what to practice, methods
and studies which should be familiarized, a description of each Band instrument, showing its compass
and possibilities, etc., etc.
The book also contains charts showing correct
seating of bands for concert purposes, proper for-
mations for marching, instrumentation of bands, of
from ten to one hundred men, a chart for tuning
purposes, a revised constitution and by-laws, rules
and regulations governing band contests, and other
subjects too numerous to mention here. Net $1.50

The Band Teacher's Assistant
A. A. Clappe Net $1.00
A complete and progressive band instruc-
tor. Rudiments of music. Valuable hints
on Band Topics, Charts, etc., etc.

The American Band Arranger
M. L. Lake Net 1.00
A complete and reliable self-instructor for
mastering the essential principles of practical and artistic arranging for military
band.

**Constitution and By-Laws for Bands and
Other Musical Organizations.** Net .10
A genuine necessity for all new bands and
others planning more elaborate organizations. (Per Dozen) Net 1.00

**Harmony and Instrumentation With Practi-
cal Instruction in Arranging Music for
Orchestras and Military Bands**
Oscar Coon Net 3.50
One of the very best and most practical
of modern books of its kind.

The Practical Band Arranger
L. P. Laureudeau Net 1.25
As its name implies, this is one of the most
desirable ‡works ever written. Clear, to
the point and full of practical ideas.

Transposition . . . . *Prof. H. Kling* Net $1.00
An invaluable little book for orchestra
players and bandsmen, with any amount
of information about transposition.

New Catechism of Music . . . . *J. S. Lobe* Net .40
A new and particularly attractive edition
of this well-known work.

**Logier's Comprehensive Course in Music
Harmony and Practical Composition. Ed-
ited by Carl Stein, Including an Abridged
Treatise on Modern Instrumentation and
Orchestration.** (Cloth) Net 3.00
(Boards) Net 2.50
One of the very best and most complete
works on the science of music in an ad-
mirable and faultless edition.

Practical Manual of Harmony
N. Rimsky-Korsakow 2.50
English translation by *Joseph Achron*
An edition in English of a work that has established itself, through its own merits, as
one of the greatest treatises of its kind in
any language. Designed for class, private
or self instruction.

Complete System of Harmony
H. E. Parkhurst Net 2.00
An entirely new book based on modern
advanced principles.

**Pocket Standard Dictionary of Musical
Terms** . . . . *Oscar Coon* (Paper) Net .25
(Cloth) Net .40
The very best and most complete of all
small dictionaries.

Manual of Harmony
E. F. Richter (Cloth) Net 1.50
The best-known of all German works on
Harmony in a splendid and faultless
English edition.

**Book of Additional Exercises to the Manual
of Harmony** . . . . *A. Richter* Net .50

Key to the Exercises by . . . . *Oscar Coon* Net .75

Text Book for the Study of Harmony
H. Weber (Cloth) Net 1.50
A concise, practical and very useful text
book. Excellent for self-instruction.

Composition . *Marx-Mendelssohn* (Cloth) Net 2.00
A complete treatise on harmony by one of
the greatest German authorities. Admirable English Edition.

THE CARL FISCHER
COMPLETE INSTRUMENT CHART

The most complete and up-to-date symposium of valuable
information ever published for musicians.

FEATURES OF THE CHART:

Illustrates complete range of all Instruments. Shows corresponding
note on the Piano of all transposing and non-transposing instruments.
Classification of wind instruments. Valuable information in regard
to pitch. Gives compass of male and female voices. Practical and
effective Band Combinations (8 to 50 players). Correct valve combinations and slide divisions for trombones, and hundreds of other
valuable hints. Size 54x45, printed on linen with wood top and bottom hangers. A most valuable addition to Studios and Bandrooms.

PRICE, Net $2.50

Carl Fischer Edition
of Methods and Studies for Wind Instruments

FLUTE

Foundation to Flute Playing by Ernest F. Wagner. An original Method for the Boehm Flute which is simple and melodious. A Great Help to Beginners and the Best Guide for Teachers. Best Method for Self-Instruction. Net $1.50.

Universal Method for the Flute with English and German Text, containing the best materials from the World's Celebrated Writers for the Flute, including Prill, Soussmann, Altes, Dorus, Gattermann, Popp and others.

Part I, Net $2.50, *Part II*, Net $2.50, *Complete, Paper*, Net $4.00, *Boards*, Net $4.50, *Cloth*, Net $5.00.

Popp-Soussmann, Complete Method for the Ordinary and Beohm System Flute (English and German).

Part I, Net $1.00, *Part II*, Net 75 cents, *Part III*, Net $1.00, *Complete, Paper*, Net $2.00, *Boards*, Net $2.50.

Deviennes, Flute Method. A Complete Method in every branch with Table of Fingering for both the Ordinary Flute and the Boehm System. Progressive Duets, Scales and Exercises, ending with Twelve Grand Studies.

Paper, Net $3.00, *Boards*, Net $3.50.

Duverge, Method for Boehm System Flute, with Table of Fingering for the Ordinary Flute. It is a complete method for the mechanical study of the instrument and comprises every variety of exercises in the art of playing. Double and Triple Tonguing, Cadenzas, concluding with several Airs with Variations.

Paper, Net $3.00, *Boards*, Net $3.50.

L'Indispensabile. A Modern School of Perfection for Flute by Leonardo De Lorenzo.

This modern flute method contains 101 extended examples covering every possible branch of flute playing, and the author has spared neither time nor exertion in his compilation of this remarkable work. It has been his special endeavor to combine the useful with the agreeable, so far as possible, through the preparation of an entirely new series of scales, arpeggios, skips, trills, preludes, and three numbers in solo form without piano accompaniment entitled; (No. 97) " Studio Caratteristico," (No. 98) " Lella," idillio oceanico, (No. 99) " Il Mulinello," Capriccio. The compilation and presentation of the major and minor scales in particular has been done in an absolutely novel and original manner. Some of the numbers have been written with a special view towards allowing them to be practiced in several inversions.

Part I, Net $2.25, *Part II*, Net $3.25, *Complete, Net* $5.00.

Paul de Ville, The Eclipse Self-Instructor for Flute. Net 50 cents.

Langey, O., Tutor for the Flute. Net $1.00.

Pares, Daily Technical Exercises and Complete Scale Studies. Net 50 cents.

PICCOLO

Paul de Ville, The Eclipse Self-Instructor for Picccolo. Net 50 cents.

Langey, O., Tutor for the Piccolo. Net $1.00.

Pares, Daily Technical Exercises and Complete Scale Studies, Net 50 cents.

CLARINET

Foundation of Clarinet Playing, by C. E. Reinecke. An Original Elementary Method which is Simple and Melodious. A Great Help to Beginners and the Best Guide for Teachers. Best Method for Self-Instruction. Net $1.50.

Klose, Complete Method for the Clarinet. This is one of the standard works for the instrument, and one that is used at the Paris Conservatory. Featuring the Boehm System more than the ordinary system.

Part I, Net $1.75, *Part II*, Net $2,00, *Complete, Paper*, Net $3.50, *Boards*, Net $4.00, *Cloth*, Net $4.75.

Lazarus New and Modern Clarinet Method. In three parts or complete in one book. This is another work that is popular among teachers and students of the Clarinet. .

Part I, Net $2.00, *Part II*, Net $2.00, *Part III*, Net $2.50, *Complete, Paper*, Net $4.50, *Boards*, Net $5.00, *Cloth*, Net $5.75.

G. Langenus, Modern Clarinet Playing. This is a new work published for the instrument and written by one of the foremost performers in the world. Net $2.00.

Labanchi, G., Progressive Method for the Clarinet (English and Italian Text). *Part II*, Net $4.00.

Baermann's Celebrated Clarinet Method. Op. 63. Division I, Net $1.00, II, Net $2.00, III, Net $1.50, Complete in one vol., Net $4.00.

Langey, O., Tutor for the Clarinet, enlarged and revised edition. Net $1.00.

The Eclipse Self-Instructor for Clarinet by Paul de Ville. Net 50 cents.

Pares, Daily Technical Exercises and Complete Scale Studies, Net 50 cents.

Cavallini, Thirty Caprices. These are exceptionally fine studies and will prove of great benefit to all students. Net $1.00.

OBOE

Langey Tutor for Oboe, emlarged and revised edition. Net $1.00.

Lebate, B., Sixteen Daily Exercises for Advanced Players. Net $1.00.

Pares, Daily Technical Exercises and Complete Scale Studies, Net 50 cents.

BASSOON

Langey Tutor for Bassoon, enlarged and revised edition. Net $1.00.

Blume, O., Thirty-Six Studies. These very important exercises are published in three volumes. Each, Net 60 cents.

Kopprasch, Sixty Studies, in two volumes. Interesting and useful. Each 75 cents.

Pares, Daily Technical Exercises and Complete Scale Studies, Net 50 cents.

Carl Fischer Edition
of Methods and Studies for Wind Instruments

SAXOPHONE

" Foundation to Saxophone Playing" by Ben. Vereecken. An Original Elementary Method which is simple and melodious. A great help to beginners and the best guide for teachers. This Method also contains the latest Chart of Fingering for all Saxophones reading in treble, tenor and bass clef. Best Method for Self-Instruction. Net $1.50.

The Saxophone Virtuoso, by Ben. Vereecken. An Advanced Method for mastery of the clefs, transposition, technical Control and every other problem of the saxophonist. Net $2.00.

Paul de Ville, Universal Method. A method containing the best material ever written for the Saxophone, by the best-known authors. A book for those who desire to study the instrument thoroughly.

Paper, Net $3.00, *Boards*, Net $3.50, *Cloth*, Net $4.00.

Mayeur's Method. Best and most complete edition published, containing diagrams and fingering for the ordinary and improved systems. This is undoubtedly the best work written for the instrument.

Paper, Net $2.00, *Boards*, Net $2.50.

Pares, Daily Technical Exercises and Complete Scale Studies, Net 50 cents.

Langey Tutor for Saxophone, enlarged and revised edition. Net $1.00.

CORNET

Arban's Complete Method, Authentic Edition. This new edition has been carefully revised and edited. It contains extra interesting features, amongst them being a picture of Arban, together with a biography of his life — a diagram of the modern cornet, giving the proper names of the various parts of the instrument, etc. The English translation has been most carefully revised and corrected from the original French Text.
This book in its present form surpasses anything of its kind ever offered to Cornetists. Prices:

Complete Edition, Paper, Net $3.50, *Boards*, Net $4.00, *Cloth*, Net $4.75.

The same in abridged edition. Net $1.50.

The World's Cornet Method. This is the most complete work published and one which has found favor with both teachers and students. It is made up of the best material from the works of Arban, St. Jacome, Gatti, etc., and is therefore a method of great value.

Parts I, II, III, Paper, Net $1.50, *Parts I, II, III, Boards*, Net $2.00, *Complete, Boards*, Net $5.00, *Cloth*, Net $5.50.

Goldman, Edw. F. Foundation to Cornet Playing. An original Elementary Method which is simple and melodious. Particularly a great help to beginners, and a guide for teachers. Each lesson thoroughly explained. Can be used for self-instruction. Net $1.50.

St. Jacome, Complete Tutor for the Cornet, in two volumes. This work by St. Jacome is a very extensive one, and contains some of the finest material for study ever written for the cornet.

Part I, Net $2.00, *Part II*, Net $2.50, *Complete, Paper*, Net $4.00, *Boards*, Net $4.50, *Cloth*, Net $5.00.

The Gatti Grand Method, for the Trumpet and Cornet. The Gatti method is used throughout Italy, and most Italian players who are well schooled have studied it. It has just been published in a new and revised edition with English and Italian text and will be found to contain exercises that are well written and very interesting.

Part I, Net $1.00, *Part II*, Net $1.50, *Part III*, Net $2.50, *Complete, Paper*, Net $4.00, *Boards*, Net $4.50.

The Expert Cornetist. A modern method for mastering the art of double and triple tonguing by Edwin Franko Goldman.
A complete, systematic and simplified course, with practical examples and thorough explanations.
Authoritative in every respect, this new work will supply players of brass instruments with the most reliable and serviceable guide ever offered. Contains valuable information, practical exercises exclusively devoted to double and triple tonguing, and presents itself as the most exhaustive method on this particular subject ever written.
Triple and Double Tonguing Made Easy.

Price, Net $1.25.

Caussinus Melodic Method for the Cornet. This is the only Method wherein every lesson is preceded by an example theoretically explaining the exact manner of executing the melodic Study which follows in form of duet, making the study more interesting and valuable.

Price, *Paper*, Net $2.75, *Boards*, Net $3.25, *Cloth*, Net $3.75

Langey, O., Tutor for the Cornet, new and revised edition. Net $1.00.

Paul de Ville, Eclipse Self-Instructor for Cornet. A popular method for those who do not have the assistance of a teacher. Net 50 cents.

Daily Studies for Strengthening the Lips, by Edwin Franko Goldman. Net 25 cents.

Pares, Daily Technical Exercises and Complete Scale Studies. Net 50 cents.

Jules Levy, Six Studies. These are excellent Studies, written by one of the greatest cornetists that ever lived. 50 cents.

Carl Fischer Edition
of Methods and Studies for Wind Instruments

E♭ CORNET

Carl Fischer's New and Revised Tutor for E♭ Cornet, enlarged by Paul De Ville. Net $1.00.

Pares, Daily Technical Exercises and Complete Scale Studies. Net 50 cents.

FRENCH HORN

The Langey Tutor for French Horn. This is a simple and practical method for the instrument. Net $1.00.

O. Franz, Grand Theoretical and Practical Method for the French Horn. This edition has been revised and translated by Gustav Saenger and is known as the "World's Edition." It has English and German text, and is the standard method for the instrument. Net $2.00.

Pares, Daily Technical Exercises and Complete Scale Studies. Net 50 cents.

E♭ ALTO

The Eclipse Self-Instructor, by Paul De Ville. The best method for beginners. Net 50 cents.

The Langey Tutor for E♭ Alto. This is probably the best work for the instrument. Net $1.00.

Daily Studies for Strengthening the Lips, by Edwin Franko Goldman. Net 25 cents.

Arban's Method. The Arban method for the Cornet can be used for the E♭ Alto with equally good results. In fact, for those who wish to study the instrument properly, nothing better can be procured. (For prices see Cornet.)

TROMBONE

Foundation of Trombone Playing. An Elementary Method by Fred L. Blodgett. Net $1.50.

This new work is written on the same lines as the Foundation to Cornet Playing, and contains many new features which cannot be found in the older methods. Starting with the very simplest exercises, the studies progress step by step, giving the pupil ample opportunity to build a solid foundation.

Every exercise has a clear and concise explanation, which besides being valuable to the student, will prove of great assistance to the teacher. This method is the best for self-instruction, and is far superior to lessons by mail.

Dieppo's Complete Method for the Slide and Valve Trombone, revised and enlarged edition with an appendix of nearly 100 pages consisting of numerous studies and duets by Dieppo, Vobaron, Carnaud, and others. This work is universally used and is probably the most popular of Trombone Methods.

Paper, Net $2.00, *Boards,* Net $2.50.

Universal Method, for either Slide or Valve Trombone, by Paul De Ville. A systematic and complete work.
Paper, Net $2.00, *Boards,* Net $2.50, *Cloth,* Net $3.00.

The Langey Tutor for either Slide or Valve Trombone. An exceptionally fine work for this instrument. Net $1.00.

Eclipse Self-Instructor. Studies for the Slide or Valve Trombone. (Bass or Treble.) Net 50 cents.

O. Blume, Thirty-six Studies for Trombone, in three books, with German and English text. Net 60 cents.

Pares, Daily Technical Exercises and Complete Scale Studies, Net 50 cents.

Kopprasch. Sixty Studies for Trombone in two books. At 75 cents.

Vobaron. Four Lessons and Seventeen Studies. 60 cents.

Daily Studies for Strengthening the Lips, by Edwin Franko Goldman. Net 25 cents.

BARITONE OR EUPHONIUM

Archimede, Alexander. Foundation to Baritone Playing (Bass or Treble). An Original Elementary Method which is simple and melodious. Particularly a great help to beginners and a guide to teachers. Each lesson thoroughly explained. Best Book for self-instruction. Net $1.50.

Universal Baritone (Euphonium) Method for three, four or five valve instrument. In bass clef, by Paul De Ville. This is without doubt the most complete work ever written, for the Baritone Players who are desirous to rank among the best performers on this instrument will find all the necessary material in this Method.
Paper, Net $4.00, *Boards,* Net $4.50, *Cloth,* Net $5.25.

Arban's Method (In Treble Clef). No Baritone or Euphonium player who desires to study his instrument seriously can afford to be without this remarkable book. Although the book was originally written for the Cornet, it is recommended and used by the leading Baritone teachers in all parts of the world. (For prices see Cornet.)

Langey's Tutor for the Baritone or Euphonium, revised and enlarged. In Bass or Treble Clef. Net $1.00.

The Eclipse Self-Instructor for Baritone in treble or bass clef by Paul De Ville. Net 50 cents.

Pares, Daily Technical Exercises and Complete Scale Studies. Net 50 cents.

Bosquet, Thirty-six Celebrated Studies. $1.25.

Collinet, Eighteen Preludes in Bass Clef. 50 cents.

Saint Jacome, Twelve Characteristic Studies. $1.00.

Daily Studies for Strengthening the Lips, by Edwin Franko Goldman. Net 25 cents.

TUBA

Eclipse Self-Instructor for E♭ Tuba, by Paul De Ville. Net 50 cents.

Langey Tutor for E♭ Tubas. This is one of the very best methods ever written for the instrument. Net $1.00.

Daily Studies for Strengthening the Lips, by Edwin Franko Goldman. Net 25 cents.

Carl Fischer's New Tutor for BB♭ Bass with three and four valves. Net $1.00.

Pares, Daily Technical Exercises and Complete Scale Studies. Net 50 cents.

Carl Fischer Edition
of Methods and Studies for Wind Instruments

Bb TENOR

Eclipse Self-Instructor for Upright Tenor in Treble or Bass Clef, by Paul De Ville. Net 50 cents.

The Langey Tutor for Bb Tenor. Net $1.00.

Arban's Method (in Treble Clef). This method will be found to be the very best that is obtainable for the instrument. It is the most complete. (For prices see Cornet.)

Daily Studies for Strengthening the Lips, by Edwin Franko Goldman. Net 25 cents.

Pares, Daily Technical Exercises and Complete Scale Studies. Net 50 cents.

DRUMS, TYMPANIES, XYLOPHONE AND CASTANETS

Gardner, Carl E., Modern Method for the Instruments of Percussion.
Part I., Drums, Cymbals, Accessories . Net $1.25
Part II, Bells Xylophone, Marimba,
Chimes .... Net 1.25
Part III, Tympani .... Net 1.25
The Three Parts, complete .... Net 3.50
This work is the most complete of its kind. Absolutely Up-to-date, teaching everything that is called for in the way of Modern Drumming, Most Effective way of using Traps, etc.

Gardner, Carl E. The Military Drummer. A Manual on Drum Playing as Practiced in the United States Army and Navy, including Drum Duties with Fife and Bugle...... Net   .75

Carl Fischer's New and Revised Tutor for Drum, Xylophone, Tympanies, and Castanets. Net $1.00.

Flockton, J. M., New Method for the Slide Drum, Xylophone, and Tympani, containing the best modern exercises for these instruments. Net $2.00.

The Eclipse Self-Instructor for Drums, by Paul De Ville. Net 50 cents.

Universal Method for the Xylophone, by Paul De Ville, "The World's Edition." The largest and most complete Method ever written for the Xylophone.
Paper, Net $2.00, *Boards*, Net $2.50, *Cloth*, Net $3.00.

BELLS (GLOCKENSPIEL)

Carl Fischer's Celebrated Tutor for Bells (Glockenspiel) and Cathedral Chimes (with Appendix of 20 Modern Solos for Bells), by Paul De Ville. Net $1.00.

250,000 Compositions, including all European Publications for the various Instruments in all forms, Methods, Studies, Solos, Duets, Trios, Quartets, etc., can be found in our enormous stock. We can supply anything in music that is published, at lowest price.

Charts and Scales

Showing the Compass, Fingering and Diagram of

WIND INSTRUMENTS

Fife, without keys .... Net	$0.15
Fife, 1 to 4 keys.................... Net	.20
Fife, 6 keys with table of shakes...... Net	.20
Flute, 6 keys with table of shakes..... Net	.20
Flute, 8 keys with table of shakes..... Net	.20
Flute, 10 and more keys, with table of shakes, explanation and examples for various keys ....Net	.35
Flute, Boehm System (closed G# key) with table of shakes................... Net	.35
Flute, Boehm System (open G key), with table of shakes .... Net	.35
Piccolo, 6 keys with table of shakes ...Net	.25
Piccolo, Boehm System, with table of shakes................................Net	.35
Oboe, 13, 15 and 16 keys, with table of shakes................................Net	.20
Clarinet, 13 keys, 2 rings, with table of shakes................................Net	.20
Clarinet, 13 keys, 2 rings, table of shakes and trills................................Net	.20
Clarinet, 15 keys, 2 rings with explanation of 4 rings and 45 examples (Klose) Albert System ....Net	.25
Clarinet, Carl Fischer Perfect Albert System, 16 keys, 6 rings, by W. F. Ambrosio...	.25
Clarinet, Boehm System, with 45 examples and shakes (Klose)....................Net	.25
Clarinet, Boehm System, Table of Fingering (G. Langenus) ....Net	.35
Clarinet, Improved Boehm System, 20 Keys, 7 Rings ....Net	.25
Bassoon, 18 keys .... Net	.25
Bassoon, 22 keys .... Net	.25
Cornet, Bb or Eb — Alto, Eb — Fluegelhorn, or Bb — Tenor Horn, Bb — Ballad Horn, — Bb Bass, bass or treble — Concert Horn (Melophone) — French Horn — Trombone, Bb (Valve), bass or treble each Net	.15
Baritone, (Euphonium) Bb 3 or 4 valves, bass clef .... Net	.15
Baritone, (Euphonium), Bb 3 valves, treble clef............................Net	.15
Trombone, Bb (slide) bass, treble and tenor clef, together with table of positions, bass or treble clef........................... Net	.20
Trombone, Bb (slide) table of positions with artificial notes....................Net	.15
Trombone, G Bass (slide or valve) bass clef ....Net	.15
Tuba, (Bass) Eb, F, CC, BBb, 3 and 4 valves............................... Net	.30
Saxophone, complete table, for all Saxophones (treble, tenor and bass clef), new improved model, by Ben. Vereecken....... Net	.50